IN SEARCH OF
THE TROJAN WAR

IN SEARCH OF
THE TROJAN WAR

MICHAEL WOOD

First published in hardback 1985
This paperback edition first published 2005
Copyright © Michael Wood 1985, 1996, 2005
The moral right of the author has been asserted

Published by BBC Books, BBC Worldwide Ltd,
Woodlands, 80 Wood Lane, London W12 0TT

ISBN 0 563 52265 8

Commissioning editors: Sheila Ableman and Sally Potter
Project editor: Martin Redfern
Designer: Linda Blakemore

Printed and bound in Great Britain by Mackays of Chatham
Colour separations by Butler & Tanner Ltd, Frome

CONTENTS

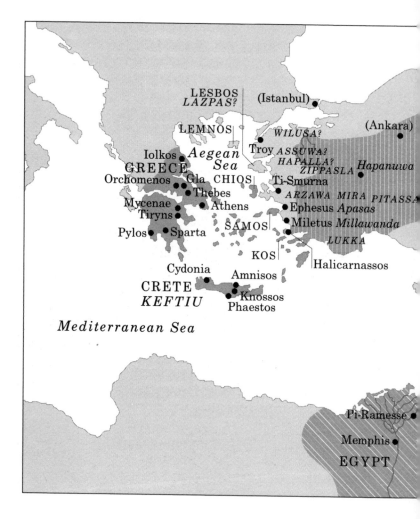

LESBOS
LAZPAS?   (Istanbul)

LEMNOS   (Ankara)
                 WILUSA?
            Troy *ASSUWA?*
Iolkos *Aegean*   *HAPALLA?*
GREECE   *Sea*   *ZIPPASLA* *Hapanuwa*
Orchomenos Gla CHIOS   Ti-Smurna
            Thebes   *ARZAWA MIRA PITASSA*
Mycenae   Athens   Ephesus *Apasas*
Tiryns   Miletus *Millawanda*
Pylos   Sparta SAMOS
                        LUKKA
                KOS
                        Halicarnassos
     Cydonia   Amnisos
CRETE
KEFTIU   Knossos
              Phaestos

Mediterranean Sea

                              Pi-Ramesse

                              Memphis
                              EGYPT

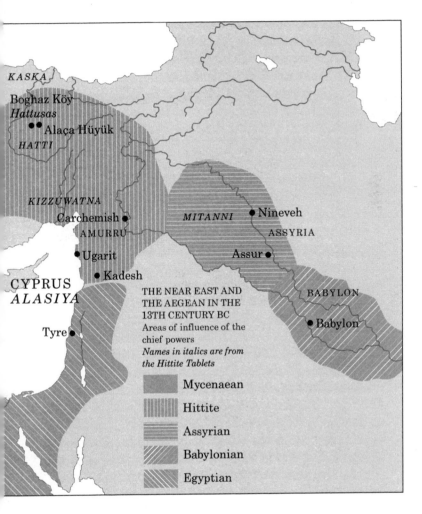

KASKA

Boghaz Köy
Hattusas
● ● Alaça Hüyük
HATTI

KIZZUWATNA
Carchemish ●
AMURRU

MITANNI   ● Nineveh
                 ASSYRIA

● Ugarit   Assur ●

CYPRUS
ALASIYA

● Kadesh

BABYLON

THE NEAR EAST AND
THE AEGEAN IN THE
13TH CENTURY BC
Areas of influence of the
chief powers
*Names in italics are from
the Hittite Tablets*

● Babylon

Tyre ●

Mycenaean

Hittite

Assyrian

Babylonian

Egyptian

*It is irrelevant how many centuries
may separate us from a bygone age.
What matters is the importance of
the past to our intellectual and
spiritual existence.*

ERNST CURTIUS, speech in memory of
Heinrich Schliemann, Berlin, 1 March 1891.

PREFACE

A HUNDRED AND THIRTY-FIVE YEARS after Heinrich Schliemann first put spade into the fabled mound of Hisarlik in northwest Turkey, the greatest archaeological mystery is still capturing the headlines. Only recently there was the dramatic reappearance of the Jewels of Helen – many had assumed that they had been destroyed during the sack of Berlin in 1945. Stored in the city's zoo in a massive concrete anti-aircraft tower, the Flakturm, the treasure (which Schliemann had associated with Helen of Troy herself) was, we now know, carried off in secret by the Soviet army; the gold ended up in Moscow and the bronzes in St Petersburg. Now at last they have been seen again, some pieces still crusted with the earth of the Trojan plain. With the prospect of exhibitions in Russia and elsewhere – possibly in Greece and Turkey – the tale has once again seized the public imagination.

Meanwhile, potentially even more exciting developments are taking place at Troy itself. For after a gap of over fifty years the site is being re-excavated and is already providing new evidence that what we call Troy – the mound of Hisarlik – is indeed the site of the legendary city sacked in the Greek epic the *Iliad*: the city of Priam and Hector.

The first edition of this book told the story of the three great excavations of the site of Troy by Schliemann, Wilhelm Dörpfeld, and Carl Blegen. Each claimed to have answered the riddle of the Trojan War, though each found a different war in a different level of the site. None has been universally accepted as solving the mystery. It was in the summer of 1938 that the last excavators, the Cincinnati expedition under Carl Blegen, closed their trenches on Hisarlik. As they admitted, they left many questions unanswered, in part because of the earlier wrecking of the site by Schliemann, but also because of the limitations of archaeological technique at that time. Like most people, Blegen concluded that the site had now been so devastated that little new evidence could ever come out of the hill. So for a long time it seemed that

Blegen's report would constitute the final word on the archaeology of Troy. However, in 1988 a major new excavation was announced, a twenty-year dig on the site of the citadel and in the lower town, where many had suspected a large Bronze Age settlement might underlie the later Roman city. Well funded by the U.S. and by Daimler-Benz in Germany, Manfred Korfmann and his international team based at Tübingen University are using the whole range of modern scientific tools to establish by survey and excavation a cultural and environmental history of the region of Troy. Already, it is safe to say, a number of outstanding problems about Troy seem likely to be resolved; the results so far are summarised here in a new final chapter.

So where do things stand now on the historicity of Troy and the Trojan War? To recapitulate, the thesis of the original edition of this book was as follows. The mound of Hisarlik was the site of the historical city which the Greek poet Homer says was sacked by the Greeks during the Heroic Age. Bronze Age Hisarlik was probably the chief seat of one of the important states of western Anatolia (Aegean Turkey). These are known from diplomatic letters written on clay tablets that have been found at a number of Bronze Age sites in Turkey. Troy was perhaps a client state of the Hittite empire, which was one of the chief Near Eastern powers at that time. This state was the cause of hostilities between Greeks and Hittites in the mid-thirteenth century BC. I also argued that the conventional dating for the Trojan War established by Carl Blegen can no longer be upheld, and that the destruction of Troy might be placed earlier in the thirteenth century BC (perhaps *c.*1275–1260) when the Mycenaean Greek world was at its height, and when the Hittites were struggling to maintain a loose overlordship in western Anatolia. This, I suggested, is the true background to the historical Trojan War, which can be adduced from first-hand primary sources, the diplomatic archives of the Hittite empire, where there is evidence for Hittite relations with a powerful 'Great King' in the Aegean world who can be identified with a mainland Greek over-king, just as legend remembered

10

Agamemnon. In short, the essential facts of Homer's story – the city, the location by the Dardanelles, the Greek expedition, the war – were all true.

Twenty years on, it is with a pardonable sense of relief that I can say that the speculations in the first edition of this book have not been disproved by the new discoveries; indeed, if anything they seem more, rather than less, likely to be correct. At that time there was a justifiable reluctance among many scholars to admit the idea that the epics have a real connection with historical events of the thirteenth century BC; indeed the feeling was fairly widespread that the Trojan War was simply a myth and had no relation to history whatsoever. When the first edition of this book came out, it had the honour of being vigorously attacked by the doyen of Troy sceptics, the late Sir Moses Finley. Elsewhere, though, Donald Easton devoted several pages to its thesis in the periodical *Antiquity*, and concluded in its favour. Since then, new discoveries in archaeology, diplomatic records and linguistics are continuing to fill in a real historical background to the Trojan War, just as they have already given us important new details about the city by the Dardanelles, which is still the most remarkable prehistoric site in all western Anatolia. Now more than ever in the 135 years since Schliemann put his first spade into Hisarlik, there appears to be a historical basis to the tale of Troy.

In this new edition of *In Search of the Trojan War*, I have added a final chapter summarising the recent discoveries made in and around Troy, with particular reference to the ongoing re-excavation of the site of Hisarlik. I have also added an update to the bibliography. I am grateful to Dr Elizabeth French for her continuing generosity in answering my queries, and for allowing me to publish the letter from Carl Blegen to her father Alan Wace quoted on pages 119–120. I would also like to thank Professor Manfred Korfmann for the details and corrections concerning his finds at Besik Tepe and at Troy itself.

Michael Wood

ACKNOWLEDGEMENTS

'I would as soon go in quest of Utopia, or of the Carib Island of Robinson Crusoe, and his Cabin; and I should return with equal emolument,' said the redoubtable Jacob Bryant of the search for Troy, which he thought never existed (1799). If I have returned from my own particular odyssey with any emolument at all, it is largely due to the many scholars and friends who have given me the benefit of their knowledge.

First, I would like to thank the friends who made the films which this book was written to accompany: Bill Lyons who produced and directed with great skill and Trojan stamina; Annette Steinhilber who was as always a tower of strength; Richard Ganniclifft, Dennis Cartwright and Alan Parker who were unfailing sources of support and good humour; Colin Adams, executive producer of the films this book accompanies, for his invaluable patience and advice during the making and editing of the series. Thanks are also due to David Jackson, Graham Veevers and Terry Bartlett, and to Pat Haggerty and Roy Newton who brought their special skills to bear on the editing. Mordo and Sevim Berker made everything possible in Turkey and were unstinting in their hospitality. In Greece I have a special debt to Maria Koumarianou-Powell. Sheila Ableman edited the book unflappably, and Viv Brearley threaded her way most accurately through a labyrinth of manuscript: to both my grateful thanks.

My depts to professional scholars working in this field are unusually large. I would like to thank Profs George Huxley, Kevin O'Nolan, John Davies, Leonard Palmer, Oliver Gurney, Peter Warren, Colin Renfrew, James Hooker and Sir Moses Finley, Drs Oliver Dickenson, Chris Mee, Mervyn Popham, Nancy Sandars, David Hawkins, John Lazenby, Jim McQueen, John Killen, Livia Morgan, Brian Hainsworth, James Jackson, Lord William Taylour and General Sir John Hackett, all of whom were kind enough to give their time to discuss points with me.

I am especially grateful to Prof. Geoffrey Kirk, Prof. R. H. Crossland and Dr John Chadwick for their help and advice, and to Drs John Bintliff, James Mellart, Donald Traill and Prof. Hans Güterbock who all allowed me to use their unpublished material. Lesley Fitton kindly located Calvert and Schliemann letters for me in the British Museum. Dr Ken Kitchen provided me with much inaccessible material, and with his typically enthusiastic encouragement, for which much thanks. Donald Easton was most generous in discussing the Troy problem with me in the light of his research into the Schliemann notebooks, and permitted me to use his unpublished material in the plans: all devotees will eagerly await the publication of his work. I would also like to thank James Candy for sharing his reminiscences of Sir Arthur Evans. It is a particularly pleasant duty to thank Sandy McGilivry, Sinclair Hood and William Taylor for a memorable evening at the 'taverna' at Knossos discussing the knotty problems of that marvellous site; in Greece too Profs Catherine Koumarianou, C. Doumas, and Spiro Jacovides, and Drs J. Sakellerakis and Alexandra Karetsou were most helpful, and to Prof. George Mylonas I owe an unforgettable day at Mycenae. I should particularly like to thank the German Schools at Athens and Istanbul for many kindnesses and especially Klaus Kilian at Tiryns who was unstintingly generous with his time and his material. In Athens Jerome Sperling shared his exciting reminiscences of the Cincinnati dig at Troy. In Turkey I am most grateful for their help to Profs Ekrem Akurgal and T. Osgüc, Dr Sedat Alp, and Mustafa Gözen Sevinç, director of the site of Troy, to the Turkish Historical Society, and to Seref Tasliova and the public bards of Kars for showing me something of the ancient traditions of the singers of tales; in the far west of Europe John Henry and the people of Kilgalligan, County Mayo, through Seamus O Cathoin's introduction, let me touch on the last of that tradition in the British Isles. Finally I should like to thank Prof. John Luce for reading my text and suggesting many improvements, and Dr Elizabeth French who suffered from being a near neighbour and endured my frequent questions with unflagging patience: to her critical eye I owe more than she will realise. However, the usual warning about blame is particularly necessary here: it cannot be too strongly emphasised that none of the above scholars can be held responsible for any errors of fact or interpretation which may be discovered in this book. In a work of synthesis it is not possible to do justice to all the differing theories in this highly contentious field – it has been well said that historians thrive on ambiguities, journalists on certainties! I hope at least that what Gladstone wrote more than a century ago on Homer is still true: 'No exertion spent upon any of the great classics of the world, and attended with any amount of real result, is really thrown away. It is better to write one word upon the rock than a thousand on the water or the sand.' (*Studies on Homer.*)

PROLOGUE

Ilium was for a considerable period to the Heathen world, what Jerusalem is now to the Christian, a 'sacred' city which attracted pilgrims by the fame of its wars and its woes, and by the shadow of ancient sanctity reposing upon it. Without abusing language, we may say that a voice speaking from this hill, three thousand years ago sent its utterances over the whole ancient world, as its echoes still reverberate over the modern.

CHARLES MACLAREN, *The Plain of Troy Described* (1863)

THE CAR FERRY from Gallipoli across the 'swift-flowing Hellespont' describes a great arc upstream to reach the bank opposite at Çanakkale, so powerful is the current which sweeps down the Dardanelles. Turquoise waves of an unnatural brilliance thump against our sides, their tops whipped into spray by the un-remitting wind. Here at the narrows, where Lord Byron swam across and Xerxes built his bridge of boats, the channel is less than a mile wide. Behind us lies the peninsula of Gallipoli, and memories of a more recent war. Ahead is the shore of Asia, the minarets of Çanakkale. This has been a crossing for armies, traders, migrating peoples since before history. And it is the way to Troy.

The way to Troy! Surely there are few other names which evoke such feelings for so many of the inhabitants of the world? In all the stories told by mankind and recorded through its history, is there a more famous place?

From the cobbled streets of Çanakkale a modern tarmac road leads southwards along the coastal strip, past the site of ancient Dardanos, now just a featureless crest above the sea, littered with sherds. On the right-hand side, pinewoods slope down to the shore, on the left is a range of low hills. Ships can be seen making their way up to the Black Sea or down to the Mediterranean – a Greek freighter, a Russian cruiser, and tiny fishing-boats gathering for the mackerel and tunny harvest just as they did in the Bronze Age. After 10 miles or so the road leaves the coast and descends from Erenköy (Intepe) into a fertile plain dotted with fields of cotton, sunflowers, valonia and wheat; there are cattle grazing, and white poplars and willows line the rivers and irrigation dykes. Here you might even see camels loaded with tobacco and ancient-looking roped storage jars on their gaily woven saddle-cloths. This is the valley of the Dumrek Su, the ancient Simois. In front of you at right angles to the road stretches a long wooded ridge, perhaps 100 feet above the plain: the road ascends it steeply, and on the top there is a sign to the right: 'Truva' – Troy.

You turn onto a narrow country road, and head along the ridge westwards, towards the sea. If you go left, after the road forks, you pass through the village of Çiplak: muddy lanes, overhanging Anatolian wood-framed houses, their plaster crumbling, wattle exposed; in the road cows being coaxed into the yard by a little boy with a long cane; a gaggle of geese. This was where Heinrich Schliemann lived at first when he started excavating the site in 1870. Then it was a village of 'ferocious' Turks, probably founded in the fifteenth or sixteenth century when life had finally died out on the nearby site of New Ilium. In 1816 travellers remembered that the village was built out of the ruins of the city, and indeed Schliemann says that in 1873 the new mosque and minaret were constructed with stones from his excavations. You drive on, past the village of Tevfikiye with its souvenir shops and its spurious 'House of Schliemann'; this place was entirely built out of the wreckage from Schliemann's dig. West of Tevfikiye the sown fields are strewn with stones, sherds and fragments of red and white veined marble. This plateau is the site of the classical city of New Ilium, 'New Troy', which existed from 700 BC to AD 500. Throughout the ancient world this place was believed to stand on the site of the city sacked in the Trojan War. The wind blows fiercely, shaking the oaks which grow around the site itself, whipping up the dust. Through the trees you catch sight of a towering timber horse, set up so that tourist parties can pose for snaps in front of 'the fierce beast of Argos' from whose belly the Greek heroes sprang to 'lick their fill of the blood of princes'. And that wind! Cold and unrelenting. (Had Homer not said that Troy was above all 'very windy'?)

Walk through the glade of pines around the site museum, through a neat little garden lined with urns, fluted column drums and statue bases inscribed in the beautiful majuscule of classical Greek: broken phrases which speak of the sense of oneness which bound the classical world together: 'Meleager greets the Council and the people of Ilium ... prompted by his veneration for the temple and by his feeling of friendship for your town....' (The definition of civilisation: 'life in a city'; 'Ask me for a true image of human existence,' wrote the Roman Seneca, 'and I will show you the sack of a great city.')

Beyond the trees you come to the site itself, a hill called Hisarlik. You see immediately that you are on the edge of the plateau. Northwards and westwards the land falls away quite sharply to the vivid green of the plain, so the city stood on an eminence, if not 'beetling', as Homer has it, then at least raised above the plain. To the south-west, beyond the Sigeum ridge which marks the coast, is the distinctive humped back of the little island of Tenedos, where Homer says the Greeks had a base during the ten years of the siege. On the north-western horizon – if the weather is fine and the sky clear (it is not often so) – you can see the Aegean Sea and, reaching into it, what seems a long promontory. This is the island of Imbros, and peeping over the top of Imbros (if the light is exceptionally good) is a vision of glory: the great mountain called Fengari on Samothrace, about 50 miles away. It was from Fengari, 'the wooded top of Thracian Samos', says Homer, that the god Poseidon watched the Trojan War; this splendid spectacle, the traveller Edward Clarke wrote in 1810,

... would baffle any attempt at delineation, it rose with prodigious grandeur; and while its aetherial summit shone with indescribable brightness in a sky without a cloud, it seemed, notwithstanding its remote situation, as if its vastness would overwhelm all Troy, should an earthquake heave it from its base.

At your feet is what we today call Troy. If your expectation is something grand, something to recall the 'topless towers of Ilium', a medieval castle perhaps, or the Cyclopean walls of Greece, you will be disappointed. The place is tiny, 200 yards by 150: the size of, say, St Paul's Churchyard or Euston Station concourse in London. In front of you is a stretch of finely built walls, behind them an overgrown maze of superimposed ruins of many ages, a jumble of gullies and ditches choked with bushes and rubble.

The first thing you notice is that the ruins exist at several levels and that there is not, as it were, one single Troy. This is compounded by the difficulty of distinguishing features of the different phases of Troy and of seeing where the surviving remains fit together; there is no coherent picture. For a start, most of the site is now destroyed: classical builders erecting a new civic centre levelled the hill and swept away much of the interior of the earlier cities. Archaeology has done the rest; of necessity archaeology destroys the very thing it examines, for to find out facts it must remove the evidence by lifting it out of the ground. So, as the visitor strolls over the site today only a few jagged pinnacles give an idea of the original height of the hill before excavators attacked it from 1870 onwards. They were: Heinrich Schliemann in six major campaigns between then and 1890; Wilhelm Dörpfeld in 1893 and 1894 and the American Carl Blegen between 1932 and 1938. There remain now only these pinnacles, and one small untouched area on the south side for future generations to check the work of earlier investigators.

From the citadel at least, then, little new evidence is now likely to emerge in the world's greatest archaeological detective story. Most of what there was left to modern times was destroyed by Schliemann, before the techniques had evolved which we use today, enabling us to distinguish the complexities of levels and to date the styles of pottery accurately.

So our picture of Troy today depends on what Schliemann, Dörpfeld and Blegen did, and how they interpreted it. The results of their work can be seen all around the site in the painted yellow signs numbered Troy I–IX, denoting the nine main phases in the lifespan of the city from before 3000 BC to the end of the Roman Empire, for the hill is a stratified mound, like the 'tells' so common in the Near East though a rarity in the west. Indeed so significant is this site that even if the tale of Troy had never existed it would still be one of the key sites in the Mediterranean world, for what it tells us about the continuity and development of human civilisation in the Aegean and Asia Minor.

The first thing to remember is that Troy (if indeed it ever bore that name before the legend named it) itself was only ever a royal citadel, home of a few dozen families and their retainers; it was a royal city on a little hill, sheltering a few hundred people with perhaps 1000 or so living around it. In its heyday, this tiny hill was still only the equivalent of a walled palace. Later it would become the acropolis of the classical city of New Ilium, situated in one corner of a small provincial town in the Roman Empire. It was never a great success, a boom town; its theatre was only built to accommodate 6000 spectators, and its population may perhaps be more accurately gauged by an inscription (third or second century BC?) which says that 3000 people had to be fed at one of the city's public feasts. That at least gives us some idea of the scale of the real city which existed on this site.

The numbers Troy I–IX are broken down into forty-seven subdivisions. These phases of human habitation one above the other were formed by the constant rebuilding which is still practised in Anatolia (in fact the arrival of modern furniture has proved so destructive that compacted earth floors are now relaid every couple of years), by human destruction (the usual fate of cities in the ancient Mediterranean world), by an earthquake, or simply by abandonment. The survivors or successors cleared up and rebuilt on top, levelling the debris, covering the refuse, the food and animal bones, the ashes or whatever with a fresh layer of earth, building new mudbrick walls, and starting again. In this way the hill of Hisarlik spread and grew, accumulating 50 feet of debris in places on the side of the hill. London, in comparison, in its 1900 years or so, has managed 20 feet of strata, in which modern archaeologists have been able to distinguish not only its general historical development but also the great events which have marked it – for instance the sack of London in AD 61 during Boudicca's revolt, the great fires of 764, 1077 and 1666, the Blitz in 1940, and so on.

A mound like Troy, then, is a paradigm of human history: end and beginning of new races and civilisations, witness to destructions and rebuildings, testimony to the sheer antlike resilience of humankind. This is 'civilisation' not in the terms of *The Last Supper* or *The Art of Fugue*, but in terms of mudbrick, bone pins, handmade pots: the long-term, slow ascent (if such it is) of Man.

Today the visitor can walk at one level over the great walls of the city contemporary with the Mycenaean Age in Greece, which was excavated by Dörpfeld in 1893–4 and whose violent end he took for the death of Homer's Troy. Across it lie walls and a theatre from Roman Ilium (Troy IX), the town which the Apostles knew. Up the street from the main gate you pass the footings of the shanties of Troy VIIa; you can still see signs of the fire which overwhelmed them and which Blegen thought marked the sack of Homer's Troy. From the top of the street you can walk over to the walls of Troy II (2500 BC) and stand at the ramp where in 1873 Schliemann found his controversial treasure, the 'Jewels of Helen', under a mass of fire debris: the fire which he thought was the sack of Troy. So in two or three minutes' walk you have gone from the time of the kings of Mycenae to the time of Jesus, to that of Alexander the Great, to the time when the Great Pyramid was built: different Troys and different sieges.

Standing in the tremendous trench which Schliemann drove through the north of the mound, steep-sided and desolate, with smashed ends of walls hanging out of what is left of the hill, it is difficult for the visitor to make the epic tale come alive in the mind's eye. Was this indeed the place of which the ancient poet sang? If so, it has been 'dug out by the mattock of Zeus', as Aeschylus says in the *Agamemnon*, consumed by a 'whirlwind of doom'; a city 'ground to dust'.

And yet Troy is a place whose memory will far outlive the last trace of its physical existence. On an unromantic reading of the evidence it was merely a small city in the Mediterranean, one of thousands of centres of human society which lived and died between the Stone Age and modern times: one city, but one which has come to stand for *all* cities. In western culture, in the languages and memory of what we call the Indo-European races, it is perhaps the most famous of all cities; and all because of one story, the story of its siege and destruction, the death of its heroes, including Hector, at the hands of Agamemnon, Achilles and the Achaian Greeks – all for the sake of Helen, 'the face that launched a thousand ships'. The tale is in the bedrock of western culture. From Homer to Virgil, Chaucer and Shakespeare, Berlioz, Yeats and the rest, it has become a metaphor. Trojan horses, Achilles' heels and Odysseys have become figures of speech in many languages; 'working like a Trojan' is still worthy of praise. From Xerxes and Alexander the Great to Mehmet the Turk it has been a political and racial exemplar, the root, as Herodotus believed, of 'the enmity between Europe and Asia'. It is a story so universal that it was used by French playwrights to evade censorship, while conveying their message, in Nazi-occupied Paris. Similarly, in exile in 1942, the Austrian novelist Hermann Broch would affirm that 'it was the fantasy of the Nazis to become the new Achaians, demolishing an old civilisation', comparing Hitler with Achilles. Inevitably the universality of the theme has lent itself to Hollywood epic movie-makers, in films like *Ulysses* and *Helen of Troy*; so too it has been amusingly satirised on television in the 'non-interventionism' of *Star Trek* (where Captain Kirk regretfully left the Trojans to their fate) and in the 'interventionism' of *Dr Who* (in which the good Doctor, who had no such scruples, was the one who gave the Greeks the idea of building the wooden horse!).

So: 'In Troy there lies the scene,' as Shakespeare said. The enduring fascination of that theme, the tale of Achilles, Hector, Helen and the rest, has led a stream of pilgrims to the Troad, the region of Troy, over three millennia; from Alexander the Great to Lord Byron they have stood and gawped on the site of the great deeds of the heroes. But did the Trojan War ever really happen? If so, where was Troy? Was it really on the site we call Troy today? Who were Homer's Achaians and Trojans, and why did they fight each other? Did Helen of Troy exist? And was there a real wooden horse? Also, *why* has the site been sought so assiduously for so long? Why the obsession with this story? And why did Schliemann, Dörpfeld and the rest come to the conclusions they did? (The search for Troy is inextricably bound up with the development of archaeology itself.) This book is aptly entitled a search, for I started it with no answers to any of these questions; indeed, if anything, I thought the whole story a myth, not a subject for serious historical inquiry. But I was convinced that the search itself was well worth undertaking, and that, if it would be a long road, as Constantine Cavafy says in his poem 'Ithaca', it would still be one 'full of adventure and instruction'. I hope some of the excitement of both comes over to the reader.

ONE

THE SEARCH FOR TROY

*Of the true and famous Troy there have been no traces for ages: not a
stone is left, to certify, where it stood. It was looked for to little purpose
as long back as the time of Strabo: and Lucan having mentioned, that
it had been in vain searched for in the time of Julius Caesar, concludes
his narrative with this melancholy observation upon the fate of this
celebrated city,* that its very ruins were annihilated.

ROBERT WOOD, *An Essay on the Original Genius and Writings of Homer* (1769)

HOMER'S STORY

FIRST, THE TALE. Homer of course is the starting point, with the
Iliad and the *Odyssey*. But it is as well to make clear at the start
that he was drawing on a vast cycle of stories which dealt with
the Trojan War. The *Iliad* in fact deals with only one episode
covering a few weeks in the tenth year of the war. In classical
times a great series of epics, now lost or in fragments, told those
parts of the story ignored by the earlier Homeric poems, and
some of these, like the epics known as the *Kypria* and the *Sack of
Ilios*, were evidently of great scope and power. They were
composed soon after Homer: if he lived in the late eighth
century BC (see Chapter 4) then his successors were probably
working around 700 BC or soon after, by which time writing
was becoming widespread in Greece. These successors to Homer
may have written down their epics, but it is clear from the
surviving fragments that they, like Homer, were drawing heavily
on a long oral tradition.

According to Greek tradition, Troy stood near the
Dardanelles. Of its general location in the story there has never
been any dispute. The topographical landmarks are all familiar
and easily placed: the Dardanelles themselves, the islands of
Imbros, Samothrace and little Tenedos, Mount Ida to the south-
east, the plain itself and the river Scamander which flowed down

through the foothills of Ida. It was an ancient city whose inhabitants were known as Teucrians or Dardanians (after legendary founders back in the mists of time) but also as Trojans or Ilians: the legends invent eponymous heroes, Tros and his uncle Ilus, to account for these two names but other accounts say with some probability that originally Troy and Ilios were two separate places (and indeed Homer's insistence on using the two names for Troy has never otherwise been satisfactorily explained). Ilus was the father of Laomedon, an important figure in the legends of Troy, for he it was who built the great walls of Troy mentioned in the tradition. In this he was helped by Apollo and Poseidon, but he tried to cheat the gods of their reward and this led to the first sack of Troy. It may be a surprise to learn of an earlier sack of Troy, but Greek legend is insistent on it. We need not go into the antecedents here – suffice it to say that Laomedon would not give up the immortal snow-white horses which were owed to Herakles (Hercules) who had helped Laomedon by destroying a sea monster sent by Poseidon. Herakles then recruited a small army in the Peloponnese – only six ships according to Homer – sailed to the Troad and attacked the city, breaching it at a place destined to be famous in the later siege, the weak spot in the western wall where the beautiful walls had not replaced the older circuit. In the sack Laomedon and his sons were killed; only the youngest, Podarces, survived, for he alone had maintained that Herakles should be given his rightful reward. Podarces was released and took a new name, Priam, meaning 'redeemed': a fateful name indeed. Herakles left Priam as a young king, and Troy was restored within the same walls.

Over a very long and successful reign, spanning three generations, Priam restored Troy to the height of its former power. He himself had fifty sons and twelve daughters; his eldest son was the great warrior Hector, the next Paris, whose other name was Alexandros – and Paris was to be the instrument of destiny in the events that followed.

For the ancients Troy was a real place, and in the Homeric epic there are a number of indications as to what the tradition thought it looked like in its heyday under Priam. Most of the descriptive epithets in Homer are stock phrases, and should not be taken too seriously, but some are at least worth remembering. Homer's Troy is 'well-walled'; it is a 'broad city', with 'lofty gates' and 'fine towers'; it has 'wide streets'. Some are applied only to Ilios, which is 'holy', 'sacred', 'steep', 'sheer', 'lovely', but 'very windy'. Like Troy it is 'well-built' but also has 'good horses' – indeed the people of Troy are several times called 'horse tamers' or 'having fine foals' (uniquely among all the people mentioned by Homer – perhaps tradition remembered that horse breeding was a characteristic of their people?). As for the layout of the town, Homer describes a great city with beautiful, strong walls, extensive enough to hold a large population. On the top of the acropolis was the palace of Priam with halls of state, a royal throne-room, fifty marble chambers for the king's sons, and royal halls for Hector and Paris; there was, says Homer, an agora where the people of the city met, a temple to Athena in the higher city, and a temple to Apollo in the citadel, the 'Pergamos' of Priam. The city seems to have had at least four gates, including the Scaean and the Dardanian gates, and at one was 'the great tower of Ilios'. Of course such descriptions cannot be taken too seriously – in some ways this is obviously a fairy-tale city, a place of the imagination, for it bears little relation to excavated towns of Homer's day – but for what it is worth, it seems reasonable to think that Homer was imagining a city far bigger than the later Aeolian colony of Ilion of his own day, 200 yards across; even the great eighth-century Ionian city of Smyrna was only 300 yards by 150. The Troy of Homer's mind's eye evidently had a sizeable acropolis and a lower walled town with a population of several thousands. This then was the great city of Troy which was the stage for the tale.

On the mainland of Greece in the time of Priam's old age the most powerful king was Agamemnon, whose residence was at Mycenae. At this time the inhabitants of Greece called themselves not Greeks or Hellenes, but Achaians, Danaans or Argives. Agamemnon's family, the Atreids, were from Lydia in western Turkey; they had married into the Perseid dynasty at Mycenae, and they controlled the Argolid with its chief fortresses at Tiryns and Midea. Their influence extended throughout southern Greece, particularly by advantageous dynastic marriages. Agamemnon himself had married Clytemnestra, daughter of Tyndareus of Sparta and sister to Helen, the most beautiful woman in the world. When Helen grew to woman-hood all the princes of Greece wanted her hand, but she went to Agamemnon's brother Menelaos, the richest and most eligible bachelor in Greece, who thus became king in Lakonia; so the two brothers from Mycenae now had a position of over-whelming power in southern Greece.

Why the Trojan War happened the legends and Homer do not agree, but a famous myth tells *how*. Eris – strife – had thrown down a golden apple 'for the fairest' at the wedding of Peleus and Thetis, and Zeus, king of the gods, could not bring himself to adjudicate in the ensuing dispute between his queen, Hera, Athena, goddess of wisdom, and Aphrodite, goddess of love. The goddesses were led to the Trojan Mount Ida where Priam's beautiful son Paris was to act as arbiter. Hera offered him the lord-ship of all Asia, and untold riches; Athena, victory in war and wisdom beyond any other man; Aphrodite promised the most beautiful woman in the world, Helen of Sparta, and of course men being men, and stories being stories, Paris gave the apple to her.

Homer does not deal with the judgement of Paris, theme of so much later art. His tale is simple and quite realistic. Paris goes on a visit to Sparta and is feasted by Menelaos in his richly adorned palace at Amyklai. On the tenth day of the celebrations, Menelaos has to leave for Crete to see Idomeneus, king of Knossos. As Aphrodite had promised, Helen immediately eloped with Paris. Their first night in each other's arms was spent on the little isle of Kranai near Githeon. Then they sailed for Troy. There are other versions of this tale which might be borne in mind. Some said that Paris carried off Helen by force, that the seizure was really a Trojan raid on Lakonia to seize treasure and women, and indeed Homer agrees that Helen left with palace treasures;

some say that other royal women and slaves were taken too, and that Paris plundered elsewhere in the Aegean before returning to Troy.

When the bad news was brought to Menelaos in Crete he hurried to Mycenae and begged his brother Agamemnon to lead an army to Troy to take revenge. This the king agreed to do, though he first sent off envoys to Troy demanding Helen's restitution, with compensation. When the envoys came back empty-handed, Menelaos and his ally, old King Nestor of Pylos, travelled over Greece, asking the independent kings of Greece to join them in the expedition. The Achaian–Greek army met at Aulis, a protected bay in the straits between Euboea and the mainland, 'where the tides come together' (as they still do). In the story the great heroes in the army were Achilles, Odysseus (Ulysses) and Ajax, but their kingdoms were insignificant: the biggest contingents were from the Peloponnese (Pylos, Sparta, Tiryns and Mycenae) and Crete (Knossos). In Homer's *Iliad* there is preserved an ancient and strange catalogue of 164 places in Greece which is said to be a list of those who sent troops to Troy. As Agamemnon was the strongest king in Greece the others acknowledged him as overlord.

At Aulis the army seer read the signs and prophesied that Troy would fall in the tenth year (that is, from this first assembly). The Greeks then set sail for Asia Minor and in error launched an attack on Teuthrania in Mysia, opposite Lesbos, devastating the land, which they had mistaken for Trojan territory. In a battle in the plain at the mouth of the Caïcus river they were driven back to their ships by Telephus, king of Mysia, and beaten into a 'shameful retreat': they retired to Greece. Tradition is uncertain over how long a time elapsed between this abortive attack and the second and famous assembly at Aulis, though some thought it was eight years; the legend does not insist on the Greeks actually spending ten years under the walls of Troy.

When the Greeks assembled again at Aulis they were windbound and unable to sail. Famine struck and still they waited. Aeschylus writes in the *Agamemnon* that 'the winds that blew from the Strymon bringing delay, hunger, evil harbourage, crazing men, rotting ships and cables ... were shredding into nothing the flower of Argos'. The army prophet Calchas then revealed that Agamemnon had offended Artemis and would never sail unless he sacrificed his most beautiful daughter to appease the goddess and change the wind. Although later tradition let her escape, early sources agree that Iphigenia (or Iphianassa as Homer calls her) was sacrificed by the generals.

So the wind veered and the fleet at last set sail. Their first landfall was in Lesbos, then Tenedos, which was visible from Troy and ruled by a dynasty related to the Trojans: here they plundered and ravaged. Now the Greeks beached their ships on the shore of Asia in a wide bay between two headlands, and here they made their camp, protecting the landward side with a wall of earth, timber and stones; here, according to Homer, they spent the years of war that followed. The Trojans also had allies, from several places in Asia Minor and Thrace, and the struggle swayed back and forth, with both sides using chariots but also fighting hand to hand on foot with bronze swords, shields and spears and wearing bronze body armour. Some elements of the story suggest that Troy was perhaps not the only objective for the Greeks; Achilles, for instance, led a great foray southwards, sacking several cities on the mainland and on the islands of Lesbos, Skyros and Tenedos. According to Homer, he brought back not only booty but 'women of skill'; some he gave to Agamemnon, but he kept the most beautiful for himself. Ajax too plundered in Teuthrania, taking women, cattle and treasure and seizing the king's daughter for his concubine.

In the tenth year of the war (the year in which it had been prophesied Troy would fall) the Greeks ceased raiding Asia Minor and attacked Troy in earnest, and the Trojans were reinforced by allies from south-west Anatolia. The Trojan hero Hector now fell in single combat with Achilles, the best Greek warrior (this incident alone is the subject of Homer's *Iliad*); this happened after the death of Achilles' friend Patroclus, in revenge for which Achilles sacrificed twelve noble Trojan captives over Hector's funeral pyre. The end was now near, though not an end to the sufferings of the Greeks, the 'pains thousandfold upon the Achaians, hurled in their multitudes to the house of Hades' of which Homer sang. After the death of the Trojan ally Memnon in battle at the Scaean gate, Paris dealt Achilles a fatal blow with a bowshot, striking him in the heel, the only place where he was vulnerable (hence we talk today of an 'Achilles' heel'). And so the greatest of all Greek heroes was burned and his ashes buried on a headland overlooking the Hellespont. Worse was to follow for the Greeks. Maddened by a dispute over his right to Achilles' arms, Ajax committed suicide with the silver-studded sword which had been given to him by Hector as a mark of respect. At this point Priam's son Paris – the cause of it all – was killed by Philoktetes, but the Trojans still refused to give Helen up. It was then that the plan was hatched to build a wooden horse to gain access to the city by stealth and trickery. The horse had a hollow belly in which armed men were hidden, among them Odysseus of Ithaca and Menelaos himself. The horse was to be left as a thank-offering to Athena, and the Greeks were to burn their camp and put to sea as if they had given up. Off Tenedos they would wait until a fire signal summoned them back.

At daybreak the Trojans found the horse and the ashes of the camp, and they pulled the horse into the city. That night, exhausted by feasting and revelry, the Trojans slept while the Greek fleet came in close to shore, waiting the signal. 'It was midnight,' says a fragment from the epic known as the *Little Iliad*, 'and full the moon was rising.' The heroes jumped down from the horse, killed the sentries and opened the gates. The Greeks poured through the streets, broke into the houses and slaughtered the Trojans wherever they found them, sparing none of the male sex. Up to the Pergamos they went, to the palace on top of the hill, and there Neoptolemus killed old Priam on the threshold of his royal house, Priam whose life spanned the four generations from the sack by Herakles, and who had witnessed the death of all his sons. Deiphobos, whom Helen had married after Paris' death, was cut down and mutilated. As for Helen herself, the object of the whole of the expedition, Arktinos of Miletus, author of the *Kypria*, told in his *Sack of Ilios* how Menelaos had determined to kill her, but he confronted her with her breasts bared in the chaos of the night, and, overwhelmed by her beauty, cast away his sword. The male children of all the Trojan heroes were slaughtered (Hector's little boy Astyanax was thrown from the walls), the women were enslaved and taken back to Greece, to be concubines in their conqueror's beds, or to card flax and draw water at the spring below the palace of Sparta.

After the massacre Agamemnon's army plundered and burned Troy, and razed its walls, 'the dying ashes spreading on the air the fat savour of wealth', as Aeschylus says. As a last act, Polyxena, the daughter of Priam, was sacrificed on the tomb of Achilles. The house of Priam was extinct. Having divided up the booty and allotted the women as chattels between the victorious chiefs, the Greeks left the Troad. The story of their various returns is told in many stories, especially the *Odyssey*. In fact their brutal victory and their lack of respect to the Trojan gods brought the victors only more suffering. They were split up by storms; our sources tell us of wanderings in the Aegean, Crete, Egypt and elsewhere; some, like Menelaos and Odysseus, took as long as ten years to find their way home; some, like the minor leader Mopsus, wandered into Anatolia and settled there; some took to piracy and attacked places in the Mediterranean; others, like Agamemnon himself, returned to political upheaval, palace coups and assassination. Agamemnon was murdered by his wife and a rival from another branch of his family; Philoktetes was expelled from Thessaly by rebels; only old Nestor died happy, a last link with the Golden Age, the heroic world shattered by the Trojan War. Greek tradition dates the collapse of the Age of Heroes to within a generation or two of the war (eighty years, thought the historian Thucydides), and tells of 'constant resettlements', party strife and large-scale migrations, of heroes like Diomedes, Philoktetes and Idomeneus finding new lands in Italy, Sicily and western Anatolia. Finally, into Greece came an influx of Greek-speaking peasantry from the north, the Dorians, and their coming marked the end of Agamemnon's world. At the end of the so-called Dark Age which followed, the poet Hesiod, farming in misery under Mount Helicon in Boeotia, looked back on the great struggles which had broken apart the heroic age, and destroyed 'that god-like race of hero-men' who lived between the Bronze Age and his own dismal Age of Iron: 'foul war and the dreadful din of battle destroyed them ... when war brought them over the great gulf of the sea to Troy for the sake of richly tressed Helen.'

The grip that this legend continued to have on the Greek imagination is shown by an extraordinary tailpiece. A lesser hero, Ajax of Lokris, was said to have defiled Athena's altar at Troy during the sack, and hence to have incurred her everlasting enmity. Belief in this story was so strong among the people of Lokris that from about 700 BC they sent each year, to serve the goddess in her temple at Troy, selected daughters who suffered indignities and even risked death in order to expiate the sin of their ancestor. Some, perhaps originally all, of the maidens stayed there until old age, cleaning the precinct, with shorn hair and bare feet, and as late as the fourth century BC the Trojans had the right – and exercised it – to kill those maidens they caught being secretly conducted to the sanctuary by their Lokrian guides. Those who got there lived out their days like slaves, in confinement and extreme poverty. This custom continued into the first century AD – an amazing testimony to the enduring potency of the legend in Hellenic society.

HISTORY OR FICTION? THE VIEW OF THE ANCIENTS

It is often said that the Greeks were the first people to deal with the events of the past in anything like a scientific manner, but it is clear that history has been far better preserved by the so-called barbarians than by the Greeks themselves.... Egyptians, Babylonians and Phoenicians by general admission have preserved the memorials of the most ancient and lasting traditions of mankind.

JOSEPHUS, *Antiquities of Judaea*

In the ancient world it was the almost uniform belief that the Trojan War was an historical event: the philosopher Anaxagoras was one of only a handful known to have doubted it, on the good grounds that there was no *proof*. But then, as now, everyone knew there was no primary source for the war; equally they *knew* that it had happened! It is a paradox unique in historiography. When the 'Father of History', Herodotus, who lived in the fifth century BC, asked Egyptian priests whether the Greek story of the war was true, he was simply asking whether they had any alternative record of it, for there were no *written* sources before the epics of Homer were committed to writing, perhaps as late as the sixth century BC, hence there were no documentary sources at all available to the historians of the fifth century BC. It is interesting to see then that those historians were prepared to give total credence to the basis of the tradition in Homer. Out of Homer Thucydides (*c.*400 BC) constructed a brilliant résumé of 'prehistoric' Greece which remains one of the most balanced and plausible accounts of how the war *might* have come about, though we cannot be certain how much is his own intuition from observable remains ('archaeological' sites) and deductions from the Homeric tale, or how much he derived from sources we do not now have – most experts would rule out this last possibility. At any rate, Thucydides thought the story of Troy was true and the 'imperial' power of Mycenae a reality:

We have no record of any action taken by Hellas as a whole before the Trojan War. Indeed, my view is that at this time the whole country was not even called Hellas.... The best evidence for this can be found in Homer, who, though he was born much later than the time of the Trojan War, nowhere uses the name 'Hellenic' for the whole force.

Thucydides then considers increased knowledge of seafaring in the Aegean, 'capital reserves' coming into existence, and the gradual construction of walled cities with acquired wealth and a more settled life. All these facts he saw as prerequisites for a united expedition such as Homer describes:

Some on the strength of their new riches built walls for their cities, the weaker put up with being governed by the stronger, and those who won superior power by acquiring capital resources brought the smaller cities under their control. Hellas had already developed some way along these lines when the expedition to Troy took place. Agamemnon it seems must have been the most powerful of the rulers of his day: this was why he was able to raise the force against Troy ... at that time he had the strongest navy; thus in my opinion fear played a greater part than loyalty in raising the expedition against Troy. Mycenae certainly was a small place, and many of the towns of that period do not seem to us today to be particularly imposing: yet that is not good evidence for rejecting what the poets and what *general tradition* have to say about the size of the expedition ... we have no right therefore to judge cities by their appearances rather than by their actual power and there is no reason why we should not believe that the Trojan expedition was the greatest that ever took place.

Thus wrote Thucydides in the fifth century BC, that is, at as long a remove from the traditional date of the sack of Troy (of which more in a moment) as the signing of Magna Carta is from the present day. The lack of anything beyond the words of the poets and 'general tradition' is noteworthy; it should be said, though, that nothing in this interpretation has been rebutted by modern archaeology or textual criticism. It still remains a *plausible* model, despite the fact that many scholars today doubt the existence of the Mycenaean 'empire', the Trojan War, and even Troy itself: plausible, but as yet incapable of proof.

How then did the ancients work out a chronology for their 'prehistoric' past? For instance, how did they date the Trojan War? In classical Greece detailed chronology went back to the first Olympiad in 776 BC. This date, we know, corresponds fairly closely to the adoption of the alphabet by the Greeks later in the eighth century, so, as we would expect, the adoption of a proper historical chronology came at about the time that written records start to exist. Hence George Grote's great *History of*

Greece, written as late as the 1840s and 1850s, begins with the first Olympiad; what lay before was for him unusable, for archaeology had not yet opened a window into prehistory. As Grote recognised, however, the ancient Greeks had a vast mass of legends, stories, genealogies and so on relating to this preclassical world and which they *thought* referred to real events just as much as Homer did: these were the 'general traditions' Thucydides mentions, and they had clearly been preserved orally. They often included detailed chronological relations – everyone for instance 'knew' that the sack of Thebes took place before the Trojan War, that the Trojan War preceded the Dorian invasion of Greece, and so on. Even from before Herodotus' time historians had tried to construct a chronology for this and rationalise it as history, difficult as that was. Later on, Diodorus Siculus says how troublesome it was to write an account of 'prehistory' because he could not find a reliable collection of dates for the period before the Trojan War. Thucydides too limited himself to the broad conjecture that, before the time of the dominance of Mycenae, Cretans from Knossos had exerted a hegemony over the Aegean. As for the date of the war itself, most calculations varied between around 1250 BC in Herodotus and 1135 BC in Ephorus; the earliest was 1334 BC in Doulis of Samos, the most influential the date arrived at by the librarian of Alexandria, Eratosthenes (1184–1183 BC). Such dates – expressed as 'so long before the First Olympiad' – were usually computed from genealogies, with estimates of the length of generations, especially of the old Dorian royal families of Sparta. A remarkable example of how accurate such records could be survives in a little country church in Chios, where a family memorial stone names fourteen generations which take us back from the fifth century BC to the tenth century BC: it is thus *possible*, at least, that such material can be accurately preserved over centuries.

The most precise ancient dating of the Trojan War is to be found on the Parian marble, a chronicle of notable events, imaginary or real, computed off the legendary genealogies of the kings of Athens coming down to the mid-third century BC.

Carved on a great slab of marble from the island of Páros, it was bought in Smyrna by an English ambassador of Charles I to the Ottoman court, who brought it to England where it became part of the Earl of Arundel's collection. The marble was damaged in the Civil War when the prehistoric portion was destroyed, but luckily it had been copied by the antiquarian John Selden; thus we know that it dated the origin of the cult at Eleusis to the early fourteenth century BC, the sack of Thebes to 1251, the foundation of Salamis in Cyprus to 1202, the first Greek settlements in Ionia to 1087, Homer's *floruit* as 907 – and the sack of Troy to 5 June 1209 BC! Unfortunately the intriguing precision of the month and day is an astronomical computation derived from a misunderstanding of a line in the *Little Iliad* – 'it was midnight and a bright moon was rising' – which was interpreted as meaning a full moon: the nearest one to midnight occurs on the last lunation before the summer solstice!

It will be immediately apparent from such material that the Jewish historian Josephus' remarks about Greek historiography, written in the first century AD and quoted on p. 31, were accurate: the classical Greeks had no good source for their prehistoric past. Oral tradition, especially in the shape of Homer, was all they had to rely on, because, as Josephus points out in his preface to the *Jewish War*, 'it was late, and with difficulty, that they came to the letters they now use.' In terms of 'archaeology' the Greeks also had little sense of the ancient past: 'as for the places they inhabit, ten thousand destructions have overtaken them and blotted out the memory of former deeds so that they were ever beginning a new way of living.' There were of course 'archaeological' digs in the ancient world; people were always finding remains, and knew the names of the cities which Homer says sent troops to Troy (remember Thucydides' remarks (p. 33) on the ruins of Mycenae in his day, which he had clearly visited). In such places many Mycenaean tombs were found in the seventh and eighth centuries BC, and were associated with Homer's heroic age, for offerings to the heroes were left in them, a practice which continued into classical times. But the way such finds were interpreted shows that the ancients had no concept of what we now call Bronze-Age history; oral transmission was their only vehicle. In one sense, then, the problem of the historicity of the Trojan War is no different today from what it was for Thucydides: Homer and the myths tell the story; the places they name were and are still visible, some clearly once powerful, some clearly utterly insignificant; similarly other myths centre on what were demonstrably Bronze-Age places – Nemea, Iolkos, Thebes and so on. If the myths of Greece actually contain a kernel of real history from the Bronze Age, as Thucydides believed, how do we prove it? In the last 100 years the new science of archaeology has attempted to provide answers. But before we turn to this attempt, we need to understand *why* the tale of Troy should have captured the imagination of our culture, for archaeology itself has not escaped that seduction. The story was clearly already the great national myth in Thucydides' Greece, but that was nothing compared to what has happened to it in the two and a half millennia which followed him. To the afterlife of the myth I now turn.

'PILGRIMS' IN THE ANCIENT WORLD

Such was the potency of the myth that a whole parade of conquerors felt drawn to stand and gaze on the plain where Achilles and Hector had fought it out. By then a small Greek colony had been founded on the overgrown ruins on Hisarlik. This was where tradition said the Trojan War had taken place, and in that belief the colonists of around 700 BC called it Ilion. When the Persian king Xerxes was poised to cross the Hellespont from Asia to Europe in 480 BC, Herodotus tells us:

He had a strong desire to see Troy. Accordingly he went up into the citadel [i.e. of the city of Ilion] and when he had seen what he wanted to see and heard the story of the place from the people there, he sacrificed a thousand oxen to the Trojan Athena and the Magi made libations of wine to the great men of old.

One hundred and fifty years later the crossing of the Dardanelles the other way, from Europe to Asia, was associated with the Trojan War in the suggestible mind of Alexander the Great. Alexander was intoxicated by the world of the gods and heroes, as they had been portrayed by his favourite poet Homer (he carried the *Iliad* with him and slept with it under his pillow). Leading his flotilla of ships to the Troad, Alexander sacrificed in mid-channel to Poseidon (so hostile to the Greeks in the Trojan War) and was the first to spring ashore on Trojan soil, throwing his spear into the ground to reinforce his claim that Asia was his, 'won by the spear' and 'given by the gods'. Then, going into the walls of Ilion itself, he dedicated his armour to the Trojan Athena and took from her shrine ancient arms and a shield which (so it was claimed) had been preserved from the Trojan War. Leaving Troy he laid a wreath at Achilles' tomb in the plain, as Arrian (*c.*AD 150) recounts, 'calling him a lucky man, in that he had Homer to proclaim his deeds and preserve his memory'.

Alexander's successors dignified little Ilion with a city wall, though it would never compete with a new city founded before 300 BC on the coast, Alexandria Troas. By Roman times the town, now known as Ilium, was semi-derelict. But once more, fired by the legend, a rich patron came along who believed in Homer's 'sacred Ilios'. Just as Alexander had claimed ancestry from the Greek hero Achilles, so Julius Caesar called the Trojan Aeneas his ancestor, and in 48 BC, according to Lucan in the *Pharsalia*, written in the first century AD, he visited the Sigeum promontory and the river Simois 'where so many heroes had died', and where now 'no stone is nameless': 'He walked around what had once been Troy, now only a name, and looked for traces of the great wall which the god Apollo had built. But he found the hill clothed with thorny scrub and decaying trees, whose aged roots were embedded in the foundations.' ('Be careful, lest you tread on Hector's ghost,' a local enjoined him.) But 'even the ruins had been destroyed'. Caesar's disappointment would be echoed by many searchers who came after him! Lucan uses the occasion to meditate on the immortality conferred by poets on egomaniac militarists: 'Yet Caesar need not have felt jealous of the heroes commemorated by Homer, because if Latin poetry has any future at all, this poem will be remembered as long as Homer's.' Posterity, thankfully, has not thought so highly of Lucan's poem as he did, but his account contains Caesar's interesting promise to rebuild Troy as the Roman capital, a story which Horace had told in his *Odes*: 'reroofing their ancestral home.'

The Roman love affair with Troy reached its consummation in the epic of the Roman state, Virgil's *Aeneid*, written in 30–19 BC, which enshrined the story of Roman descent from Aeneas and the Trojans. The affair was to experience a strange afterglow in the fourth century AD when Constantine the Great first tried to build his new capital of the Roman Empire on the Sigeum ridge at Troy before turning his attention to Constantinople. At a place still called Yenisehir ('New City') the gates were said to have been visible to seafarers approaching the Dardanelles over a century after Constantine's day, and parts of the walls were still seen by Elizabethan and eighteenth-century travellers. Today a walk along the ridge reveals not a trace remaining. The situation would have offered as much natural beauty as that of Constantinople, and been more convenient. But the reason why it was abandoned after the erection of great buildings is obvious: by then, the great bay which had been the reason for Troy's existence for over 3000 years had silted up and ceased to exist – Troy no longer had a harbour.

My last story of Troy from the classical period comes from a wonderfully vivid letter from the Emperor Julian, written before his reign in the winter of AD 354–5. As is well known, Julian worshipped the 'old gods', that is the pagan pantheon to which classical man had sacrificed since before Homer, and this despite the fact that his uncle Constantine had adopted Christianity as the official 'state' religion in the early years of the century. Julian entertained hopes that the hated 'Galilean' (as he called Jesus) would not in the end conquer – indeed Julian would try to do something practical about it when he became emperor.

That winter Julian's ship put into Alexandria Troas opposite Tenedos, and being an ardent Hellenist, not to say besotted with Homer, Julian took the opportunity to walk up to Troy, the city of Ilium Novum, though his friends gloomily predicted that he would find the shrine desecrated by the Christians, and the tomb of Achilles vandalised. First on the tour was the shrine to Hector, and there to his astonishment Julian found a fire still burning on the altar and the cult statue still glistening with offering-oil. 'What is this? Do the people of Ilium still give sacrifices?' he asked the Christian bishop, who replied: 'Are you surprised that they should show respect for their distinguished fellow citizen, just as we show ours for the martyrs?' They walked up to the temple of Athena and again Julian saw that offerings had been made; nor, he noticed, did the bishop make the sign of the cross as Christians did 'on their impious foreheads', or hiss between his teeth to ward off the evil spirits which were thought to inhabit such places. The tomb of Achilles, too, was intact. Julian soon realised that it was the bishop himself who was keeping the flame burning. The two men walked around the city and discoursed on its antiquities and ancient glories, swapping (one imagines) Homeric tags. When Julian returned to his ship that evening it was with a sense of deep relief and barely suppressed joy: the old world was, if momentarily, still intact, the memory maintained, the correct observances performed.

Of course the old world, the world which had invented the tale of Troy and the Homeric heroes, and which made them a precipitate of its own beliefs, was about to end, at least in terms of the classical tradition of education and culture (though not, perhaps, in those deeper structures of Mediterranean life which – as we shall see – changed imperceptibly only over centuries). The Roman Empire in the west was about to disintegrate, and its new breed of witnesses did not find any moral succour for such cataclysms in the works of Homer: *their* Bible was Christian. The young Augustine of Hippo, the future saint, born in the year of Julian's journey to Ilium, was taught the classics as part of his education in North Africa, but admits to being bored to distraction by Homer (in fact he never bothered to learn Greek): evidently Hellenism was on the way out in fourth-century Christian (North African) Thagaste. Augustine and his like would soon inherit the earth, or at least its western part. The Christian father Basil, an older contemporary of Augustine (he had briefly been a fellow student with Julian at Athens), made a point of denying that the Trojan War ever happened: what was it, after all, but a mere pagan tale? It was a sign of the times. There were of course still Homeric scholars in fifth-century Byzantium, but their Greek studies were directed to a new end: the Empress Eudoxia, wife of Theodosius II, for instance, wrote a *Life of Jesus* in Homeric verse!

Our last glimpse into the extraordinary hold which Homer maintained on the classical imagination for 1000 years is provided by a remarkable last testament of civilised Hellenism, the *Saturnalia* of Macrobius (early fifth century AD) which portrays literate and civilised Roman gentlemen, who still do know their Attic Greek, spending a dinner party making the most elaborate parallels between Homer's and Virgil's treatment of the story of Troy. To the very end the intelligentsia and political élite of the ancient world lived by Homer: Macrobius' diners clearly knew huge chunks off by heart.

But when the table had been cleared from that particular banquet, the early Middle Ages would be left more austere fare, a diet of Christian exegesis which usually rejected such stuff as Homer and called it devil's entertainment. In the orthodox east, Byzantium (as a Christian empire) was an enemy of Hellenism and equated Homer and the rest with paganism and polytheism. In the west knowledge of Greek nearly vanished altogether, and not until the nineteenth century did the kind of obsessive cultivation of Homer reappear of which Julian and Macrobius would have approved. But that, as it were, is another story: in the west the *story* of Troy, in whatever form it came, never ceased to be told.

THE TRANSMISSION OF THE TALE,
FROM SAXON STORIES AND TUDOR MYTHS
TO FIRST-WORLD-WAR POETS

Four hundred and thirty winters before Rome was founded [i.e. 1183 BC] it happened that Alexander son of Priam the king of the *burh* of Troy abducted Helen, the wife of king Menelaus of Lacedaemonia, a Greek city. Over her was fought that great and famous war between the Greeks and the Trojans. The Greeks had a thousand ships of what we call the big longship type, and they swore an oath to each other that they would never return to their native land until they had avenged their wrongs. And for ten years they besieged that town and fought around it. Who can say how many men were killed on either side, of which the bard Homer has told! There is no need for me to tell it, says Orosius, for it is a long story and in any case everybody knows it. Nevertheless whoever wishes to know it can read in his books what evils took place, and what victims by manslaughter, by hunger, by shipwreck and by various misdeeds, as is told in the stories. For full ten years the war was waged between these people. Think then on those times, and on our own, which are the best to live in!

An Anglo-Saxon account of the Trojan War, from a translation of Orosius made *c.*AD 895 in the circle of Alfred the Great

The story of Troy never lost its appeal in the millennium between the fall of Rome and the Renaissance. It fascinated the thegns of Alfred the Great around the firesides of Viking-Age Wessex, and with an added dash of love interest it was a hit in the courtly societies of twelfth-century Europe; indeed it was at this time that a most influential vernacular poetic version was made by Benoît de Sainte-Maure, an Anglo-Norman trouvère at the court of Henry II (*Roman de Troie, c.*1160). The tale translated well to the world of chivalry, of *vaillants chevaliers* and *bons vassaus*. It was, incidentally, Benoît's fickle Briseida (*trop est mes cuers muable et fel*) who provided Shakespeare with his model for 'false Cressid' through that landmark in English translation, Caxton's

41

Recuyell of the Historyes of Troye (*c.*1475), a prose version from Benoît via the French of Raoul le Fèvre. In framing his account Benoît in his turn had used the late Roman stories of Dares and Dictys, the former allegedly a translation of the *Iliad* story older than Homer, the latter supposed to have been unearthed at Knossos in Nero's time. It is one of the curiosities of historiography that during this period these two worthless pieces of fiction had pride of place as authorities for the Trojan War, which they were thought to have actually witnessed. This was especially pertinent as several western nations followed the Virgilian idea of tracing their ancestry back to Aeneas and those Trojans who were thought to have escaped the sack and emigrated to Italy and further west. Strangely enough, it was in Britain that the Trojan theme was particularly tenacious.

Back in the declining days of the late Roman Empire we first find evidence of the Troy tale being appropriated by the invading barbarians as a way of getting themselves more closely identified with the ancient and superior Roman culture they were to inherit. Not long before the fall of Rome the historian Ammianus Marcellinus tells us that fugitive Trojans had settled in Gaul (now France), and soon enough the story was made to serve political ends. In about AD 550 Cassiodorus' *History of the Goths* claimed Trojan descent for Theodoric, the Ostrogothic king of Italy. The Franks next appropriated the tale, inventing their mythical eponymous ancestor, Francus the Trojan. It was a good story, and from France it soon came to Britain. In Dark-Age Wales, as related by Nennius, it was told that the founder of Britain was one Brutus, who was descended from 'Ilius' who 'first founded Ilium, that is Troy'. This story was popularised by Geoffrey of Monmouth in his famous story of Brutus' founding of London as Troynovant, or New Troy. Though dismissed by the historian Polydore Vergil, this story was accepted by most Elizabethan poets as part of the Tudor myth, and it became a commonplace of Elizabethan thought. The Tudors, it was argued, were of Welsh or ancient British descent, and therefore, when they ascended the throne of England after the battle of Bosworth in 1485, so ran the myth, the ancient Trojan–British race of monarchs once more assumed imperial power and would usher in the Golden Age. Hence in Armada year Elizabeth could be greeted at Gray's Inn as 'that sweet remain of Priam's state: that hope of springing Troy', and in the famous painting of 1569 in Hampton Court she, not Athena, Aphrodite or Hera, receives the golden apple in the judgement of Paris! So when in *Henry V* Shakespeare's Pistol says to the Welshman Fluellen, 'Base Trojan, thou shalt die', he was assuming in his audience familiarity with an old story: one more curious reverberation of the tale of Troy!

The place of the tale of Troy in the Tudor myth perhaps helps account for the number of translations of the *Iliad* in sixteenth-century England, as the original text was increasingly studied in early manuscripts. Hall's version of ten books appeared in 1581, Chapman's famous rendering in 1598. But it is interesting that Caxton's *Recuyell* was still popular, running through five editions before 1600: it was used by Shakespeare as a source for *Troilus and Cressida* and was still in demand until Pope's time. Chapman's and Pope's works have always been regarded as the greatest English translations of Homer; Pope's in particular is still a classic ('a performance which no age or nation can pretend to equal,' said Samuel Johnson, though as the scholar Richard Bentley said, 'It is a pretty poem Mr Pope but you must not call it Homer').

But it was in the nineteenth century that Homer came into his own as a popular 'classic', the most influential of all the attempts being William Morris's *Odyssey* (1887), part Norse saga, part Tennyson, and Andrew Lang's strangely effective late Victorian *Iliad*, which was reprinted eighteen times between 1882 and 1914. It was in the minds of the ruling class that Homer was pre-eminent. Typically, on the Albert Memorial itself it is Homer who is enthroned in the place of honour among the great artists of the world at Albert's feet.

The unrivalled popularity of Homer in the late Victorian and Edwardian imagination perhaps reflects the role of the *Iliad* in the English public-school system. At the height of the British Empire Homer was perhaps the poet who spoke most feelingly to the British imperialists, for his 'gentlemanliness' and his 'stiff upper lip' in the face of death (not forgetting his emphasis on athletics and hardiness) as much as for his glorification of courage in war. Whether it was on the South African veld, in the trenches of Flanders or even in the skies above Picardy, Homer evoked the most powerful images in those brought up to see themselves as the new Athenians. During the First World War, Maurice Baring wrote of:

> Such fighting as blind Homer never sung,
> No Hector nor Achilles never knew;
> High in the empty blue.

But inevitably it was at Gallipoli that Homer most struck home, for Troy and Cape Helles face each other across the Dardanelles. There it was impossible for the young poets and writers of the British Empire – John Masefield, A. P. Herbert, Patrick Shaw-Stewart, Compton Mackenzie – not to think of the *Iliad*. For the young Frenchman Jean Giraudoux, too, seeing his friends die in the trenches at Suvla, himself badly wounded, the trauma gave terrible inspiration for his art (*The Trojan War will not take place*): 'Why against us?' says Hector. 'Troy is famous for her arts, her justice, her humanity.' Rupert Brooke died before he heard the guns, but as he sailed to his fate he promised to recite Homer through the Cyclades and 'the winds of history will follow us all the way'. Fragments scribbled on that last voyage show how Brooke imagined it:

> They say Achilles in the darkness stirred....
> And Priam and his fifty sons
> Wake all amazed, and hear the guns.
> And shake for Troy again.

Patrick Shaw-Stewart, who reread the *Iliad* on the way to Gallipoli, felt a dreadful sense of *déjà vu* at the sight of Imbros, of Troy and these 'association-saturated spots':

O hell of ships and cities
Hell of men like me,
Fatal second Helen,
Why must I follow thee?

Achilles came to Troyland
And I to Chersonese:
He turned from wrath to battle,
And I from three days' peace.

Was it so hard, Achilles,
So very hard to die?
Thou knowest and I know not –
So much the happier I.

I will go back this morning
From Imbros over the sea;
Stand in the trench, Achilles,
Flame-capped, and fight for me.

So for the young public-school chaps who sailed to Gallipoli – 'the youth whom to the spot their schoolboy feelings bear' as Byron had so keenly put it – associations of the place produced overwhelming nostalgia: the islands, the plain, the hill of 'holy Ilios'. Perhaps the experience of the war destroyed all that. After 1915 memories of a more terrible war took their place, of the *common* heroes who died, from 'wide-wayed Liverpool' and 'hundred-gated Leeds'. (Homer's world is predominantly aristocratic, it must be remembered.) And now, ninety years on, the intense identification of the English ruling class with the stern morality of Homer strikes us as oddly obsessional. In the proletarian world of the early twenty-first century, there is, however, no denying the spell still worked by the story over generations of Britons, Americans, Germans, Greeks and the rest, brought up on such ideas, and paradoxically this is especially true of the professional scholars and archaeologists who still interpret these ideas today for the general audience. Difficult as this makes objective discussion of the evidence, the myth (or legend) has become a fact; it is precisely its power as a myth which has excited belief in its historicity – the story moves us so much that it must be true. Many archaeologists, professed scientists, have nevertheless been able to encompass this within their scientific 'truth'!

I have tried briefly to summarise the history of Homer in English culture. It would take a whole book – and a long one – even to outline its effect in other languages and cultures, but to conclude let me mention one last version, a Gaelic one by John McHale, Primate of all Ireland in the mid-nineteenth century. This striking assimilation of the Trojan tale into the ancient heroic traditions of Celtic epic (Agamemnon is *ard-ri*, and the Achaians *Feanna*) reminds us that Homer's epics are the first great works of European literature, composed in a language whose roots are shared by the languages of the Celtic and Germanic peoples who moved westwards towards their present homes after the Indo-European peoples came into Europe in the early second millennium BC, at which time the Greeks moved southwards into the Balkans. Homer's texts are a dim reverberation of those events, written in a language which has a continuity going back to the second millennium BC. The Greek you hear today in the tavernas of Corfu or Crete was written in the Bronze Age in palaces like Mycenae and Knossos. No other European language can say that and none has written texts going back so far. In that sense Homer's epics constitute the root text of all western culture.

THE SEARCHERS

While the story of the Trojan War was cultivated so obsessively in medieval Europe, the general site of Troy itself was never forgotten. Many travellers' accounts survive from the Middle Ages and early modern times which show that the locality of the classical cities of New Ilium and Alexandria Troas was still pointed out as the site of Homer's city. Some Greeks on board the boat which bore the Anglo-Saxon pilgrim Saewulf from Chios to Constantinople, a generation or so after the Norman Conquest, pointed out the 'very ancient and famous city of Troy' on the coast near Tenedos where 'you can still see the ruins extended over many miles' (probably Alexandria Troas?). Others were interested enough to go ashore and try to piece together the events of the *Iliad* on the ground. A Spanish ambassador on his way to meet Tamerlane the Great in October 1403, Ruy Gonzales de Clavijo, saw the ruins and the plain extending as far as the foothills of Ida and commented that 'the circuit of Troy appeared to extend over many miles of country, and at one point above the ancient city rose a high steep hill on the summit of which, it is said, stood the castle known of old as Ilion'. At Kumkale on the Dardanelles, Clavijo wrote, 'the Greek camp was set. Here too they had dug great trenches to lie between them and Troy, to prevent the Trojans in their attack coming to destroy the Greek ships. These trenches are seen to be three in number and lie one behind the other.' Such stories came from Greeks in Tenedos, who even then acted as guides to the site, and from people in the still Greek-speaking villages of the Troad. In the journal of his adventures a more sceptical traveller, the Spaniard Pero Tafur, speaks of Greeks of Tenedos who could give account of Troy; having survived a shipwreck in Chios harbour at Christmas 1435 he was stuck for three weeks with nothing to do, so, obtaining a lift to the mainland, he hired a guide and horses and rode north to Troy. Tafur's trip (like that of many who came after) was disappointing:

So many ruined buildings, so many marbles and stones, that shore and the harbour of Tenedos over against it, and a great hill which seemed to have been made by the fall of some huge building. But I could learn nothing further and returned to Chios.

It is very likely that Tafur only saw the remains of Alexandria Troas.

Tafur's visit only just preceded one by the most remarkable of all early travellers and antiquarians, Cyriac of Ancona. Archetype of the peripatetic early Renaissance antiquary, and one of the most influential – perhaps more than anyone he deserves the title of the first archaeologist, though the word would not be coined for another 400 years.

In October 1444, having walked the Trojan plain, Cyriac set sail for Imbros and saw Samothrace peeping over the top just as Homer says. So the famous nineteenth-century travel writer Alexander Kinglake was not the first to note from personal observation (in *Eothen*) that Homer spoke truly: 'Aloft over Imbros – aloft in a far-away heaven – Samothrace, the watchtower of Neptune – so Homer had appointed it, and so it was.' Cyriac's note is scribbled into his copy of the works of the ancient geographer Strabo (now in Eton College Library). Coming from the region of Troy, from where the towering outline of Samothrace can be seen hovering in the distance, Cyriac recalled the passage in the *Iliad* where Poseidon watches the battle between Greeks and Trojans from the 'top of the highest summit of timbered Samothrace'. Homer had told the truth!

A former shipping clerk, glorified commercial traveller and unofficial political consultant, Cyriac wandered the eastern Mediterranean for fifty years, clambering over ruins, sketching monuments, copying inscriptions, haranguing the citizens of sleepy Mediterranean towns to save their 'half buried glories'. For Cyriac, the ruins of antiquity were living voices crying out for the torn fabric of that ancient world to be reknit, by both the 'sons of Greece' and the 'sons of Troy' – the Turks.

Cyriac's hopes for the 'sons of Greece and Troy' and the rebirth of the ancient world remind us how peculiarly the story of archaeology in Greece is bound up with the rebirth of Hellenism and the idea of Greek nationhood. The Byzantines who ruled the Eastern Roman Empire until the fall of Constantinople did not call themselves Hellenes, the word Greeks use today to describe themselves (as did Thucydides). They were 'Roman', and moreover throughout their history as a Christian empire they were generally hostile to what became known as Hellenism – the philosophical, moral and religious conceptions of ancient Greece. To them it was pagan and polytheistic: in the eleventh century, Michael Psellus relates,

Greek monks habitually crossed themselves at Plato's name, that 'Hellenic Satan'.

The Hellenising movement came to a head in the first half of the fifteenth century in the years immediately preceding the fall of Constantinople. The idea now emerged that the inhabitants of the Peloponnese and the adjacent mainland and islands were the direct descendants of the ancient Greeks, and should re-establish the national state in the lands once occupied by the Hellenes of old. This was the climate in which men like Cyriac of Ancona made their pioneering attempts to gather and record the archaeological evidence for Hellenistic civilisation, and in this the Trojan War had special significance for, as Thucydides had said, it was the first recorded action by a *united* Hellenic power. But in 1453 Constantinople fell to the Turks under Mehmet II and Greece soon followed – Athens in 1456, the Morea in 1460. The dream – for the moment – was dissipated.

There is an ironic tailpiece to Cyriac's mystical mingling of ancient and modern, his desire somehow to make the Trojan tale serve contemporary political ends. In 1462 his friend Mehmet II visited the site of 'Troy'. The scene is described by the Greek Critoboulos of Imbros who, like many Greeks, favoured Mehmet out of hatred of 'the Latins', the Catholic Church. Mehmet walked the circuit of the city,

inspected its ruins, saw its topographical advantages, and its favourable position close to the sea and the opposite continent. Then he asked to be shown the tombs of the heroes Achilles, Hector and Ajax, and like other great conquerors before him he made offerings at the tomb of Achilles, congratulated him on his fame and his great deeds, and on having found the poet Homer (whom Cyriac had read to Mehmet) to celebrate them. Then, it is said, he pronounced these words: 'It is to me that Allah has given to avenge this city and its people: I have overcome their enemies, ravaged their cities and made a Mysian prey of *their* riches. Indeed it was the Greeks who before devastated this city, and it is their descendants who after so many years have paid me the debt which their boundless pride [*hubris*] had contracted – and often afterwards – towards us, the peoples of Asia.'

So in sacking Constantinople Mehmet had avenged the Fall of Troy! It was a pilgrimage which re-enacted other pilgrimages by world conquerors at great moments of confrontation; it is clearly modelled on that of Alexander. The wheel had come full circle: even if Mehmet never said those words, one feels he ought to have!

In the fifteenth and sixteenth centuries the Turkish and Christian worlds were opposed, and travel was dangerous and difficult. But from the late sixteenth century a change is noticeable, with new commercial relations developing between east and west. At this time the visits of a number of western visitors, starting with the naturalist Pierre Belon (who mistook Alexandria Troas for Troy), rekindled interest in Troy, aided by the spread of printing which enabled the dissemination of Homer in translation for the first time, and also of the accounts of the travellers themselves. From the 1580s, indeed, there is a continuous record of western visitors to Troy, the bulk of them English.

When William Shakespeare sat in London in 1602 writing *Troilus and Cressida*, and imagined the 'Dardan plains' and the 'strong immures' of Troy, 'Priam's six-gated city', he was not reflecting topographical knowledge about Troy and its environs; merely using the book on his desk, Caxton's *Recuyell*. But it was in his lifetime that English travellers first made their mark in the search for Troy on the ground. From the sixteenth century English and French merchants replaced Venetians and Genoese in the courts of Ottoman Turkey, and the first commercial treaty and diplomatic exchanges between England and Turkey were established in 1580. Elizabeth's ambassador, John Sanderson, twice 'put into Troy', in 1584 and 1591, and Richard Wragg, taking the queen's second present, saw the two big mounds on Cape Yenisehir in 1594: 'not unlikely the tombs of Achilles and Ajax,' he thought. Others followed: Thomas Dallam, the organ-builder, taking an elaborate hydraulic organ to the Sultan, put into the same place and saw ruins which he took to be Troy (probably the foundations of Constantine's abortive city on the

Sigeum ridge); and in the winter of 1609–10 William Lithgow was shown round a ruined site in the Troad by a Greek guide. Some, like William Biddulph in 1600 and Thomas Coryate in 1603, published their accounts, the latter being the first detailed modern description of the plain. Most of these early visitors, however, were misled into thinking that Alexandria Troas, or the Sigeum ruins, were the site of Homeric Troy, though even in the early seventeenth century, as George Sandys said, the problem of the location of Ilium, the 'glory of Asia', had 'afforded to rarest wits so plentiful an argument'. Sandys, in 1627, was the first to identify the rivers Scamander and Simois with the Menderes and Dumrek Su. By this time it is clear that little trace remained of the site of New Ilium, for it was ignored by all early travellers.

It was not until the eighteenth century that the first scholarly attempts were made to pin down the exact location of the city of Homer and the events of the *Iliad*. On two visits in 1742 and 1750, at a time when travel in bandit-ridden Asia Minor was still a dangerous business, Robert Wood laid the foundations for the modern topographical study of the Trojan problem. Wood has claims to be considered the first 'pilgrim' to Greece. His book *Essay … on the original genius of Homer*, published in 1769, came to no conclusion about the exact site of the city (he thought it had been utterly obliterated) but made some excellent deductions about the topography of the plain which he thought very different from Homer's day. Wood reckoned that 'a great part' of the plain had been formed of river silt since antiquity (he compared it with the mouth of the river Maeander at Miletus, formerly a great port which is now high and dry), that there had been a wide bay in front of Troy at the time of the war, 'some miles' nearer the city than at present, and that the courses of the rivers had moved considerably over the intervening centuries. These conclusions were abandoned by most other scholars right up to the present, but we now know they were correct (see p. 160; another important assertion of Wood's was that Homer's account had not been composed in writing, but 'sung and retained by memory'). Wood's basic premise, that the location of

51

Troy and the historicity of the Trojan War could be determined by patient field research, set the tone for future treatment of the theme, and his book marks the start of a famous controversy which shows no sign of abating: it went through five editions and was translated into four languages.

It was with Wood's book in his hand – along with the *Iliad*, of course – that the Frenchman Jean Baptiste Lechevalier went to the Troad in 1785, and with him modern topographical exploration of the Troad began. Over three visits he walked the whole area from Ida to the Dardanelles and rapidly became convinced that the Troad exactly accorded with the description in Homer. The city itself, Lechevalier thought, had lain not near the sea, but up the valley of the river Scamander (Menderes) at a place called Bunarbashi where there was a prominent, acropolis-like hill above a well-known local landmark, the 'Forty Eyes' springs, which Lechevalier identified with Homer's hot and cold springs at Troy.

Exiled by the French Revolution, Lechevalier first announced his theory in a lecture in French to the Royal Society of Edinburgh in February 1791, and it was published there in English the same year with a preface testifying to the 'vivacity of his conversation and the agreeableness of his manners'. In the light of his researches, Lechevalier also gave his opinion on the vexed question of the historicity of the Trojan War: it was, he thought,

not poetical fiction but historical fact. ... For the space of ten years the Greeks were employed in laying waste the coast of Asia, together with adjacent islands. The capital of the Trojan territory was not always the immediate subject of their disputes ... they do not appear to have attacked it in full force till the tenth year of the war. Whether it was really taken or ... baffled all the efforts of the Greeks I cannot take it upon me to decide.

Now the controversy really took off, with some, like Jacob Bryant, not only denying that the war had taken place but vehemently asserting that Troy itself had never existed. Armchair critics fired off scholarly brickbats, arguing hotly over the minutest problem of

52

the disposition of the Greek ships (or even the likely number of babies born to the camp whores over ten years!).

It was in the midst of this famous and heated dispute that Lord Byron spent seventeen days at anchor off the Troad in 1810 and walked the plain, which he found 'a fine field for conjecture and snipe hunting'. The romantic associations of the place, however, were too much even for Byron and he roundly dismissed the 'unbelievers' for their pedantry. Later, in *Don Juan*, he would make fun of Bryant and his supporters and wax eloquent on both the intense sense of the past he had felt there, and on its irretrievable distance from him:

> High barrows without marble or a name,
> A vast, untilled and mountain-skirted plain,
> And Ida in the distance, still the same,
> And old Scamander (if 'tis he) remain:
> The situation seems still formed for fame –
> A hundred thousand men might fight again
> With ease; but where I sought for Ilion's walls,
> The quiet sheep feeds, and the tortoise crawls.
>
> Canto IV, 77

'It is one thing to read the *Iliad* with Mount Ida above you,' he wrote (with a touch of smugness – he actually spent more time on the plain than most scholars before or since!), 'another to trim your taper over it in a snug library – this I *know*.' Byron's parting shot in *Don Juan* takes on the religious fervour of a true Homerist:

> ... I've stood upon Achilles' tomb,
> And heard Troy doubted; time will doubt of Rome.

Years after his visit to the Troad, and not long before he died fighting for that same romantic Hellenism, Byron returned to the great theme in 1821, in his diary: 'We *do* care about the authenticity of the tale of Troy ... I venerate the grand original as *the truth of history* ... and of place; otherwise it would have given me no delight.' Byron's remark is, characteristically, central to the whole search: why *should* it matter to us whether Troy really existed?

FRANK CALVERT: DISCOVERER OF TROY?

It mattered to someone else: Frank Calvert, who has claims to be regarded as the discoverer of Troy. In fact the Troy mystery was something of a family fascination. The Calvert family were English, but had been in the Troad since Byron's day and did not leave until the onset of the Second World War (they are still remembered in those parts). Three Calvert brothers are con- cerned with the story of Troy: Frederick was British consul in the Dardanelles in 1846–62 (he appears in Russell's *Despatches from the Crimea*), while James was American consul, a job he handed on to Frank who lived at Erenköy (Intepe). The family wheeler-dealed in commerce and local business in a rather seigneurial way, but they were continually helpful to outsiders, giving advice, medicine and loans to travellers. Frank's work as American consul has left only a handful of records, but he went out of his way to help people. All the brothers were interested in antiquities, and all were intrigued by the Trojan question. Frederick (who conceived the plan of forming a museum of the Troad) thought Homer's Troy was about 5 miles up the Scamander valley from the site of New Ilium, at a place called Akça Köy, where until 1939 the family had a farm, and later he discussed this with Schliemann. James Calvert, too, offered Schliemann his theories on Troy. But Frank was the moving force; he knew the Troad better than anyone, before or since; he identified many of the ancient sites there, reported on them laconically in learned journals, and formed a collection the bulk of which is in the new museum at Çanakkale. Frank had explored from an early age. Schliemann mentions that Frank pointed out a site to the British cartographer Spratt in 1839, when young Calvert was in his teens; one wonders whether Schliemann, who turned his own life into an inextricable tangle of fantasy and truth, appropriated Frank's childhood fascination with the Troy story? (See p. 59)

In the 1850s Frank had supported the theory that Troy had been at Bunarbashi, but a series of unpublished letters in the British Museum show that before 1864 he had turned to Hisarlik, the site of Ilion and the acropolis of New Ilium. Others had thought the same. Frank was aware, for example, of *A Dissertation on the Topography of the Plain of Troy* by Charles Maclaren (founder of *The Scotsman* and prophet of the railways) which argued that Troy must lie at New Ilium, but Maclaren had written from his desk in Edinburgh without seeing the plain, and his theory went unnoticed for many years. Maclaren deserves first credit for the identification, and it may be that he met the Calverts on his first visit there in 1847.

Another of the visitors to the Calverts' farm was Charles Newton, who later became one of the British Museum's greatest keepers. Newton was seconded to the consular service for the furtherance of the Museum's interests in Asia Minor, and came to the Troad in 1853, where he consulted Calvert over local sites. At this time Calvert took him to Bunarbashi which they rejected as Troy on the grounds that there were no surface potsherds such as littered the surface at Mycenae and Tiryns. At Hisarlik, however, Calvert showed Newton that extensive ruins lay hidden under the soil. Calvert and Newton corresponded fairly regularly after this ('I have been following up the ancient geography of the Troad and identified many sites,' Calvert wrote in 1863). By 1863, supported by Newton, Calvert had formulated plans to excavate New Ilium for the British Museum, and Newton recommended that £100 should be sent to Calvert for preliminary work. The Museum committee, however, dithered and asked for more information. Calvert was disappointed: 'I am anxiously waiting to learn the result,' he wrote to Newton. 'I will be sorry if my proposal be not fortunately received, for such another favourable opportunity of carrying on excavations at Ilium Novum could be found only with difficulty.' In fact so anxious was Calvert that, on hearing Newton was on a French boat in the Dardanelles on the night of 11 December 1863, he rowed out and climbed aboard, only to be rebuffed by an unhelpful captain who did not wish to wake his passengers.

Thus I was prevented from having the pleasure of a talk with you on archaeological subjects and discuss my proposals to the British Museum for excavating at Ilium Novum. You would much oblige me by letting me know the decision of the British Museum on this subject of excavations so as to enable me to make my plans accordingly.

Believe me dear Sir very truly yours

Frank Calvert

And so the chance passed. Meanwhile German excavations at Bunarbashi in 1864 confirmed Calvert and Newton in their belief that Homer's Troy had not been there. Calvert now bought the northern part of Hisarlik, and in the following year, 1865, conducted trial excavations in four places. On the north his trenches located the remains of the classical temple of Athena and the Hellenistic city wall erected by Lysimachus, one of Alexander the Great's generals; he came within yards of the great north-eastern bastion of what we now call Troy VI, and on the south, part of the city wall, which he probably thought classical. It is also certain that he exposed Bronze-Age levels on the north, immediately below the Athena temple, though the classical builders had cut away the walls of the ancient cities below them except for the massive underpinnings of the prehistoric walls, which were not recognised for what they were until the 1930s. Still, the dig had been a notable success. Calvert had seen enough to know that the mound was deeply stratified and that an excavation on the scale necessary to do it carefully would require the kind of money he did not possess. Nevertheless Calvert felt sure that Hisarlik was the site of the epic story and that an archaeological dig could 'settle the ground question "*ubi Troja fuit*".... All the ancient authors (subsequent to Homer) place the site of Troy at Ilium Novum until Strabo's time,' he wrote in 1868. It was left to another to gain the glory: Heinrich Schliemann.

TWO
HEINRICH SCHLIEMANN

Imagination is a very important qualification for an archaeologist
to possess … but in proportion to the strength of this power,
a counterpoise of judgement is necessary, otherwise the imagination
gets loose and runs riot. Dr Schliemann is, undoubtedly, an able man;
but he must be credited with a vast amount of this sort of unbalanced
imagination in order to explain the creations which he has produced
out of the explorations of Hisarlik.

WILLIAM BORLASE, *Fraser's Review* (1878)

IN THE SUMMER of 1868, at five in the morning on 14 August, to
be precise, an unlikely-looking visitor picked his way on horseback through the sandy riverbed and marshy thickets of the
Menderes river in the north-west corner of Turkey, by the
Dardanelles. He was a little man with a round, bullet-like head
(as a friend described him), very little hair and a reddish face with
spectacles; 'round-headed, round-faced, round-hatted, great-
round-goggle eyes', as another said. At 10 a.m. he came to an
extensive rubble-strewn plateau, the site of the classical city of
New Ilium. He walked its 1½-mile circumference, noting the
traces of its circuit wall. Finally he ascended a smaller hill, called
Hisarlik, 'place of the fort', in the north-western corner, about 100
feet above the plain, 30 feet above the spur of the plateau; there he
inspected an excavation made earlier by its owner, who had laid
bare part of the podium of a temple. The site, he later wrote,

fully agrees with the description Homer gives of Ilium and I will
add that, as soon as one sets foot on the Trojan plain, the view of
the beautiful hill of Hisarlik grips one with astonishment. That hill
seems destined by nature to carry a great city … there is no other
place in the whole region to compare with it.

As the afternoon sun started to sink over the Dardanelles he headed for the coast to find lodgings for the night, trudging his way on foot through the marshy flats along the lower river.

On leaving Hisarlik I moved on to the town of Yenitsheri at Cape Sigeum … here one can take in a splendid panorama of the entire Trojan plain. When, with the *Iliad* in hand, I sat on the roof of a house and looked around me, I imagined seeing below me the fleet, camp and assemblies of the Greeks; Troy and its Pergamus fortress on the plateau of Hisarlik; troops marching to and fro and battling each other in the lowland between city and camp. For two hours the main events of the *Iliad* passed before my eyes until darkness and violent hunger forced me to leave the roof.… I had become fully convinced that it was here that ancient Troy had stood.

This account, which we now know is largely a fiction, was written in Paris that autumn. It marks the start of the most amazing story in archaeology.

A BIOGRAPHICAL PROBLEM

It is often said that we know so much about Troy today because of one man's obsession, indeed of his childhood dream which he made come true. However, this is only so if we can believe his personal account of his early life. Schliemann's is the most romantic story in archaeology and should be read in his own words in his great books *Ilios, Mycenae, Tiryns*, but it should be read with a large pinch of salt, for with Schliemann, as with the story of Troy, it is not always possible to distinguish myth from reality. The material about his life is copious, for like many geniuses Schliemann was a compulsive hoarder of all the out-pourings of his life. There are eleven books, the so-called autobiography, eighteen travel diaries, 20,000 papers, 60,000 letters, business records, postcards, telegrams and all sorts of other ephemera; and there are also 175 volumes of excavation note-books, though forty-six more are missing, including important ones from Troy, Orchomenos and Tiryns (three lost albums of plans, drawings and photographs from Mycenae came into the hands of an Athens bookseller some years ago). Add to all this the vast amount of parallel material in the work of scholars who knew him, collaborated with him or argued with him, the newspaper files, the inevitable new finds (like the five letters found in 1982 in Belfast, of all places) and you have an idea of the size of the task involved in trying to disentangle fact from fiction in Schliemann's life. It is a task beyond the scope of one lifetime, for Schliemann was a man of colossal energy, addicted to words and ideas, a correspondent in a dozen languages. Many books have been written about him since he began his dig at Troy–Hisarlik, but as yet there is no reliable biography; it is the main gap in our imperfect knowledge of Troy, and clearly now it will take a prodigious effort to reconstitute his finds. So the reader who is fascinated by the remarkable story of one of the most extraordinary people of the nineteenth century – a genius, let no one be in any doubt over that – needs to be wary of accepting the myth Schliemann put forward about himself, and which the world swallowed so willingly, for, as he himself admitted, 'my biggest fault, being a braggart and a bluffer … yielded countless advantages.' Addicted to hyperbole, braggadocio, and often downright lies, Schliemann presents us with the curious paradox of being at once the 'father of archaeology' and a teller of tall stories.

We cannot, for instance, even be sure of the truth of his famous tale about his childhood, which is accepted unquestioningly even by his critics. At the age of eight, he recounts in *Ilios*, published in 1880, he received from his father a Christmas present of Jerrer's *Universal History* which contained the story of Troy with an engraving of Aeneas escaping from the burning towers of Troy.

'Father, Jerrer must have seen Troy,' [Schliemann *says* he said] 'otherwise he could not have represented it here.'

'My son,' he replied, 'that is merely a fanciful picture' …

'Father!' retorted I, 'if such walls once existed they cannot have been completely destroyed: vast ruins of them must still remain, but hidden away beneath the dust of ages' ...

In the end we both agreed that I should one day excavate Troy.

This story first appears in a less developed form, and with differences of fact, in *Ithaque, le Péloponnèse et Troie*, written in 1868 when Schliemann was forty-six: this is the first mention in *any* source of what Schliemann claimed had been a lifelong obsession, namely to uncover the ruins of Troy and prove the truth of Homer's story. But is it true? In December 1868 he wrote a letter to his eighty-eight-year-old father regarding the new book:

In the foreword I have given my biography, I have said that when I was ten ... I heard the tale of the Trojan War from you ... I have said that you were the cause of this [i.e. the thirty-six-year obsession] because you often told me of the Homeric heroes, and because that first impression received by me as a child lasted throughout my life.

The sceptic might infer that this was the first old Schliemann had heard of it, and indeed a cool look at his son's correspondence suggests that the story of Schliemann's obsession is indeed an invention. After a childhood in Mecklenburg Schliemann became a wealthy businessman in St Petersburg and the United States. He was often involved in unscrupulous dealings – for instance he cornered the saltpetre market for gunpowder in the Crimean War, bought gold off prospectors in the California gold-rush, and dealt in cotton during the American Civil War – at least, that was his story. In the late 1850s he seems to have wanted to break away from his business career into more intellectual pursuits in order to gain respectability. His first hopes were to become a landed proprietor, devoting himself to agriculture. When this failed, he wanted to turn to some sort of activity in a scientific field, perhaps philology, but was soon discouraged: 'It is too late for me to turn to a scientific career,' he wrote.... 'I have been working too long as a merchant to hope I can still achieve something in the scientific field.' (*Letters*, I, nos 62 and 67,

1858–9.) Like many European people in the nineteenth century he knew Homer and loved his tale, but it was probably only his visit to Greece and Troy in the summer of 1868 – and his meeting with Frank Calvert – which gave Schliemann the inspiration to turn to archaeology, and the idea of discovering Homer's Troy by excavation.

This kind of textual criticism has revealed other discrepancies about incidents in Schliemann's career; for instance his story of the San Francisco fire (which he says he witnessed), his alleged meeting with President Fillmore, and now even the find of the so-called 'Jewels of Helen' at Troy, which Schliemann has been accused of forging or buying on the black market and planting on site. These doubts have now reached such fever pitch that a request was submitted in 1983 to the National Museum in Athens to test the gold of one of the masks Schliemann found at Mycenae, implicitly suggesting that he faked part of the Mycenae treasures too. It must be said that such allegations are not new: in his own lifetime he was accused of 'fixing' his evidence, and some who met him were suspicious. The poet Matthew Arnold thought him 'devious' and Gobineau, a French diplomat, called him a 'charlatan'. Ernst Curtius, the excavator of Olympia, thought him 'a swindler'. However, these criticisms do not tell the whole truth, as, for example, in the case of the 'Jewels of Helen', whose find circumstances can be plausibly established. But there are still some serious discrepancies which make a proper biography all the more desirable. For instance, one question bearing on the archaeology is the disturbing revelation by his contemporary William Borlase that Sophie Schliemann was not present, as her husband alleged, at the discovery of the 'Treasure of Priam'. She was not even in Turkey! If Schliemann could lie (or fantasise) about this – he said he did it 'to encourage her interest in archaeology by including her' – could he have lied about the finds themselves? We know enough about him to say that he could indeed be unscrupulous; he cheated and lied to get his way; he was surreptitious and conniving; he sometimes dug in secret and purloined material; he smuggled his Trojan treasures abroad rather than give them to the

Turks; he desperately craved acceptance by the academic world as a serious scholar and archaeologist, and yet, we now know, he lied about something as trivial as the provenance of some inscriptions he had bought in Athens. All this is admitted – and may be thought damning enough. But set against this are the record of the finds in the books and journals and the brilliant letters to *The Times*, and of course the amazing finds themselves in the Mycenaean room in Athens Museum. Wayward, naïve, enthusiastic, unashamedly romantic, easy to hurt and anxious to learn, Schliemann is a bundle of contradictions; but judgement on him should be made on the basis of his finds. It was his luck – or skill – to achieve the greatest archaeological discoveries ever made by one person. But before we turn to the tale of Schliemann's incredible finds there is one more question we must ask: why did he turn to archaeology in particular, rather than, say, philology? The story of the search for Troy is inextricably bound up with the beginnings of archaeology as a science.

ARCHAEOLOGY: THE BEGINNINGS OF A NEW SCIENCE

In Schliemann's time the very word 'archaeology' had only recently begun to be used in its present meaning. It would need a whole book to sketch the intellectual background of mid-nineteenth-century prehistoric scholarship. Without a definitive biography of Schliemann we remain uncertain as to how much contemporary scholarship he had imbibed. For instance, what was he reading in Paris when he was a 'mature student' there in the late 1860s? Certainly in the following twenty years he shows an astonishing breadth of reading, especially in archaeological and antiquarian studies, but also ranging far and wide in linguistics and comparative ethnology. He also made it his business to visit all the major museum collections for the purpose of comparison with the often perplexing finds at Troy. If his thought lacked true scholarly discipline ('industrious but not clear-thinking,' said his schoolmaster) and if his theories were often far-fetched, he was usually thinking in the right direction. His ideas became clearer as his career progressed because he enlisted the help of specialists – Virchow, Sayce, Müller, Dörpfeld and so on, many of them the most distinguished scholars in their own field. Today it is customary to deride Schliemann's archaeological technique as well as his character, but it is worth remembering that, in terms of the general study of the past, the period of Schliemann's adult life, 1850–90, was perhaps the most revolutionary in the history of science. In 1859, the year of Schliemann's first visit to Athens and the islands (a brief account of his travels appears in *The Times* of 27 May that year), Charles Darwin published *The Origin of Species* and created an entirely new climate for the study of man, history and the development of civilisation. (Interestingly enough, one of the first scholars to praise Darwin's work in public was the English antiquary John Evans, father of the excavator of Knossos – Schliemann, incidentally, would come to know them both.) At this stage the very idea of prehistory had barely entered into the language of science. The word itself only came into common currency in Europe with Daniel Wilson's *Prehistoric Annals* (1851) and John Lubbock's *Prehistoric Times*, published in 1865: it was Lubbock who coined the words Paleolithic and Neolithic to describe phases in prehistory. Lubbock visited Schliemann at Troy in 1873 and Schliemann used his book when writing *Ilios*, of 1880. Lubbock's crowning work, *The Origin of Civilisation* (a title intended to echo Darwin), came out in 1870, six years before Schliemann's dig at Mycenae would alter forever our perceptions about the origins of European, and especially Aegean, civilisation.

At the time of Schliemann's maturity, before he dug Troy, most western intellectuals viewed 'civilisation' as meaning their own culture: a Christian, western, capitalist, bourgeois, imperialist democracy. Their texts were the classical writers and the Bible, and empires such as the British and German were seen as the logical culmination of ancient culture, whose traditional components were Rome (for its government and law), Israel (for religion and morals) and Greece (for intellectual, artistic and democratic ideals). This was 'civilisation', and hence 'history' was simply a matter of the Greek, Roman and Hebrew ideas shaping the western tradition. But from the middle of the century archaeology started to reveal the riches of civilisations far more ancient – Egyptian, Assyrian, Babylonian and Sumerian – which, when their languages were deciphered, turned out to have had an incalculable influence on the development of the 'younger' civilisations of the Mediterranean. In the century that followed *The Origin of Species* we became almost blasé about our state of knowledge: the discovery of the Mesopotamians, Egyptians, Hittites and Minoans were all important steps forward, to be followed by the non-western civilisations of India, China and pre-Columbian America. And so was born the science of archaeology, an old word which in the seventeenth century referred to the study of history in general, but which appears in the strict modern sense, as the scientific study of the material remains of prehistory, in Wilson's *Prehistoric Annals* in 1851. Only thirty years later, in 1880, R. Dawkins could write in *Early Man*: 'The archaeologists have raised the study of antiquities to the rank of a science.' This was essentially the achievement of Schliemann, as Virchow wrote: 'Today it is pointless to ask whether Schliemann started from right or false premises when he began his studies. Not only did success decide in his favour but also his scientific method proved a success.'

SCHLIEMANN AND ROMANTICISM

Juxtaposed with Schliemann's craving to be a serious scholar was another aspect of his intellectual and temperamental make-up which deserves mention. Indeed if we read him right, it was his crucial emotional 'trigger' – it was romantic philhellenism, the love of things Greek. This may seem hard to understand now, but Schliemann's birth and youth coincided with an event which had a decisive effect on many European artists and thinkers: the Greek War of Independence.

Between the day in 1453 when Cyriac of Ancona rode into Constantinople by the side of Mehmet II when the city was conquered by the Turks, and the day Lord Byron died in the malarial swamps of Missolonghi, an extraordinary development had taken place in western European culture, whose effects are still very much with us. Of course the liberation from the Turks was chiefly achieved by the Greeks themselves, inspired by western-educated Greeks who worked in European intellectual circles. But it was not simply a matter of the way Greeks looked at themselves; the way the west looked at Greece was also important. Such was the incredible impact in the Renaissance of the rediscovery of classical Greek civilisation that, as we have seen, the idea of the rebirth of a Hellenic nation was first conceived *in Greece* in the fifteenth century. But it was precisely then that Greece fell to the Ottoman Empire and became one of its most impoverished provinces, economically and culturally. From that time the idea of Hellas reborn was maintained outside Greece and it is fascinating to see how the War of Independence in the 1820s was preceded by a great outpouring of books by western Hellenists on the history and culture of ancient Greece. As perceived by Pletho and Cyriac in the fifteenth century, the development of nationalism and that of archaeology went hand in hand. So to read what travellers and artists of the time wrote – a poet like Byron, or, slightly later, a musician like Berlioz, composer of *The Trojans* – is to sense some of the romantic philhellenism which evidently inspired the self-educated Schliemann, even if he actually acquired it late in life in the classroom in Paris; 'making my beloved Greece live again', as he put it, was a common goal for nineteenth-century intellectuals and artists, and inevitably the new science of archaeology did not escape such feelings – how could it? At one level it is the most romantic of all sciences since it involves the actual physical reconstitution of the lost past. In a sense, then, the physical recovery of ancient Greece, which began with the digs at the classical sites of Olympia and Samothrace in the 1860s and was followed by Troy, Mycenae and the rest under Schliemann in the 1870s, was the logical culmination of nineteenth-century philhellenism; only this can explain Schliemann's seemingly genuine desire to 'prove the truth' of the ancient stories, even more than to find treasure. His time, after all, was deeply troubled, plagued by revolutions and war, by colonialism and imperialism, culminating in the terrible Franco-Prussian War of 1870–1 (of which Schliemann had a first-hand glimpse – neighbouring houses in his street in Paris were blasted by gunfire). The great practical achievements of nineteenth-century 'civilisation' were in the eyes of many tainted by the prospect of future horrors. What more enticing idea than to discover an almost limitless prospect: a recoverable history stretching back deep into lost time? Progress – that great goal of nineteenth-century thinkers – progress to a culture of noble aspirations, simple moral grandeur, could indeed be made, but by journeying backwards. Though outside the scope of this book, this aspect of Schliemann and his contemporaries should not be overlooked: 'I have lived my life with this race of demigods; I know them so well that I feel they must have known me,' wrote Berlioz of the Homeric heroes; many passages in Schliemann's books show that he felt exactly the same.

WHERE WAS HOMER'S TROY?

No stone there is without a name.
LUCAN

The site of classical Ilion (in Latin Ilium Novum) occupies the north-west corner of a low plateau between the Menderes river (classical Scamander) and the Dumrek Su (Simois). The Greek and Roman city was quite extensive – its walls enclosed an area of about 1200 by 800 yards – but at its north-west extremity there is a mound about 700 feet square which falls away sharply to the plain on the west and north; this mound rose about 30 feet above the adjacent plateau and about 130 feet above the plain before Schliemann began his dig, though it may have been higher and steeper in the Bronze Age before classical builders levelled it off. This mound, known as Hisarlik, the 'place of the fort', had been the acropolis of the classical city, site of civic buildings and a temple of Athena. No one had paid it much attention in the debate over the lost site of Homer's Troy; it was first noticed by travellers in the 1740s, when part of the circuit wall built in Alexander the Great's day was still visible amid the undergrowth and olive trees. By 1801, when Edward Clarke went to the spot, the foundation blocks were being plundered by local Turks; they had gone by the 1850s and now even the line of the circuit is difficult to trace. From these signs, and from the coins he found there, Clarke rightly concluded that this 'ancient citadel on its elevated spot of ground, surrounded on all sides by a level plain', was 'evidently the remains of New Ilium'. But although some scholars accepted the proposition made by the armchair topographer Maclaren in 1822, that this must also be the site of Homeric Troy, no attempt was made to test the hypothesis by the spade until Frank Calvert and Schliemann.

Such was the meagre archaeological background to this famous place when Frank Calvert turned to it. At this stage the Troy–Bunarbashi theory still held the field, but after excavations there in 1864 had drawn a blank, Frank Calvert was finally able to dig on Hisarlik. It was a site he must have known since childhood, and he acquired from a local farmer a field which contained the northern part of the mound. As we have seen, he began to excavate in 1865 and immediately uncovered remains of the Athena temple and the wall of Lysimachus, the beautifully built classical city wall whose remains were to be swept away by Schliemann. Calvert also struck Bronze-Age levels, and realised that Hisarlik was deeply stratified, in places with 40 or 50 feet of accumulated debris.

Schliemann first visited the Troad in August 1868. From Calvert's letters we can be certain that at this time Schliemann espoused Lechevalier's Bunarbashi theory, and he poked around there for a couple of days. Hisarlik evidently had made no impression on him – contrary to the fiction on page 57. It was only when he met Calvert at Çanakkale on his way back to Constantinople that he heard details of Calvert's excavation, and his theory that Hisarlik was an artificial mound with 'the ruins and debris of temples and palaces which succeeded each other over long centuries', a theory Calvert had formulated as long ago as Newton's visit in 1853. Schliemann was immediately convinced by Calvert that this was the site of Homer's Troy, as he says in his first book, published in French the next year: 'After carefully examining the Trojan plain on two occasions, I fully agree with the conviction of this *savant* [Calvert] that the high plateau of Hisarlik is the position of ancient Troy, and that this hill is the site of its Pergamos.' In fact Schliemann entirely owed this idea to Calvert, and an extraordinary letter written to Calvert from Paris that October shows that Schliemann had only the dimmest recollection of what Hisarlik had actually *looked like*! So much had his attention focused on Bunarbashi. In passing, he asked Calvert everything from why he thought the hill artificial to what was the best type of hat to wear, and 'Should I take an iron bedstead and pillow with me?' Calvert provided all the answers to the questionnaire with patient detail. Later Schliemann would deny Calvert's inspiration and help, and in 1875, in a letter to the *Manchester Guardian*, Calvert was forced to quote Schliemann against himself: 'Had anyone else proposed for me to dig away a hill at my cost, I would not even have listened to him!' So Calvert was the 'onlie begetter' of the idea, and Schliemann was later unwilling to share his glory.

There was still the problem of permission. Schliemann was in an independent country and from the mid-1860s, when their imperial museum was founded, the Turkish government were increasingly concerned to preserve their ancient remains. Persuasive as ever, Schliemann had no trouble getting his firman, his permit; but its conditions were clear: the finds would be divided, with half going to the Turkish archaeological museum; ruins he uncovered should be left in the state in which they were found, and existing structures should not be demolished; lastly, Schliemann should foot the bill. The last of these was the only one he observed; indeed his cavalier treatment of the Turks, his destruction of many walls on the site, and especially his theft of treasure from Troy, have resulted in a permanent mistrust of foreign archaeologists in Turkey. Clearly Schliemann found it difficult to abandon a lifetime's habit of fast operating, and often practised deception to get his own way.

He began a preliminary excavation in April 1870, and over 1871–3 made three major campaigns totalling over nine months' work with anything from eighty to 160 workmen on site each day. Although Calvert counselled a network of smaller trenches, rather than immense platforms, Schliemann decided to drive vast trenches through the mound, removing hundreds of tons of earth and rubble, demolishing earlier structures which stood in his way. Among the walls which went forever were, as we have seen, parts of the beautiful limestone city wall of Lysimachus, and, in two places behind it, an earlier wall of finely worked limestone blocks which Schliemann considered too fine to be early; in fact, we now know Schliemann had unwittingly struck part of the city which, if anything, was Homeric Troy.

The results of Schliemann's initial depredations can still be seen today; what is left is the ruin of a ruin. By 1872 Calvert had withdrawn his agreement for Schliemann to dig his part of the mound, and the two had – temporarily – fallen out. It is not hard to see why.

The fact is that Schliemann was completely perplexed by the complexity of the mound, baffled by the stratification. Fortunately he was wise enough to accept advice: '*Only the exact findspot* of an object in the excavation can accurately indicate the epoch. Take good heed of that!' the French architect Burnouf wrote to him in 1872. He did well to insist, for nothing so complex had ever been excavated, and Schliemann had to learn his technique as he went along. It is futile to criticise Schliemann for this: other digs of the time were simpler sites, as at Samothrace, or done like 'digging for potatoes', as Müller said of the British dig at Carchemish, near the Syrian border, in 1878–81. Gradually, however, in the course of these three seasons he succeeded in identifying four successive strata or 'cities' below the classical Ilium, and he came to the conclusion that the Homeric one was the second city from the bottom, which had been destroyed in a great conflagration. His claim that this tiny place – 100 yards across – was the Homeric Ilium, with its towers and 'great walls', did not excite much belief, despite his enthusiastic exaggerations in his reports and letters. Schliemann was especially infuriated by an article by Frank Calvert in the *Levant Herald* (4 February 1873) in which Calvert acknowledged Schliemann's prehistoric strata below the Roman, but brilliantly observed that 'a most important link is missing between 1800 and 700 BC, a gap of over 1000 years, including the date of the Trojan War, 1193–1184 BC, no relics of the intervening epoch having yet been discovered between that indicated by the prehistoric stone implements and that of pottery of the Archaic style'. In other words the Trojan War was not there! Blind to the implications of Calvert's argument, Schliemann lashed out hysterically, accusing Calvert of stabbing him in the back, and later calling him a 'foul fiend … a libeller and a liar'. Within weeks, however, Schliemann found his justification, in *his* Troy (II), when at the very end of his final season, probably 31 May 1873, he made the first, and most controversial, of his famous discoveries of treasure – the so-called 'Treasure of Priam'.

I came upon a large copper article of the most remarkable form, which attracted my attention all the more and I thought I saw gold behind it…. I cut out the treasure with a large knife, which it was impossible to do without the very greatest exertion and the most fearful risk of my life, for the great fortification-wall, beneath which I had to dig, threatened every moment to fall down on me. But the sight of so many objects, every one of which is of inestimable value to archaeology, made me foolhardy, and I never thought of any danger. It would, however, have been impossible for me to have removed the treasure without the help of my dear wife, who stood by me ready to pack the things which I cut out in her shawl and to carry them away.

The 'treasure', so Schliemann alleged, comprised copper salvers and cauldrons inside which were cups in gold, silver, electrum and bronze, a gold 'sauceboat', vases, thirteen copper lanceheads, and, most beautiful of all, a mass of several thousand small gold rings and decorative pieces, with gold bracelets, a gold headband, four beautiful earrings, and two splendid gold diadems, one of which comprised over 16,000 tiny pieces of gold threaded on gold wire. This last, which became known as the 'Jewels of Helen', was the headdress in which Sophie Schliemann was later photographed, one of the most famous images of the nineteenth century.

The find caused a sensation: in fact it was this more than anything that helped Schliemann's claims to be taken seriously. But we now know that, at the very best, Schliemann greatly embellished his account for effect. Recently some scholars have even argued that the treasure itself was fabricated and planted, but it was certainly of the right date for its context, which recent research suggests was possibly a cist grave dug into Troy II layers from Troy III, though Schliemann's account is too imprecise to be sure. We also now know that gold had been found sporadically at this level earlier in the year, including a major find of similar jewellery in illicit digging by his workmen. Also, when the Americans re-excavated this area in the 1930s they found scattered gold in almost every room, as if the inhabitants of Troy II had fled in panic before the onslaught which engulfed their city: so Troy II remains a possibility for the 'Jewels of Helen'. There seems reason, then, to believe that Schliemann did find these marvellous things, but probably over several weeks rather than in one sensational hoard. This he had kept under wraps to smuggle out of Turkey at the end of excavation, and he wrote it up in Athens where the confused postdating in his journal led modern investigators to think the whole thing a concoction. As for Sophie's help, she was in Athens at the time, as Schliemann admitted to the English visitor Borlase, but this white lie need not (in my opinion at least) vitiate the find as a whole. Unfortunately, the treasure itself, which might have provided a few more answers, vanished in Berlin in 1945, so today the paltry survivors of the gold of Troy are a pair of beautiful earrings, a necklace, rings and pins, part of the finds made later by Schliemann in 1878 and 1882; these can still be seen in Istanbul Museum, along with misshapen gold ingots, the remains of a priceless treasure of the third millennium BC. Other gold finds from the 1870s were doubtless melted down in the villages near Hisarlik. And that, we must assume now, is the fate of the Berlin treasure, the 'Jewels of Helen' and the rest: ironic, for had the British Museum coughed up the £100 to Calvert (see p. 55), the treasure might still be safe in Bloomsbury!

Back in Athens, with furious Turkish agents on his trail, Schliemann was jubilant. The treasure was the kind of luck he had needed in his campaign to persuade the world of scholarship that his costly obsession was well-founded, that he had located the world of the heroes, and that it did indeed have high material culture – and gold, as Homer said. For him the wall where the treasure lay was clearly Priam's palace, and the pieces themselves 'hurriedly packed into the chest by some member of the palace of the family of King Priam'. He could not resist a jibe at the doubters: 'This treasure of the *supposed mythical* King Priam, of the *mythical* heroic age which I discovered at a great depth in the ruins of the *supposed mythical Troy*, is at all events an event which stands alone in archaeology.'

It was, but writing in English to Newton he was more circumspect:

Troy is not large; but Homer is an epic poet and no historian. He never saw either the great tower of Ilium, nor the divine wall, nor Priam's palace, because when he visited Troy 300 years after its destruction all those monuments were for 300 years couched with its ten feet thick layers of the red ashes and ruins of Troy, and another city stood upon that layer, a city which in its turn must have undergone great convulsions and increased that layer considerably. Homer made no excavations to bring these monuments to light, but he knew them by tradition for Troy's tragical fate had ever since its destruction been in the mouth of the rhapsodes. Ancient Troy has no Acropolis and the *Pergamos is a pure invention of the poet*. (My italics.) Such would not have been the impression gained by the public from Schliemann's book.

72

As he admitted privately, what still nagged Schliemann was the question: was this indeed Homer's Troy? Two facts in particular perturbed him. First, the size of the prehistoric settlement – 100 yards by 80 at the maximum – seemed far too small for the great city Homer portrays. Where were the wide streets, towers and gates depicted by the poet? Moreover there was no sign that the settlement extended on to the plateau as he and Calvert had expected. Second, deep though they were, the prehistoric strata had produced obscure and primitive pottery which seemed far too primitive for the age of heroes to which Schliemann would assign them: where, for instance, was the elaborate palace decoration Homer mentions? Of course much of it had only ever existed in Homer's imagination, but Schliemann had also been unlucky. Much, though not all, of the top of the hill, with its Bronze-Age layers, had been sliced off in antiquity by the builders of Ilium Novum; so, attacking from the north, Schliemann had virtually no chance of finding Mycenaean material which might have given him – or a visitor like Newton – a 'fix' against pottery already found in Rhodes and Attica. He was confused and confounded, so much so that as early as 1871, when a party of eminent German scholars had visited the site and declared that Homer's Troy was not here but at Bunarbashi after all, Schliemann bowed to their wisdom (with his habitual deference to professional scholars) and came to doubt his intuition after all. That autumn he wrote in his journal that he had 'given up all hope of finding Troy'. Perhaps, he thought, it had only ever existed in the mind of the poet. In November he went so far as to open an excavation at Akça Köy, the site proposed by Frank's brother Frederick: Hisarlik 'perplexes me more and more every day,' he wrote to James Calvert. 'I can dig there [Akça] more next spring in order to see whether I cannot discover there Troy if I do not find it at Hisarlik.'

So much of what Schliemann found was new to scholarship as a whole, not just to him, that his confusion was understandable: he begged everyone for advice. His first major publication of his finds in 1874 consisted of field reports with a great loose album of over 200 sketches, plans and photographs 'in the hope that my colleagues might be able to explain points obscure to me … [for] everything appeared strange and mysterious to me'. Such was the reality of Schliemann's 'new world of archaeology'! That, and the discomfort, the malaria, the scorpions and insects, the fevers when the rains came, the fierce wind from the north which 'drives the dust into our eyes' and blew through the chinks in the dig hut at night (it soon ceased to be gratifying to the romantic Schliemann that Troy was indeed as Homer said, 'very windy'). He fought off constipation with a 'bottle of best English stout every day', but he and Sophie were often so ill that 'we cannot undertake the direction [of the dig] throughout the day in the terrible heat of the sun'. Such physical hardships simply do not happen in archaeology today, and Schliemann stuck it for twelve seasons over the next twenty years at huge personal expense. The motive was hardly fame. Or gold. Even if Schliemann himself took time to realise it, he kept going back because he still had questions to answer.

Schliemann had considered the 1873 dig his last on the site. In his initial flush of enthusiasm he claimed the 'Treasure of Priam' as proof that he had indeed found Homer's Troy. But true to his underlying honesty, he realised that he had not solved the key problems satisfactorily, and his thoughts soon went back to Hisarlik. He began to negotiate for a new permit to dig there. But the Turks, furious about the theft and smuggling of the treasure, turned him down. When he finally got permission in 1876 (with a large cash payment) his mind was elsewhere. He had decided to dig at the site of the stronghold of Agamemnon, leader of the Greek forces at Troy: Mycenae.

MYCENAE RICH IN GOLD

Though it had been deserted for well over 2000 years, Mycenae had never been forgotten. As we have seen, Thucydides had visited its ruins and was happy to agree with Homer's account of its pre-eminence at the time of the Trojan War – as the 'capital' of the Mycenaean 'empire'. In the ancient world everybody accepted that this was the place to which Agamemnon had returned to be murdered after the sack of Troy, and it was the general belief that he and the other kings of the Atreid dynasty had been buried there. Although abandoned after the destruction by Argos in 468 BC, Mycenae still had impressive ruins to show, its Cyclopean walls and the tremendous 'beehive' or tholos tombs which were thought to be the burial places of the ancient kings. These were visited by the Greek traveller Pausanias in the second century AD, and he describes the Lion Gate and the tholos tombs said to be of Atreus and Agamemnon. But in comparison with Troy and many of the sites of Greece and Crete, Mycenae was unvisited by postclassical travellers and there seems to be no first-hand account of it between Pausanias and the Frenchman Fauvel in 1780. The site, though, was never lost, appearing on Italian maps from the seventeenth century onwards, and the remains of its great walls were always visible above ground.

When John Morritt of Rokeby, Walter Scott's friend, went there early in 1795 after visiting the Troad to participate in the Bryant controversy (see p. 52), his is the first detailed account since Pausanias (in fact he used Pausanias' writings as his guide!). Morritt was a keen traveller, ignoring hardships at a time when few travelled and fewer explored. Led by a 'country labourer', he reached the Lion Gate, admiring its 'rudely carved bas-rilievo'. Mycenae, he thought, could have changed but little since Pausanias; in that he was probably right. Morritt also forced his way into the choked Treasury of Atreus and described the massive lintel block ('beyond anything we have seen') which he compared to the lintel at Orchomenos, another tholos tomb associated with the Homeric Age.

Morritt's journal was made available to a number of scholars who followed him to Mycenae in the next thirty years. First and most controversial was Thomas Bruce, Lord Elgin, now notorious for his removal of the Elgin marbles. In the summer of 1802, while the marbles were being taken down from the Parthenon in Athens, Elgin made a tour of Greece searching for other antiquities; when he visited Mycenae he was so impressed by the ruins that he immediately began excavation there under cover of a permit from the Turkish government, which then controlled Greece. In the half-blocked entrance to the Treasury of Atreus he uncovered a number of pieces of the red and green marble friezes which had fallen from the façade of the tomb; he also found (perhaps in one of the other tholos tombs) two massive monumental fragments of a bull relief in hard black limestone which can be seen today in the British Museum. Elgin also removed the main portions of the green marble decorated zigzag half-columns which in 1802 still flanked the door of the tomb; the remainder were taken by the Marquis of Sligo in 1810 and set up at Westport House in County Mayo, to be given to the British Museum in 1905; that they are not today on the monument for which they were created (and of which they were an integral part) is greatly to be regretted. Elgin even cast covetous eyes on the magnificent relief on the Lion Gate itself, but decided reluctantly that it was too heavy and too far from the sea to be transported away.

Other visitors in those last two decades before Greek independence took a more constructive attitude towards the antiquities of the prehistoric age. Chief among them were English scholars, who examined, measured and drew the Treasury and the Lion Gate. Edward Clarke, whom we have already met at Troy, went there. William Leake, in his *Travels in the Morea*, set the standards for nineteenth-century classical topography with what is still one of the best descriptions of the site. Charles Cockerell made a small excavation on the outside of the roof of the Treasury of Atreus to establish the nature of its 'beehive construction'. Edward Dodwell attempted to define Cyclopean architecture in a lavish folio volume which included the first illustrations of the walls and tholoi of Mycenae and Tiryns. William Gell, in the course of extensive itineraries all over Greece, sought out further fragments of the decorations and described the Lion Gate as the 'earliest authenticated specimen of sculpture in Europe'. All these were significant steps in the growth of modern understanding of the Mycenaean civilisation; some, like Leake and Clarke, still deserve reading in their own right as marvellously observant travel books: Leake's indeed is one of the best archaeological travel books ever written. These writers knew their classical sources, their Homer and Thucydides; it is thanks to them that, from the start of modern archaeological inquiry, these ruins were assumed to date from the prehistoric, 'heroic' age of Greece, and also that progress had already been made in piecing together ideas about the style of 'Cyclopean' architecture. The way had been prepared for Schliemann, and he carefully studied all these books before and during his dig at Mycenae.

Before we go to Mycenae with Schliemann, though, two other visitors who preceded him should be noted, for their discoveries were potentially of the greatest importance in the progress of Mycenaean studies. In 1809 Thomas Burgon visited Mycenae 'south of the southernmost angle of the wall of the acropolis', and picked up some fragments of Mycenaean pottery which he published with a colour plate in 1847 as 'An attempt to point out the Vases of Greece proper which belong to the Heroic and Homeric Age'. It was this simple but revolutionary article which Charles Newton had in mind when he visited Lechevalier's Troy at Bunarbashi in 1853 with Frank Calvert (see p. 55):

If this hill has ever been an acropolis we might expect to find those fragments of very early pottery which, as was first remarked by the late Mr Burgon, are so abundant on the Homeric sites of Mycenae and Tiryns. Of such pottery I saw not a vestige....

Burgon and Newton's observations lie at the root of all the present-day studies of the chronology of the Mycenaean world, and in fact when he saw Schliemann's pottery from Mycenae Newton was also able to advance a rough *absolute* chronology for the Heroic Age at Mycenae, by the simple device of a comparison with similar pottery found in Egypt which could be dated to around 1375 BC. It was Schliemann's discussions Newton which made him assert his dependence on pottery dating (as in *Mycenae*, 1880), though the implications of Newton's conclusions for his Troy dig seem to have eluded him to the last.

It was natural that the Lion Gate and the Treasury of Atreus should have attracted the main attention of the nineteenth-century investigators just as they had done in Pausanias' day. But of course it was the interior of the citadel, if anywhere, which was likely to provide answers about the early history of the place, and this had attracted little interest before Schliemann. Few travellers had even bothered to look around it, though Leake provided a rough map and described the overgrown slopes inside the gate, with traces of terraces and walling. Dodwell's engraving suggests that the whole area was overgrown, with no major structures visible; likewise a watercolour done in 1834 shows that even the Lion Gate itself was completely choked with rubble and bushes, the bastions on either side ruined and covered with earth. This is what Schliemann had seen when in 1868 he first set eyes on the legendary stronghold of Agamemnon, the city 'rich in gold', as Homer had said. Schliemann's guides from Corinth had never heard of Mycenae, but a farm boy from Charvati who took him to the site knew the citadel as 'the fortress of Agamemnon' and the Treasury of Atreus as 'Agamemnon's tomb'. For Schliemann this was virtual confirmation of the ancient myths. Eternal romantic that he was, his response to such stories was no different from that of the musicians and artists of his day, as for example the artist von Stackelberg, who actually went to Mycenae to paint:

I sat for hours in solemn solitude in front of the gigantic ruins, and while my pen reproduced their bold outlines I thought about the gigantic figures of the Greek heroes in this memorable place, the heroes who, murdering and murdered, were sacrificed to their inexorable fate.

Now in the summer of 1876 Schliemann was about to cap the imaginings of his fellow romantics. At Mycenae he would do no less than bring the Heroic Age to life.

THE MASK OF AGAMEMNON

The key to Schliemann's incredible success at Mycenae lay in a passage in Pausanias' book describing the tombs of the murdered Agamemnon and his companions as lying inside rather than outside the walls. Scholars had always assumed that Pausanias was referring to the great tholos tombs, including what we today call the Treasury of Atreus, and therefore that the walls of which he spoke were those of the outer circuit which lies well beyond the citadel. Schliemann was certain the scholars were wrong, and had been laughed at for saying so in print in the book he wrote after his 1868 trip. He insisted that Pausanias meant the great Cyclopean defences of the citadel, and that the heroes of Troy lay inside the Lion Gate itself. Preposterous said the scholars – where was there room for a cemetery within this small citadel on its steep hill, and in any case, they argued, since when did the ancients bury their dead within their cities? Determined to prove his point, in early September 1876, with a permit from the Greek government, Schliemann started digging a trench just inside the Lion Gate, cutting through several feet of wreckage that had fallen or been washed down the hillside. The end of Schliemann's trench can still be seen gouged into the side of the hill at the foot of the stairs which face the visitor immediately inside the gate. This trench he drove westwards across a small flat terraced area inside the Cyclopean walls; there he immediately struck the remains of a series of upright stone markers which formed a circle nearly 90 feet in diameter. The ground had clearly been carefully levelled in antiquity, and within this space Schliemann found a carved upright stone resembling a grave monument; his excitement grew as others soon followed, bearing the clearly distinguishable images of warriors in chariots. The sensational discoveries which ensued are now part of archaeological legend, but the fresh breath of discovery can still be read in Schliemann's letters to *The Times* (reprinted in English in *Briefwechsel* II) and in his great book *Mycenae*.

By now the November rains were turning Schliemann's trenches to mud. When he reached the bedrock he found the top of a shaft cut down into the rock. It was the first of five rectangular grave shafts in which he uncovered the remains of nineteen men and women and two infants: they were literally covered in gold. The men's faces were covered with magnificent gold masks so distinctively modelled as to suggest portraits; on their breasts were extraordinary decorated 'sunbursts' of thick gold leaf impressed with rosettes; two women wore gold frontlets and one of them a diadem; around the bodies lay bronze swords and daggers, with elaborate gold hilts and gold and silver inlay on the hilts and blades – in two cases wonderfully vivid scenes of hunting and fighting were inlaid in gold, silver and lapis lazuli on the ridges of the dagger blades. There were gold and silver drinking cups, gold boxes, ivory containers and plaques, and hundreds of gold discs decorated with rosettes, spirals, animals and fish: these had perhaps been sewn on to the clothes and the shrouds. The artistic accomplishment was simply dazzling – exemplified best, perhaps, in some of the least significant articles, such as a deco-rated ostrich egg or (to choose an item from a later excavation) an exquisite little bowl of rock crystal adorned with a bird's head and neck: a thing of fragile, translucent beauty to set beside the grim, golden, bearded warlords and their arsenal of weapons.

For Schliemann, of course, there was no doubt: this was the world of Homer and the *Iliad*, and these were the graves of Agamemnon and his companions. Pausanias had mentioned five graves and Schliemann had dug five; tradition even insisted that Cassandra had two infant twins who were killed with her – and there were two infant burials in one of the shafts! The climax of his search came in the fifth and, for him, last tomb, where, as with the 'Jewels of Helen', Schliemann found exactly what he had wished so passionately to find. There were three male bodies, richly adorned with inlaid war accoutrements, gold coverings on their breasts, and gold face masks. The first two skulls were in such a state of decomposition that they could not be saved, but the third

had been wonderfully preserved under its ponderous golden mask … both eyes perfectly visible, also the mouth, which owing to the enormous weight that had pressed upon it was wide open and showed thirty-two beautiful teeth … the man must have died at the early age of thirty-five…. The news that the tolerably well preserved body of a man of the mythic heroic age had been found … spread like wildfire through the Argolid, and people came by thousands from Argos, Nauplia, and the villages to see the wonder.

So ran Schliemann's own thrillingly evocative account, published in 1880 in *Mycenae*. As usual it was probably embellished in the retelling. The dispatch to *The Times* dated 25 November 1876 is more prosaic: 'In one of these [the gold masks] has remained a large part of the skull it covered.' Nothing more! As for the famous and often told story, that he sent the King of Greece a telegram saying: 'I have gazed upon the face of Agamemnon,' we can at least say that, though he did not say it, the sentiment was in character. (Schliemann, incidentally, made efforts to preserve the body by pouring on it alcohol containing dissolved gum, but it has not survived. The painting made at the time by a local artist has, however, recently resurfaced in one of Schliemann's lost albums.) Schliemann's interpretation of this discovery, perhaps the single most remarkable one in the history of archaeology, was characteristically to the point:

For my part, I have always firmly believed in the Trojan War; my full faith in the tradition has never been shaken by mode and criticism, and to this faith of mine I am indebted for the discovery of Troy and its treasure…. My firm faith in the traditions made me undertake my late excavations in the acropolis [of Mycenae] and led to the discovery of the five tombs with their immense treasures…. I have not the slightest objection to admitting that the tradition which assigns the tombs to Agamemnon and his companions may be perfectly correct.

81

Needless to say, the finds at Mycenae caused a sensation and also brought Schliemann world fame. He was fêted in the high society of Europe; the British Prime Minister Gladstone, a classical scholar himself, wrote the preface to the English edition of *Mycenae*; Schliemann lectured to learned societies all over Europe. There were, of course, still many critics: some claimed the graves were a post-Roman, barbarian cemetery with 'Scythian' masks; others even said they were Christian, Byzantine; but most accepted them as 'Homeric', that is, pertaining to a Bronze-Age heroic world which had some connection with Homer's tale – for had not Schliemann found depictions of boar's-tusk helmets such as Homer had described? On the inlaid dagger blades there were representations of 'tower shields' such as Ajax carries in the *Iliad*; there were, too, 'silver-studded' swords like the one given by Hector to Ajax. At last the new science of archaeology had done what had previously been impossible: it had demonstrated some kind of connection between the world of Homer and real history. And Schliemann could no longer be dismissed as a mere crank. The great Oxford Sanskrit scholar Max Müller wrote:

I am delighted to hear of your success, you fully deserve it. Never mind the attacks of the Press in Germany.... Your discoveries are open to different interpretations – you know how much I differ from your own interpretation – still more from Gladstone's. But that does not affect my gratitude to you for your indefatigable perseverance. I admire enthusiasm for its own sake, and depend upon it the large majority of the world does the same. You are envied – that is all, and I do not wonder it.

Had Schliemann really found Agamemnon? Alas, no! This is not the place to analyse Schliemann's finds and their real dating. Sufficient to say that the shaft graves date from the sixteenth century BC, long before the possible date for the Trojan War in the thirteenth or twelfth century BC – it is not even certain that they are from the same dynasty as Agamemnon's, if he existed, though they may be. Nor were the six shaft graves (the last found by Stamatakis in 1877) all from the same time, as Schliemann thought; rather, they were added to over a number of generations. (A second grave circle was found in 1950 with equally fabulous riches.) We now know that the great architectural achievements of the Mycenaean period – the Lion Gate, the Cyclopean walls and the great 'treasuries' of Atreus and Clytemnestra – date from the thirteenth century BC, and that it was at this time that the area of ancient royal tombs of the shaft graves was refurbished and enclosed as an object of public cult. Some of Schliemann's misconceptions were evident at the time; as we have seen, it was Charles Newton who brilliantly observed to Schliemann that the thousands of fragments of stirrup jars – the most typical Mycenaean pottery – found by Schliemann in 1876 could be compared with pottery found at Ialysus in Rhodes, which by association with Egyptian material found in the same levels could be dated to the early fourteenth century BC; near enough to the traditional dating of the Trojan War. In his publication of his finds Schliemann very fully and commendably set out the comparisons with the Rhodes material. But as far as the connections he really wanted were concerned, connections between his finds at Mycenae and at Troy, all he could point to was the 'champagne glass' of a kind he had here, and had seen at Tiryns (and from the Rhodian tomb), and the goblets 'found by me in Troy at a depth of 50 feet'. The more he found, the more *his* 'Homeric Troy' appeared backward and strangely isolated.

GOLDEN ORCHOMENOS

Of all the hundreds of places mentioned in the *Iliad*, Homer singles out only three as being 'rich in gold'. For Schliemann, two of them, Troy and Mycenae, had lived up to the epithet sensationally. It was inevitable that he should be drawn next to the third 'golden city', and with the permission of the Greek government he undertook a small excavation at Orchomenos, a ruined site in central Greece which had occupied a long hill above Lake Copais. According to the legends Orchomenos had once ruled even mighty Thebes, the city of Oedipus. Pausanias told how in the Heroic Age the people of Orchomenos – the Minyans – had constructed a great dyke system to drain Lake Copais; it was one of the chief centres which sent ships to Troy, according to Homer's catalogue of the ships; its wealth was proverbial – 'not for the riches of Orchomenos,' says Achilles in the *Iliad*. Furthermore there was Pausanias' reference to the great tholos tomb there:

The Treasure House of Minyas is one of the greatest wonders of the world, and of Greece. It is built in stone, circular in shape … they say the topmost stone is a keystone holding the entire building in place. Greeks are terribly prone to be wonderstruck by the exotic at the expense of home products: distinguished historians have explained the Pyramids of Egypt in the greatest detail and not made the slightest mention of the Treasure House of Minyas, or the walls of Tiryns, which are by no means less marvellous!

The site of Orchomenos had never been lost, neither had the name: we find it in the journal of Cyriac of Ancona who sniffed around there in the 1440s. In more recent times Gell, Morritt and Leake had searched out the place, a five-hour horse ride from Athens, along the malarial plain of Copais; Lord Elgin too had come, looking for *objets d'art*.

Like those before him Schliemann found the great tholos collapsed, though enough survives today to see what a masterpiece it was; virtually identical in measurement to the Treasury of Atreus at Mycenae, it may well have been planned by the same architect (as was suggested to Schliemann on site by the twenty-seven-year-old Wilhelm Dörpfeld, then the architect for the German archaeological team at Olympia, soon to become Schliemann's invaluable collaborator). But trial excavations on the citadel brought Schliemann no gold this time; in fact there was tantalisingly little sign of the legendary wealth of Homeric Orchomenos, and Schliemann soon gave up. There was, however, one bonus. In the tomb chamber of the tholos Schliemann and Sophie found many fragments of carved greenish slate plates which seemed to have covered the ceiling of the tomb, which had collapsed only years before. The relief comprised beautifully interwoven spirals of leaves and rosettes which the Schliemanns were able to reconstruct, and today's visitor to Orchomenos may once again walk into the tomb chamber and see the ceiling in place. It is, incidentally, likely that the entire chamber was originally decorated in this way: inspection of the earth debris in the corners of the chamber shows that small fragments of the slate plaques are still in position on the side walls.

So Schliemann left Orchomenos after a few weeks. One enigma about his dig there remains unsolved. It is, we now know, supremely important in the search for Troy and the Trojans. He had turned up large quantities of a strange monochrome grey pottery – thrown and glazed – which he called Grey Minyan, after the ancient people of the site. He had already found a very similar kind of pottery in an upper level of Troy, far above his 'Homeric Ilium'. Why did Schliemann not see the significance of the parallels between them? Had he known it, the answer to the riddle of Troy lay there. But Schliemann's eyes were elsewhere, on a site he had known for some years: Tiryns.

'TIRYNS OF THE GREAT WALLS'

Rising like a ship from the plain of Argos, Tiryns lies 9 miles south of Mycenae, on a low, rocky promontory now about a mile from the sea. In the Bronze Age the sea came only 100 yards from the western walls, and Tiryns must have been a port. From here, says Homer, King Diomedes took eighty black ships to Troy. Tiryns' position probably enabled it to dominate the plain, for from its gates prehistoric roads went south to Nauplia, south-east to Asine, east to Kasarma and Epidavros, north-east to Midea, north to Mycenae and Corinth, and north-west to Argos. From the top Tiryns is seen to be completely encircled by mountains, in the foothills of which the great natural fortresses of Argos and Midea stand out; Mycenae is tucked away in its valley to the north. The panorama is splendid, as Schliemann himself remarked:

I confess that the prospect from the citadel of Tiryns far exceeds all of natural beauty which I have elsewhere seen. Indeed the magic of the scene becomes quite overpowering when in spirit one recalls the mighty deeds of which the theatre was this plain of Argos with its encircling hills.

Like Mycenae, Tiryns was a ruin in classical times, deserted when Pausanias came there and made his famous remark about the Cyclopean walls – 'by no means less marvellous' than the Pyramids of Egypt. In medieval times there was an impoverished little village below the acropolis, doubtless the reason for the existence of a small Byzantine church and cemetery on top of the ruins, the traces of which Schliemann removed in his excavation. The medieval settlement lasted from the tenth century to around 1400. Many early travellers found their way to Tiryns when the Morea became open to foreigners in the seventeenth century; since it lay on the road from the main port, Nauplion, to Argos, the site was easily accessible where Mycenae was less so. The first modern visitor was a Frenchman, Des Mouceaux, in 1668, who described the vaulted galleries and the construction of the Cyclopean walls. After him came the Venetian Pacifico, but it was again the English travellers, Gell, Leake, Clarke and Dodwell, who laid the foundations for modern archaeology, and Dodwell in particular who made the first plan and engravings of the fortification.

Despite the increase of interest in these monuments there was no attempt to dig at Tiryns before Schliemann, apart from a one-day affair by the German Thiersch in 1831. For Schliemann it was an obvious choice: unable to locate Homeric Pylos or Sparta, it was the other great mainland palace in Homeric tradition. Schliemann had inspected the place on his visit to Greece and the Troad in 1868, and to him its great history in legend betokened a truly ancient centre, possibly, as he would assert, 'the oldest town in Greece'. He dug trial shafts in the summer of 1876 (causing much damage), and in 1884 set about the place in earnest. Unfortunately, once again, his finds were vitiated by his failure to record findspots, depth and context. It may be that he was led more by architectural considerations: having uncovered 'palace' or 'temple' buildings at Troy, he hoped to compare them with a Mycenaean citadel which he thought contemporaneous. Fortunately, however, Dörpfeld was with him, otherwise he would very possibly have demolished the Mycenaean palace buildings on top, which were immediately below the Byzantine church. In the event Schliemann seems to have left Dörpfeld to it, and as a result the vast building complex the visitor can see today emerged without being wrecked. If anything Tiryns represents Schliemann's archaeological maturity, egged on by Dörpfeld, and their publication, *Tiryns*, was very much a joint effort. It is interesting that at this time Schliemann and Dörpfeld still supported the widely held view that the Phoenicians were the founders and builders of the Mycenaean citadels. Adler, co-director of the excavations at Olympia, wrote an appendix to Schliemann's book in which he denied this, saying that he was convinced that these were Bronze-Age Greeks. Though Schliemann himself was privately attracted to this idea, he was perhaps reluctant to go publicly against the academic orthodoxy, the Phoenician theory.

What was remarkable about Tiryns was that here Mycenaean palace civilisation came to life with some very close parallels with Homer's descriptions, and it is somewhat surprising that Schliemann refrained from evolving them (perhaps he was being encouraged to be less hasty in jumping to conclusions!). As any visitor to the site today knows, Tiryns gives a particularly vivid impression of the world of the Bronze-Age warlords: the ascent up the ramp to the main entrance, flanked on the right by an immense tower of Cyclopean stones, and on the left by corbelled galleries to give covering fire; the massive entrance passage leading to a main gate which must have looked much as the Lion Gate at Mycenae; then the colonnaded outer hall and courtyard which led into a magnificent columned inner court facing the royal hall, the megaron (royal hall) with its porch, anteroom and throne-room; the throne-room itself with a large circular hearth in the centre, its walls decorated with alabaster and inlaid with a bordering of blue glass paste (just as Homer mentions); all this could be recovered from the foundations and debris which lay only inches below the remains of the Byzantine church. Particularly exciting for Schliemann were fragments of frescoes showing battle and hunting scenes, and one extraordinary depiction of a youth leaping a bull (a theme already known from signet rings). The layout of the palace, the hearth, the bathroom, the blue glass kyanos, all seemed reflected in Homer's portrayal of the Heroic Age. 'I have brought to light the great palace of the legendary kings of Tiryns,' wrote Schliemann, 'so that from now until the end of time … it will be impossible ever to publish a book on ancient art that does not contain my plan of the palace of Tiryns.' Typical Schliemann hyperbole – but he was not, this time, indulging in pure fantasy: one learned critic called his book 'the most important contribution to archaeological science that has been published this century'.

THE 'PALACE OF MINOS' AT KNOSSOS: 'THE ORIGINAL HOME OF MYCENAEAN CIVILISATION'?

After the deserved success of the Tiryns dig, with the book finished and ready to come out, Schliemann fretted after other fields to conquer, and wrote in March 1885:

I am fatigued and have an immense desire to withdraw from excavations and to pass the rest of my life quietly. I feel I cannot stand any longer this tremendous work. Besides, wherever I hitherto put the spade into the ground, I always discovered new worlds for archaeology at Troy, Mycenae, Orchomenos, Tiryns – each of them have brought to light wonders. But fortune is a capricious woman, perhaps she would now turn me her back; perhaps I should henceforwards only find fiascos! I ought to imitate Rossini, who stopped after having composed a few but splendid operas, which can never be excelled.

And it must be said that the last ten years of Schliemann's career form an anticlimax to the sensational discoveries of the 1870s. How could they not? In the main, though, it was a question of luck, as so much archaeology is. Schliemann's instinct did not fail him. Behind it, as always, lay the simple assumption that behind the Homeric world was a real prehistoric Aegean world; that the places Homer says were important dynastic centres were in fact palace sites of the Bronze Age. This simple assumption may seem obvious now, but it is only through archaeology that it has been possible to demonstrate it. (Remember, too, that in the nineteenth century no one knew, as we have since 1952, that Greek was the language of the palaces: very few scholars would have bet on this in Schliemann's day.)

Late in 1888 Schliemann headed for the southern Peloponnese and searched in vain for King Nestor's palace at Pylos, which had provided the second biggest contingent in the Trojan War. He had already visited the area in 1874, looking for the 'cave of Nestor' on the steep acropolis of Koryphasion near Pylos Bay; there in a cavern he found sherds of the 'so-called Mycenaean type', the first such find on the western coast. But at Pylos he found no royal graves, and the location of the palace itself – a famous conundrum since antiquity – evaded Schliemann. It was not until roadmaking activities started in the year of his death that the first hints were gathered of the whereabouts of the palace on Englianos hill; subsequently tholos tombs were found in the vicinity in 1912 and 1926, prior to the dramatic uncovering of the palace in 1939 (see p. 128).

Following the track of the heroes, Schliemann explored the Evrótas valley in Sparta, looking for the palace of Menelaos and Helen herself. He ascended the Menelaion hill at Therapne, overlooking the modern town of Sparta, where the massive plinth of the later classical shrine to Helen and Menelaos still stands. Again disappointed, Schliemann declared that there were no remains from the Bronze Age on the site. Ironically enough, it was only months afterwards that the Greek archaeologist Tsountas (who had followed Schliemann at Mycenae) noted signs which did indeed point to Mycenaean occupation of the Menelaion site; in 1910 an important building was excavated by the British only 100 yards from the shrine, and dramatic new finds in the 1970s suggest that the main palace site in Lakonia at the time of the Trojan War was indeed on this site (see p. 164): Helen, if she existed, may well have lived here.

Many other sites were suggested to Schliemann by his growing army of admirers. Perhaps the most interesting in the light of future discoveries was that of the English scholar Boscawen who was working on Hittite inscriptions, then an absolutely new field. On 14 January 1881 he wrote to Schliemann: 'We have often expressed the wish that some day you would cast a favourable eye on the pre-Hellenic remains in Asia Minor, especially those at Boghaz Keui and [Alaça] eyuk on the Halys.' Boghaz Köy indeed would turn out to be one of the greatest of all Bronze-Age sites in the Mediterranean (see p. 195). But Schliemann's eye was on Crete. There he hoped to crown his achievement.

Many scholars of the time thought Crete might provide the link between the Aegean world and the great civilisations of the Near East. For Schliemann the attempt to obtain permission to dig there became one of the obsessions of the last ten years of his life. 'My days are numbered,' he wrote as early as 1883, 'and I would love to explore Crete before I am gone.' His collaborator Virchow agreed: 'No other place is apt to yield a way station between Mycenae and the East.' So Schliemann's visit to Knossos in the spring of 1886 was exciting, even for him (legend has it that on his landfall he scandalised the local Turks by falling on his knees and offering a prayer of thanks to Dictaean Zeus!).

There had in fact already been an excavation at Knossos in 1878 by a local man, the aptly named Minos Kalokairinos, who was probably inspired by Schliemann's dig at Mycenae. Schliemann knew of his finds, for they had been published by his correspondent Fabricius and had provoked much interest.

Kalokairinos showed Schliemann the finds in his house in Heraklion and then took him out to the site, where rooms were still exposed to a height of 6 or 7 feet, one still 'coated with two broad bands of deep red colour'. What he saw there so excited Schliemann that he wrote from the spot to his friend Max Müller (in English), on 22 May 1886:

Dr Dörpfeld and I have examined most carefully the site of Knossos which is marked by potsherds and ruins of the Roman time. Nothing is visible above ground, which might be referred to the so-called heroic age – not even a fragment of terracotta – except on a hillock, almost the size of the Pergamos of Troy, which is situated in the middle of the town and appears to us to be altogether artificial. Two large well-wrought blocks of hard limestone, which were peeping out from the ground induced Mr Minos Kalokairinos of Heracleion to dig here five holes in which came to light an outer wall and parts of walls with antae of a vast edifice *similar* to the prehistoric palace of Tiryns, and apparently of the same age, for the pottery in it is perfectly identical with that found in Tiryns....

Schliemann resolved to dig there:

By its splendid situation close to the Asiatic coast, its delicious climate and its exuberant fertility, Crete must have been coveted from the first by the peoples of the coastlands; besides the most ancient myths refer to Crete and especially to Knossos, I should therefore not at all wonder if I found here on the virgin soil the remnants of a civilisation, in comparison to which even the Trojan War is an event of yesterday.

Schliemann once again could hardly have been closer to the mark, for this was precisely what Arthur Evans would uncover in 1900. Max Müller's reply to this remarkable letter, written from Oxford on 5 June, gives an added twist: 'Crete is a perfect rookery of nations, and there, if anywhere, *you ought to find the first attempts at writing, as adapted to Western wants.*' (My italics.)

There have been few more brilliant predictions in the history of archaeology, for it was at Knossos that Linear B was discovered, the script of the Aegean Late Bronze Age. Indeed it is possible that before he died Schliemann saw a single Linear B tablet which was found in Kalokairinos' excavation, the first known find in modern times.

The fascinating material in Kalokairinos' collection (which was destroyed in the liberation of Crete in 1898) only fuelled Schliemann's ambitions: 'I would like to conclude my life's work with a great undertaking in the to me familiar field of Homeric geography, that is to say, with the excavation of the prehistoric palace of Knossos.' He was back in Crete negotiating for the purchase of the site in spring 1889, still hoping to dig 'this palace so similar to that of Tiryns'. But the following year, unable to agree terms, he abandoned the project and returned to Troy. He was never to return to Crete, and deeply regretted his failure; writing in the last months of his life he admitted that it had been at Knossos that 'I hoped to discover the original home of Mycenaean civilisation'.

RETURN TO TROY

During these years Troy was still the central theme of Schliemann's career as an excavator. Twenty years had now elapsed since he had first set foot in the Troad, and still the central driving mystery remained unsolved. Had Homer's Troy stood at Hisarlik? If so, which level was it? Where were the indications of cultural contact with the world he had uncovered at Mycenae? Where *was* the Heroic Age? To examine these questions we must go back in time.

Flushed with his triumphs at Mycenae, Schliemann had returned to Troy in 1878 and 1879 for two major campaigns. He surveyed the plain and believed that he had 'blown up' the ancient and modern theory 'that at the time of the Trojan War there was a deep gulf in the plain of Troy'. As for the city itself, closer inspection of the strata enabled Schliemann to recognise two further 'cities': one, the sixth, he hesitantly thought a pre-Greek settlement founded by the Lydians (this was the level of the Grey Minyan pottery like that at Orchomenos); the other was in the older, prehistoric, levels and caused him to raise his Homeric city from second to third from bottom. The basic stratification had now taken shape and Schliemann seems to have felt his work on Hisarlik done: 'I think my mission accomplished and in a week hence I shall stop forever excavating Troy,' he wrote on 25 May 1879. The 1879 campaign was followed by the book which has justly been called his masterpiece, *Ilios*, remarkable not merely for its description of the finds and its thoroughgoing account of the literary sources, but for its scientific appendices by Schliemann's friends and collaborators. It was, by the standards of the time, a considerable achievement by one who had on his own admission started out an amateur. As Rudolf Virchow wrote in the preface, 'The treasure digger has become a scholar.'

With typical *élan* Schliemann wrote to his American publisher: 'There is no other Troy to excavate … this my present work will remain in demand as long as there are admirers of Homer in the world, nay as long as this globe will be inhabited by men.' But privately his doubts were still there. Had he really found Priam's palace? If Mycenae and his Troy were contemporary, where were the connections? Now that he had excavated a mainland Mycenaean royal cemetery and knew what its culture looked like, the cultural isolation and backwardness of his Troy seemed all the stranger. So though his book claimed finality – such are the demands of publishers as well as Schliemann's own bent – he could not disguise his own underlying concern. The facts simply did not fit. Indeed the only solution was that Homer had lived so long after the event that he had magnified a tiny kernel of fact into the great legend:

The imagination of the bards had full play; the small Ilium grew great in their songs…. I wish I could prove Homer to have been an eyewitness of the Trojan War! Alas, I cannot do it! … My excavations have reduced the Homeric Ilium to its real proportion.

In November 1879 he wrote to his German publisher, 'Now the only question is whether Troy has *only existed in the poet's imagination,* or in reality. If the latter is accepted, Hisarlik must and will be universally acknowledged to mark its site....' (My italics.) But of course, to admit that the glaring discrepancy between Homer and the archaeological fact was the product of poetic fantasy was but a short step from suggesting the whole thing was fiction. Within three years of the 1878–9 dig he wrote,

I thought I had settled the Trojan question forever ... but my doubts increased as time wore on.... Had Troy been merely a small fortified borough, a few hundred men might have taken it in a few days and the whole Trojan War would either have been a total fiction, or it would have had but a slender foundation.

In the back of his mind was the thought that either Hisarlik was refusing to give up its secrets, or he had got the wrong place.

Still perplexed by the mystery that he had found no apparent relationship between the Mycenaean world and Troy, he went back to Turkey in May 1881 and spent fifteen days trekking on horseback, alone but for local guides, re-examining all the other sites in the Troad; if he was looking for another possible site for Troy he did not say, nor did he find one. But in 1882 he came back for another season. This time, as we have seen, he had lured Wilhelm Dörpfeld away from the team at Olympia, and the young man's fine eye for architectural detail soon clarified the mess Schliemann had left from earlier campaigns. 'I regret now not having such architects with me from the beginning,' he wrote, 'but even now it is not too late.'

Schliemann now thought – going back on his previous dig – that Troy II, the burned city, was after all 'perfectly identical with Homer's Troy'. Dörpfeld had been able to distinguish the circuit wall of Troy II, identify two of its gates, and show that it had been a fortified prehistoric palace-residence with megaron-type buildings and formidable ramparts, parts of which are still standing today. Schliemann jumped at this and at the end of 1882 pronounced:

I have proved that in remote antiquity there was in the plain of Troy a large city, destroyed of old by a fearful catastrophe ... this city answers perfectly to the Homeric description of the site of sacred Ilios.... My work at Troy is now ended forever.... How it has been performed I now leave finally to the judgement of candid readers and honest students....

More than ten years had passed since Schliemann's siege of Troy had begun in earnest.

No more than on previous occasions, however, was Schliemann's work at Troy finished. This time his detractors drove him back. From 1883 an army captain, Ernst Bötticher, had been producing pamphlets claiming that Hisarlik was not a city at all, but a necropolis, a city of the dead, and that, worse, Schliemann and Dörpfeld had misled the public by withholding and faking evidence. The charge was preposterous (though interesting, as such allegations are emerging once more), but Schliemann felt he had to acquit himself by digging a new sector of Hisarlik with independent witnesses. As early as January 1887 he was writing to Calvert about preparations for his last great campaign, which lasted from autumn 1889 to August 1890, and it was then, with Schliemann tired and ill, that the crucial discovery was made.

Near the western border of the mound, 25 yards *outside* the great ramp of Troy II, the excavators uncovered a large building closely resembling the megaron (the royal hall) found at Tiryns. Here Dörpfeld's assistant Brückner found the peculiar Grey Minyan pottery of the mysterious sixth city which Schliemann had never been able to identify for certain; but here too he found pottery with the unmistakable Mycenaean shapes and decorations so familiar to them from Mycenae and Tiryns, especially the now well-known stirrup jars. In retrospect this discovery was truly sensational and epoch-making. In fact (for those who believed that the event happened at all) this would be seen as the long-awaited sign that Hisarlik was indeed Troy. For Schliemann the discovery must have been tremendously exciting, and yet a great shock, for it forced him to reconsider all that he had thought and published about the Homeric city; indeed it called into question the validity of all the conclusions he had reached about the chronology of the seven cities, and of course his identification of Priam's Troy. His 'Lydian' city had been the one in touch with Mycenaean Greece; the burned city of Troy II, *his* city of Priam, was not merely earlier but 1000 years earlier!

For a sick man it must have been a staggering blow to face the collapse of the whole intellectual structure he had built up with so much toil, discomfort and expenditure in 'this pestilential plain'. But he took it with fortitude and, typically, resolved to continue his excavations in 1891 on a still more ambitious scale in a determined effort to discover the truth. In any plea for a more balanced appreciation of Schliemann it is surely greatly to his credit that he continued to wrestle with the problems of this complex site for twenty years, trying to solve them by excavation, often in great physical hardship: after all, the needs of fame and status had long been satisfied. So 1891 was to be the final attempt. Schliemann never lived to fulfil his plans. At Christmas 1890, while Dörpfeld was at his desk penning the last words of their joint report on the new discoveries, Schliemann died miserably in Naples, collapsing in the street with a stroke and carried speechless and apparently penniless into a hotel foyer on the Piazza Umberto where, by one of those quirks of history, the Polish novelist Sienkiewicz observed a scene which, if Schliemann had told it of himself, we would doubtless have accused him of fabricating. Homer's Troy – and with it the Trojan War – eluded his perturbed spirit to the last.

That evening, a dying man was brought into the hotel. His head bowed down to his chest, eyes closed, arms hanging limp, and his face ashen, he was carried in by four people…. The manager of the hotel approached me and asked, 'Do you know, Sir, who that sick man is?' 'No.' 'That is the great Schliemann!' Poor 'great Schliemann'! He had excavated Troy and Mycenae, earned immortality for himself, and – was dying …

Letters from Africa (1901)

WILHELM DÖRPFELD: HOMER'S TROY FOUND?

Just over two years after Schliemann's death, in spring 1893, Wilhelm Dörpfeld returned to Troy; he was now in charge of the excavations, which were paid for by Sophie Schliemann and by the Kaiser. The dig of 1893–4 is one of the landmarks in archaeology. Acting on the assumption that the house found in 1890 lay inside a Bronze-Age city which lay far *outside* Schliemann's city, Dörpfeld opened up the southern side of Hisarlik in a great curve around the hill, and immediately struck walls far more magnificent than anything Schliemann had found. Over those two seasons he uncovered 300 yards of the city wall, sometimes buried under as much as 50 feet of earth and debris and overlain by the ruins of later cities. In the north-east corner there was an impressive angular watchtower, still standing 25 feet above the rock; originally it had been at least 30 feet tall with a vertical superstructure of brick or stone as high again. Sticking up like the prow of an old battleship, this must have dominated the plain of the Dumrek Su. Built of well-dressed blocks of limestone, this bastion was astonishingly like later classical work, which helps explain why Schliemann had demolished similar walling on the northern side. The city wall itself was beautifully made in sections, each of which ended in a distinctive offset, and each of which had a pronounced batter – perhaps, thought Dörpfeld, the 'batter' or 'angle' of the wall mentioned in Homer when Patroclus tries to scale the face of the wall. There was a gate on the east, protected by a long overlapping wall, near to which was the base of a large square tower built of beautifully fitted limestone blocks. On the south was an important gate with another massive tower fronted by stone bases – presumably where idols of the gods were displayed; on the western side, immediately below the house discovered in 1890, Dörpfeld found that one inferior section of the previous circuit had not been replaced by the city's builders, and even the most cynical critic did not blame him for pointing out that Homer describes one section of the wall being weaker than the rest, 'where the city is easiest to attack'.

Inside the city Dörpfeld found the remains of five large, noble houses whose ground plans could be recovered, and others that were more badly damaged, and from this he was able to deduce that the city had risen in concentric terraces with the front outer faces of the houses slightly wider than their backs, as if to achieve an effect of perspective narrowing towards the summit; this impression was reinforced by a beautiful house whose outer face reproduced the offsets of the city wall. Certainly, thought Dörpfeld, a master architect had planned the city and his scheme had been followed in the gradual replacement of almost the whole circuit: the latest additions to the beautiful walls were the great north-eastern bastion and the towers on the south and south-east, whose masonry is of the highest quality. Everywhere he found Mycenaean pottery: in its last phase this city, Troy VI, clearly had close contacts with the Mycenaean world. It had lasted, so Dörpfeld thought, from around 1500 to 1000 BC, near enough to the traditional date of the Trojan War in the twelfth century BC, and it had ended in violence: in many places debris was heaped up, walls had fallen, and there had been a 'great fire'. Surely, this was the city reflected in the epic – a 'well-built' city with wide streets, beautiful walls and great gates just as the *Iliad* had told. Even the weak wall and the 'angle' fitted. This, at last, must be the Troy of the Trojan War.

Our master Schliemann would never have believed, or even dared to hope, that the walls of Sacred Ilios of which Homer sang, and the dwellings of Priam and his companions, had been preserved to so great an extent as was actually the case.... The long dispute over the existence of Troy and over its site is at an end. The Trojans have triumphed ... Schliemann has been vindicated ... the countless books which in both ancient and modern times have been published against Troy have become meaningless. The appearance of the citadel must have been known to the singers of the *Iliad*, though perhaps only the singers of the older layers of the *Iliad* actually saw the citadel of Troy.

Troja und Ilion, 1902

The academic world was full of passionate philhellenes and lovers of Homer who were all too ready to agree. The English Homerist Walter Leaf wrote in *Homer and History*:

A fortress was found to have stood on the very spot where Homeric tradition placed it, a fortress which had been sacked and almost levelled by enemies.... From it follows the historical reality of the Trojan War.... We shall therefore not hesitate, starting from the fact that the Trojan War was a real war fought out in the place, and at least generally in the manner, described in Homer, to draw the further conclusion that some at least of the heroes whom Homer names as having played a prominent part in that war were real persons named by Homer's names, who did actually fight in that war.

Of course the 'proofs' furnished by archaeology were actually very much more limited than Leaf's declaration of faith would have us believe; such conclusions did not, could not, 'follow' from Dörpfeld's discoveries, but of course these discoveries caused a sensation at the time. Leaf was only voicing the general view when he declared that this was the long-awaited proof that Hisarlik was Troy: 'The discovery of the Mycenaean Troy was ... the definitive epoch in the history of the Homeric question.' And indeed, whatever the truth of that (there were doubters), a revolution had overtaken the history of the Bronze-Age Aegean in a very short time. George Grote's *History of Greece*, 1846–56, perhaps still the greatest work of its kind, could show no authority for the Bronze Age in Greece, the 'Heroic Age'; its myths were an unchronicled chasm unusable by the historian. Yet in 1884 the English scholar Sayce could write that 'hardly ten years have passed since the veil of an impenetrable seemed to hang over the beginnings of Greek history'. Now, with Troy, Mycenae and Orchomenos, Schliemann's energy and perseverance had begun the recovery of the lost past:

The heroes of the *Iliad* and *Odyssey* have become to us men of flesh and blood.... It is little wonder if so marvellous a recovery of the past, *in which we had ceased to believe*, should have awakened many controversies and wrought a silent revolution in our conceptions of Greek history. (My italics.)

As for the 'controversies', and Schliemann's many critics, Sayce continued,

It is little wonder if at first the discoverer who had so rudely shocked the settled prejudices of the historians should have met with a storm of indignant opposition or covert attack … [but] today no trained archaeologist in Greece or Western Europe doubts the main facts which Dr Schliemann's excavations have established; we can never again return to the ideas of ten years ago.

For Walter Leaf, too, Schliemann was epoch-making in this branch of study,

… and it is not for epoch-making men to see the rounding off and completion of their task. That must be the labour of a generation at least. A man who can state to the world a completely new problem must be content to let the final solution of it wait for those that come after him.

Indeed today the work Schliemann began is still nowhere near completed, though a coherent picture has emerged.

However, pleasant as it is to give Schliemann credit where credit is due over 100 years on, when he is once more under a storm of opposition as a charlatan and a faker, in 1894 the Trojan question was not finished, as Dörpfeld thought it was. In fact, even before Dörpfeld's finds at Hisarlik were published, they were overtaken by sensational discoveries at the site Schliemann had coveted for so long: Knossos.

THREE

THE COMING OF
THE GREEKS

Out in the wine-dark sea there is a rich and lovely island
called Crete, washed by the waves on every side, densely populated
with ninety cities … one of the ninety cities is a great town called
Knossos, and there for nine years King Minos ruled and enjoyed
the friendship of almighty Zeus.

HOMER, *Odyssey*

CRETE: THE KNOSSOS STORY

CRETE HAS BEEN OF PARAMOUNT IMPORTANCE throughout history, for it is a stepping-stone between Europe, Asia Minor and Africa. It is part of the chain of islands leading eastwards throughout Karpathos and Rhodes to south-west Anatolia (the Minoans were evidently of the same speech as the people of that region). North-westwards through Kythera, Crete has also had close connections for millennia with the southern Peloponnese (Crete was first inhabited by Greek speakers in around 1400 BC, and still is Greek). But looking southwards Crete is only 200 miles from the coast of Africa, and sponge fishermen from Kommos still go there to ply their trade: though European, Knossos is on the same latitude as Kairouan in central Tunisia, or Jablah in the Lebanon. The history of Crete has always reflected its geography: colonised in turn by Neolithic peoples, Minoans, Achaian Greeks, Dorians, Romans, Arabs, Byzantines, Venetians and Turks, it was the meeting place in the Late Bronze Age of mainlanders, Minoans, Anatolians and Egyptians.

The island, 160 miles long, is dominated by its great back-bone of mountains, the White Mountains, Ida and Dicti, the highest rising to over 8000 feet and often covered with snow in early summer. In these inaccessible peaks, sanctuaries existed from Neolithic times and gave rise to Minoan and early Greek cults of peculiar tenacity and old-fashionedness; here sacred caves were venerated for millennia, and in one, on Dicti, the birthplace of Zeus was said to be; here too a form of 'Dionysiac' ecstatic religion existed which, in the 1980s, became tangible with new archaeological evidence of human sacrifice and ritual cannibalism as late as the fifteenth century BC. The memory of these dark rituals survived vividly in later classical myths.

But Crete was also in classical times a repository of more 'historical' myths. One in particular, the myth of the lawgiver Minos, was believed to reflect real events. Homer mentions Minos and his just rule in Crete: he was later remembered as one of the great lawgivers in Hades. The historical tradition recorded by the fifth-century historian Thucydides was that Minos was the first person to establish a navy, that he dominated the Aegean and ruled the Cyclades

... in most of which he sent the first colonies, expelling the Carians and appointing his own sons as governors; and thus did his best to cut down piracy in those waters, a necessary step to secure the revenues for his own use.... As soon as Minos formed his navy, communication by sea became easier, and he colonised most of the islands.

It is with this period that Thucydides associates the building of the first walled cities in the Aegean world and, at a somewhat later stage, the expedition against Troy. Thucydides' perceptive account represents the rational classical Greek's interpretation of the many legends about Minos and his rule at Knossos (and interestingly it can now be paralleled by growing evidence of Minoan 'colonies' in the Cyclades, and on the coast of Asia Minor). According to Homer, it was Minos' grandson Idomeneus who led eighty ships to Troy with Agamemnon of Mycenae, but we should probably take that genealogical relation as symbolic; the ancients distinguished two kings called Minos, one in the fifteenth and one in the thirteenth century BC, and if we wish to take Thucydides' account at all seriously, it might be seen as implying one Minos ruling a Cretan ('Minoan') empire in the Aegean in the fifteenth century, and a king of Knossos in the thirteenth, perhaps calling himself a descendant of Minos, who was part of the Mycenaean world at the time of the Trojan War.

Of the many other Cretan legends which involve Minos, only one need detain us: it is the most famous, popularised by Mary Renault in her novel *The King Must Die*. According to this story, Minos was so powerful that even the mainlanders paid him tribute: each year the Athenians sent him seven young noblemen and seven young women as a tribute to be given to the Minotaur (literally the 'Bull of Minos'), a monstrous half-man half-bull which was kept in a labyrinth under the palace at Knossos. The story of how the young prince Theseus killed the Minotaur and was saved by his love for Minos' daughter Ariadne (and by her thread) need not be retold here, but the labyrinth (a non-Greek word from the root *labrys* = 'double axe') was one of the most constant features of the Knossos myth in later centuries – it appears in the classical coinage of the city, and it was the labyrinth in particular which attracted travellers who alighted in Crete. In fact it seems that the modern mismeaning of the word labyrinth must have arisen at Knossos itself.

Crete remained a 'famous island' even to Anglo-Saxon travellers who used it as a stopping place going eastwards (Crete was only occupied for a century by the Arabs, and was taken back by the Byzantines in 962); they knew of the position of *Creto thaet igland* halfway to Africa, and of its size (*hit is an hund mila long*). (Orosius' *History*.) All these early travellers were fascinated by Minos and the labyrinth, but opinions differed as to where it had been. The first modern survey of the island, made by Cristoforo Buondelmonti who spent nearly eleven weeks travelling there in 1415, identified ancient mine workings in the hills behind Gortys as being the site of the labyrinth, and this story we find repeated right up to the nineteenth century, for instance by Lord Elgin's associate Charles Cockerell. However the observant Spanish traveller Pero Tafur, whom we met at Troy, gives us a fascinating short description of Crete in 1435 in which he places the labyrinth made by Daedalus at Knossos, outside Candia, 'with many other antiquities'. Discerning travellers who knew their sources agreed. Richard Pococke published his account in *A Description of the East* in 1745, noting an 'eminence to the south' of the classical ruins of Knossos which may be the hill of Kefala where the palace stands. It was left to two nineteenth-century English travellers to put the map of early Crete on a firm footing, identifying most of the main sites with an accuracy which has not been challenged. The first was Richard Pashley, still only in his twenties when he spent seven months labouring over the Cretan mountains in 1834, and produced an illustrated account of his travels. When he reached and located Knossos, he thought that the tangle of ruins in the neighbourhood 'calls to mind the well-known ancient legend respecting the Cretan labyrinth.... There is however no sufficient reason for believing that the Cretan labyrinth ever had a more real existence than its fabled occupant.' The second observer was the naval surveyor Thomas Spratt. In 1865 he published *Travels in Crete*, which is still useful today. Spratt visited Knossos and rightly deduced that the legendary prehistoric palace was on the same site by the river Kairatos. At this time the area had been heavily quarried for building stone for Heraklion, and was still being plundered.

The memory of the site of Knossos had survived then, and the time would soon be ripe to see whether the legends about Minos contained a kernel of truth. Schliemann's digs at Troy and then Mycenae in the early and mid-1870s had revolutionised the view of Aegean prehistory, indeed revealed a world no one believed had existed. They also inspired many Greeks to delve into their prehistory.

PRELUDE TO KNOSSOS

Today Knossos is one of the best-known tourist sites in the Aegean; with its rebuilt halls, courtyards and stairways it is a goal for all visitors to Crete, a place where, courtesy of Sir Arthur

Evans' reconstructions, the modern visitor can momentarily enter a lost world which seems to combine innocence and sophistication. Evans is the great figure of the second stage of our search, and, as with Schliemann at Troy, the story of Knossos is inextricably bound up with Evans' own 'myth'.

No more than Schliemann at Troy was Evans the 'discoverer' of Knossos; he was not even the first excavator. In fact the specific site had been identified by the 1860s at the latest, and trial excavations were made there in December 1878 by the Heraklion merchant Minos Kalokairinos; his were the finds we saw with Schliemann and Dörpfeld in Chapter 2, and they were extensively commented on at the time – 'the most important of all the digs made in Crete', wrote the eminent German scholar Fabricius prior to Evans' dig. Born in 1843, Kalokairinos came from a well-to-do Cretan family. He says he had first wanted to dig the site of Knossos in 1864, but was prevented from doing so by the revolt against the Turks in 1866 (unlike Greece, Crete was still under Turkish rule). His chance came in 1878, when he was probably inspired to try again by Schliemann's success at Mycenae two years before, and impressed by the close similarity of vases dug up at Knossos to those found at Mycenae. Such pottery was already known, could be freely bought in Heraklion and had found its way into collections in Athens; it was no secret that it came from the Kefala hill at Knossos.

Kalokairinos made twelve trenches in the hill, each about 6 feet deep, and he immediately struck massive buildings. He realised he had a palatial complex about 60 yards by 45: in fact we now know that this was simply the west wing of the palace, the throne-room apartments. He hit the curved corner of the antechamber of the throne-room, exposing red painted walls; he uncovered part of the west front, which greets visitors today as they come from the entrance kiosk (here could be seen evidence of the fire which finally destroyed the palace); he also cleared the third magazine of its twelve pithoi (storage jars) which still contained peas, barley and broad beans. In the debris in the corridor outside the magazine he may have found the Linear B tablet seen by Evans in Heraklion in 1894, the first known in modern times. So Kalokairinos made quite an extensive trial dig and he took sample pottery throughout the west wing of the palace, including stirrup jars, amphorae and jugs, possibly of the thirteenth century BC, as well as 'champagne glasses' (kylices) and decorated one-handled cups certainly of a thirteenth-century date – in other words of the same period as Schliemann's finds at Tiryns.

The success of this trial dig was Kalokairinos' undoing. In February 1879 the native Cretan parliament refused him permission to dig further, for fear that the finds might be expatriated by the Turks to the Imperial Museum in Istanbul. Nevertheless the finds were widely reported and created great scholarly interest. Kalokairinos sent pithoi to London, Paris and Rome, hoping to interest archaeologists and institutions in the site (the pithos he gave to the British Museum can still be seen, in the corridor to the Mycenaean room). Among those he showed round the site were Schliemann and Dörpfeld, the American consul Stillman, and the Englishman Arthur Evans who had been intrigued by Schliemann's finds on the mainland. All were agreed that this was a palace remarkably like that at Tiryns – the pottery, as the Frenchman Haussoullier said, was 'so similar to finds at Mycenae, Rhodes and Spáta [in Attica]'.

When Evans examined Kalokairinos' collection at his home in March 1894 he swiftly formulated plans to excavate the palace: he said he hoped to be the preferred candidate for permission to dig the site, and in that year he bought a quarter of it, 'where the Palace of Minos stands which I found', notes Kalokairinos in his diary. In 1898 Evans came back again, a few days before the burnings and fighting in Heraklion which preceded the liberation. They went out together to the site where 'I showed him the double axehead engraved on the stones, and the axes on the upper part of the labyrinth.' Unfortunately Kalokairinos' collection was destroyed when his house was burned down in the fighting against the Turks, and his excavation notes went with it (rebuilt in 1903, the house, which is near the old harbour, is now the Local History Museum of Crete). After the liberation Evans was able to buy the rest of the site of Knossos, where he started excavation in 1900. Evans' dramatic finds gave Kalokairinos much joy, being a loyal Cretan: 'These new discoveries will make the Heraklion Museum richer and worthy of admiration: people from all over Europe and America are coming to visit the palace and see the artefacts.'

We should be grateful that Evans and not Kalokairinos was able to dig the site, for the Cretan was not a professional excavator: his was a messy dig as far as Evans was concerned (he says so in one of his grudging references to his predecessor in his book *The Palace of Minos*). But it is pleasing that a Cretan played his part in the search. There is a touching endpiece to the story. In 1902, by which time Evans' fame was worldwide, Kalokairinos was fifty-nine, his business had collapsed, and he turned again to the law, in which he had taken a degree as a young man. His thesis was entitled 'The legal system of King Minos and its influence on Roman legislators'!

Ironically our comparatively meagre record of Kalokairinos' dig is now proving of value to historians attempting to recover a picture of the palace as it was when Evans found it, because, for good or ill, Evans was to change the site at Knossos permanently and irreparably. Indeed it is unlikely now that firm agreement will ever be reached on the nature of the last palace of Knossos, the palace from which, if the Homeric catalogue of ships is correct, King Idomeneus sailed with eighty vessels to help Agamemnon of Mycenae sack Troy.

ARTHUR EVANS

Evans was born in 1851, at which time Schliemann was on the way to making his first fortune in California, buying gold-dust from prospectors. The background of the two men could hardly have been more different. Evans was Oxford-educated; his father, John, was a well-known antiquary and collector, treasurer of the Royal Society, and one of that group of men we have already met, Sir John Lubbock among them, who established the new studies of anthropology and prehistory on a scientific basis in Britain. Evans was brought up steeped in antiquities, and he had a brilliant eye for their tiniest detail. Tough, obstinate and determined to the point of dogmatism, Evans was also an exceptionally good field researcher – like Schliemann in this respect – who loved to travel, especially when roughing it, and who from his late teens until well into middle age liked to make long journeys on foot or horseback into difficult and primitive country: his minute examinations of the local terrain in eastern and central Crete remain the basis of all modern topographical study.

After a holiday in the Balkans when he was twenty years old, he developed a particular interest in Bosnia, then under Turkish rule. He was in Sarajevo during the 1875 rising and produced a book, which Gladstone quoted in Parliament, on the subject of Turkish atrocities. In 1877 Evans was appointed special correspondent to the *Manchester Guardian* by the editor, C.P. Scott, and in the next few years Evans lived a cloak-and-dagger life of extraordinary adventure and risk, a career which in most people's eyes would have been quite enough for one lifetime (his dispatches were later published as *Letters to the Manchester Guardian*).

But in all this Evans maintained his interest in archaeology and antiquities; he was able, for instance, to be in England to see the Kensington exhibition of Schliemann's treasures from Troy in 1878, and was electrified by what he saw. In 1883, shortly before he became keeper of the Ashmolean Museum at Oxford, he went to Greece, saw Mycenae and Tiryns, and visited Schliemann in Athens. There he spent some hours examining the treasure from Mycenae. Their conversation, unfortunately, is unrecorded. That Evans was already of the opinion that Mycenaean civilisation originated in Crete seems unlikely, but the idea was not a new one; Schliemann had already been to Knossos, and Virchow and Müller, as we have seen, would soon be urging Schliemann to look to Crete for the source of the civilisation of the shaft graves. *Ex oriente lux* had long been the guiding dictum of continental scholarship: in other words, the characteristic features of western and Greek civilisation came as 'light from the east', from Egypt and Mesopotamia, incomparably older and richer cultures. Schliemann and his followers were following this in assuming that Mycenae and Tiryns were built by Phoenicians, that the Greeks only arrived in the 'Dark Age' after the collapse of Mycenaean civilisation. But there was a growing reaction to this viewpoint which contended that the west had always shown a measure of creativity and originality of its own (Reinach's book on this, *The Oriental Mirage* of 1893, made a particular impression on Evans).

The crux came in 1893 (a tragic year for Evans, for his wife died). In the spring of that year, searching among the trays of the antiquity dealers in the Athens flea market, he came across a number of tiny three- and four-sided stones engraved with what appeared to be an unknown system of writing. Evans had seen similar stones in Oxford: now he was told they came from Crete. At that time, the idea that a hieroglyphic system of writing could have existed in any part of prehistoric Europe seemed far-fetched, but this appears to have been what impelled Evans in spring 1894 to go to Crete, where he met Kalokairinos, saw the site at Knossos, and was shown the single Linear B tablet preserved from debris at the magazines. That decided him: 'The great days of Crete were those of which we still find a reflection in the Homeric poems – the period of Mycenaean culture, to which here at least we would fain attach the name Minoan,' he wrote, before he had even set spade to soil at Knossos. 'The golden age of Crete lies far back beyond the limits of the historical period [i.e. Greece and Rome]; its culture … is practically identical with that of the Peloponnese and a large part of the Aegean world.'

On 23 March 1900 the excavation started in the area where Kalokairinos had dug twenty years before. By an extraordinary accident the building had been left virtually untouched since the day over three millennia before when it had been consumed by fire – only a few inches below the grass, parts of walls appeared with frescoes still adhering to them. The chamber laid bare had red-painted walls up to 7 feet high, surrounded by gypsum benches with some sort of sunken tank on one side, and on the other – incredibly – a gypsum throne still in position, undamaged but bearing on its back the marks of the fire which finally destroyed the palace. Scattered on the floor were beautiful alabaster ritual containers which Evans thought the last king of Knossos had been using in a desperate rite of propitiation before the final blow fell. The finds were truly sensational, but it was their great antiquity which immediately made Knossos the focus of Aegean archaeology, for here was a high civilisation which went back into the fourth millennium BC, far beyond anything known from the mainland. As early as 27 March 1900 Evans could write in his diary:

The extraordinary phenomenon – nothing Greek – nothing Roman – perhaps one single fragment of late black varnished ware among tens of thousands. Even Geometrical pottery [seventh century BC] fails us – though … a flourishing Knossos existed lower down [the valley] … nay, its great period goes well back to the pre-Mycenaean period.

Evans had in fact discovered a hitherto unknown civilisation.

THE DIG OF 1900 AT KNOSSOS

It is worth spending little time over Evans' excavation at Knossos, for it was one of the most famous and significant digs in archaeology; on it still rests our whole view of the structure and chronology of the Aegean Bronze Age. It is also worthwhile because hundreds of thousands of tourists visit the site every year and they are not always well served by either the guides to the site or the books available to tourists. Additional difficulty is caused by Evans' reconstructions, which have destroyed or masked many key features. To be fair to Evans, he was immediately faced with conservation problems: as can be seen from the 1900 photograph, the throne-room with its damaged frescoes was far too delicate to leave unprotected – it suffered rain damage that first winter, in fact – and Evans roofed it over in 1901. Similarly it was entirely justifiable to support and restore the many-storeyed Grand Staircase, all of whose architectural elements were found burnt and fallen in on themselves below ground level – surely anyone who has experienced the thrill of walking down those stairs into the truly labyrinthine lower corridors of the palace will be grateful to Evans for giving that opportunity; nor can there be any doubt about the basic correctness of the restoration: the Grand Staircase definitely was there. But Evans went far beyond this. Although the palace nowhere survived above head height at the level of the central court, he gradually came to want to restore many parts of the palace to show what it might have looked like. This work was mainly done between 1922 and 1930, in which year the throne-room complex reached its present state.

A first point: in the 1900 dig, in which Evans uncovered the main part of the west wing where Kalokairinos had dug, he was on site for nine weeks and his workforce numbered anything from fifty to 180 men. In that time 2 acres were uncovered. It is fair to say that such a complex site would take years today, so Evans' technique, for all his undoubted skill and his wonderful eye for detail, is nearer to that of Schliemann than to that of our own day. Also, though Evans had been interested in archaeology since his youth, this was his first proper excavation, at the age of forty-nine, and he was never to excavate a mainland site. The main work took place over the first four seasons, so it is important to establish what Evans thought he had found *at the time*, for, as is the practice in archaeology, most of the millions of sherds found at Knossos were thrown away; only a sample, about 1 per cent (but that is still scores of baskets!), were retained. Archaeology then, in destruction.

Fortunately the main elements were recorded at the time in the day books of Evans' assistant Mackenzie, which, along with

Evans' notebooks, photographs (some of which appear in this book) and architects' plans, are kept in the Ashmolean Museum at Oxford, where the interested reader who cannot get to Knossos can see the best Cretan collection outside Greece. Out of this raw material Evans constructed his annual reports, published by the British School of Athens from 1900 onwards, and this record was brought together in the *Palace of Minos*. But Evans was an old man when he wrote the later volumes of this great work, and it is best to go back to the annual reports to see what they made of it actually at the time.

Evans' report for 1900 shows that he agreed with Schliemann and Dörpfeld about Knossos. His first impressions are of a 'Mycenaean' palace just like that at Tiryns. He makes several stylistic parallels with Tiryns: the bathroom adjoining the 'Central Clay Area' in the west wing was like that at Tiryns, for instance; the brown and green reliefs with carved rosettes from the southern entrance he compared with marble decoration found by Elgin and Schliemann at Mycenae; the latest changes in the layout of the palace he attributed to the work of Mycenaean overlords, for this final phase was full of 'pottery of the mature Mycenaean class, analogous to that found at Mycenae, Ialysus [Rhodes] and Tell el Amarna [in Egypt]'. The Egyptian parallels, which included enamelled roundels which had been fixed to the throne-room ceiling, suggested to Evans a thirteenth-century-BC date for the throne-room, which was from the 'latest phase of the palace'; by then, Evans thought, 'the Mycenaean Lords of Knossos had achieved the conquest of the Eteocretan population'; on the whole, he argued, 'it is difficult to bring down the period of the destruction of the Palace later than the thirteenth century BC'.

The interpretation, then, could hardly be clearer. Evans thought he had found a great and ancient Minoan culture which in its last stage of existence, in the fourteenth to thirteenth centuries BC, had been conquered and occupied by mainland Mycenaeans who had refurbished the place, decorating it with mainland palace-style designs, filling it with Mycenaean pottery and even inserting within it a Mycenaean throne-room. There had even been, it appears, a mainland megaron or royal hall, which Evans initially termed a 'Pelasgian megaron' but later deemed (almost certainly wrongly) to be a classical intrusion – its foundations were subsequently demolished and used in one of his more fanciful reconstructions. Evans' interpretation was thus entirely consistent with the analysis of the pottery found by Kalokairinos which had been examined and published by Fabricius, Haussoullier, Furtwängler and Löschke, as well as commented on by Schliemann and Dörpfeld. All these experts agreed on the style and approximate date of this pottery, and as illustrations of it were published we can be sure they (and Evans) were right: the palace was indeed occupied by a Greek dynast in the thirteenth century BC, just as Homeric tradition had it: the Achaian Idomeneus could indeed have taken an army from his palace around the traditional date of the Trojan War.

However, Evans soon abandoned his initial impressions. He announced a new theory of the relationship between Crete and the mainland as early as his 1901 report. (The main work on the palace was over by 1905, though further explorations were done before the First World War, and in the early 1920s. The last year of large-scale work at Knossos was 1930.)

The new theory Evans had evolved was as follows. It appears in his *Palace of Minos*, published in four massive volumes between 1921 and 1936, one of the greatest works of archaeological scholarship ever written, unrivalled in its astonishing reach, its grasp of parallel evidence in other civilisations. If my account appears to be overcritical of Evans, it is only because, in the area of his work which is relevant to our search – the problem of the last palace of Knossos – a growing body of evidence suggests that Evans got it completely wrong in his final version. It should be pointed out, though, that many experts still agree with much of Evans' analysis, and the interested reader who wishes to look further into this fascinating but treacherous material is recommended to consult the appropriate part of the bibliography on p. 308.

Evans found that the hill of Knossos had been inhabited since Neolithic times, and that a sophisticated palace civilisation had existed from 1900 or 1800 BC with not one but two forms of writing, both unknown. This civilisation had evidently dominated the Cyclades and much of the rest of the Aegean world until the burning of Knossos, which Evans dated to around 1420 BC. This 'Minoan' empire must have had a powerful fleet, both naval and mercantile, for Knossos differed conspicuously from the known mainland sites in having no fortifications whatsoever; clearly, thought Evans, there had been a kind of *Pax Minoica* imparting peace to the whole region. Such archaeological evidence therefore seemed to corroborate the outline of Thucydides' account of Greek prehistory which we have already seen regarding the Trojan story:

The first person known to us by tradition as having established a navy is Minos. He made himself master of what is now called the Hellenic sea, and ruled over the Cyclades, into most of which he sent the first colonies ... and he did his best to put down piracy in those waters, a necessary step to secure the revenues for his own use.

The Minos legends inevitably made a great impression on Evans, and he soon asserted that the Mycenaean civilisation found by Schliemann at Mycenae and Tiryns was merely a barbarian offshoot, colonised and 'civilised' by Minoans, employing Minoan artists and craftsmen (as for instance in the masterpieces of the shaft graves and the friezes of the Treasury of Atreus). In his presidential address to the Hellenic Society in 1912 Evans expressed his certainty in the 'absolute continuity' of Minoan and Mycenaean civilisation, a unity which on the mainland and in Crete 'imposes the conclusion that there was continuity of race'. He was equally sure that this world was not Greek, though he was prepared to admit that Greek speakers may already have been present in Greece before the 'Dorian invasion' at the end of the Bronze Age, as a kind of submerged lower class. Homer's heroic world he thought definitely post-Mycenaean: 'Homer, though professedly commemorating the deeds of Achaian heroes, is able to picture them among surroundings which, in view of the *absolute continuity* of Minoan and Mycenaean history we may *definitely set down as non-Hellenic.*' (My italics.) In other words the Homeric poems, though written in Greek, were, according to Evans, merely pale reflections of the great non-Greek Minoan–Mycenaean culture. The Trojan War itself was nothing more than a revamped Cretan myth. It is remarkable that Evans was so dogmatic about this matter when he had 2000 Linear B tablets in his own possession, *untranslated*: 'If the inhabitants of the latest palace structures are to be regarded as "Achaians" the Greek occupation of Crete must, on this showing, be carried back to Neolithic times.' The very idea of it! Evans was asserting here that there was no sign in the archaeology of Knossos which could indicate the arrival of a new race, the Mycenaeans, despite his clear initial impression precisely to this effect! It is a mark of Evans' sway, the grand, proprietorial manner with which until his death in 1941 he controlled the interpretation of his finds at Knossos (which, after all, he owned!) that he was able to push through ideas which many competent authorities saw as more than questionable. The premise of continuity of race and culture was particularly dubious: '*I* do not presume to dispute it,' wrote Walter Leaf in 1915, but 'many good authorities believe that they can detect a wholly new influence entering with LM III [i.e. after 1400].' And of course they were right: as Evans had originally thought, the destruction shortly before 1400 BC heralded the arrival of conquerors from mainland Greece who smashed the society of Minoan Crete and imposed on it their own militarist bureaucracy (see Chapter 5); this is now generally accepted. An even more revolutionary rewrite of Evans' thesis would return us to the state of affairs as Evans saw it in 1900: Greek rule at Knossos lasting until a final destruction around 1200 BC or a little later. The last palace at Knossos was, after all, Greek; its art and its Linear B archive characteristic of the Mycenaean world of the thirteenth century BC.

WHY DID EVANS COME TO THE
CONCLUSIONS HE DID?

In the evolution of modern thought about the Bronze-Age Aegean there have been two crucial stages. The pioneering work of Schliemann, driven by his passionate faith in the truth of Homer, engendered a state of mind which tended to consider all relics of this Mycenaean culture as illustrating Homer's poetry, and Homer as reflecting an actual heroic world. Arthur Evans' epoch-making discoveries at Knossos, however, and the reconstitution of the earlier Minoan civilisation, put Schliemann's finds in an entirely new perspective. The state of mind which grew out of the tremendous (not to say dogmatic) grasp of ideas with which Evans publicised his finds has been equally pervasive – namely the unswerving conviction that every cultural manifestation on the mainland was introduced, if not actually made, by Minoans who had conquered and colonised Greece and imposed on it their own civilisation. In short Evans was to assert that the world of Homer never existed except as a distant reflection of a Minoan world. These two mental attitudes, the Schliemann and Evans schools, have dominated the field of research, even when both were proved in part misguided.

Evans was influenced in arriving at his viewpoint by the key discovery of writing – it was what he had been after all along. Masses of Linear B tablets came to light first in the magazines where Kalokairinos had dug, and later all over the palace: the Bronze Age had been literate after all. But a problem immediately arose. The writing was found in the *last phase* of the palace, the phase with which Evans initially associated not only the tablets, but the throne-room and most of the painted frescoes, those so-called masterpieces of Minoan art: the phase which he later termed the 'reoccupation' by 'squatters'. As he evolved his ideas about the basic structure of the Bronze Age this became an intractable problem, and so he altered his opinion that the tablets were of the reoccupation period, asserting instead that the last phase had been illiterate. For how could such a sophisticated civilisation have been illiterate, and yet the 'squatter phase' literate? It went against all the contemporary ideas of historical progress. And so Evans put forward his theory of the structure of Bronze-Age chronology: Early, Middle and Late Bronze Age and their subdivisions (what experts call Early, Middle and Late Minoan for Crete, Helladic for the mainland, Cycladic for the islands, with their subdivisions, e.g. MM II, LH III B). The basic idea of Evans' chronology rested on a comparison with the Old, Middle and New Kingdoms of ancient Egypt, but there was perhaps an equally important analogy behind it in late-nineteenth-century ideas about art and civilisation. This was the assumption that all civilisations had a period of beginnings, a period of flowering, and a period of decadence, and it was clearly the model behind Evans' picture of Cretan civilisation. Even in 1935, after renewed excavations at Mycenae and Tiryns had cast doubts on his interpretation of the Late Bronze Age, the eighty-four-year-old Evans attacked Alan Wace's correct (as we now know) dating of the Treasury of Atreus to the thirteenth century BC (LH III B) – how, he asked, could he possibly date the finest example of Mycenaean architecture to 'the last age of decadence?' Much of Evans' work has triumphantly stood the test of time, and there is no denying his great stature in the annals of archaeology, but on the history of relations between Crete and the mainland in the Late Bronze Age it now appears he was wrong, and it is worth asking why: how did Evans' theories come about?

As with Schliemann, we should try to put ourselves in Evans' shoes. To do so, we need to know something about the intellectual climate of the time when Evans first announced his theory of tripartite chronology to the Anthropology section of the British Association, in 1904. As mentioned earlier, Evans was born in 1851 and his father was a noted antiquarian, the first British scholar to embrace Darwin's ideas and apply them to the study of prehistory. Darwin's theories of human evolution, as we have seen, strongly influenced human disciplines and especially prehistory and archaeology in the late nineteenth century. A formidable scholar, far more so than Schliemann, Evans could hardly have been better equipped, temperamentally and intellectually, to evolve a system of classification for Aegean prehistory, and this is what he did: ample models existed already, as in Lubbock's coining of the terms of Palaeolithic and Neolithic (see p. 63). However in broader matters of cultural change in art and civilisation it was German scholars who were most influential. In particular Winckelmann's famous dictum on the phases of ancient art (the necessary, the beautiful, and the superfluous or decadent) had been a prime model in nineteenth-century scholarship as it had been for artists like Goethe. Broad theories like this were applied to sociology and anthropology in the 1830s and 1840s by scholars like Auguste Comte. Let us again remember the conjuncture of politics and ideology at this time, especially in Britain. Evans' father had warmly welcomed Darwin's great book in 1859; to many scholars the idea that Man had descended from animals had become impossible to resist even before this, as archaeological evidence accumulated in the 1850s – the apelike skull of Neanderthal Man, for instance, was found in 1856. The relevance of such ideas to history was obvious. The leading landmark of 'cultural anthropology' in England, Tylor's *Primitive Culture* of 1871, saw the evolution of culture in three broad stages, from primitive 'animism' (a word coined by Tylor), to the higher monotheistic religions, to the eventual triumph of science, which late-nineteenth-century intellectuals saw as capable of explaining increasingly wide areas of human experience without reference to the spiritual world. The tendency, then, was to think that a 'systematic law' could be worked out in history.

Such theories convinced Evans that there was a close relationship between art and archaeology, just as there was no boundary between archaeology and anthropology: 'The same object is showed by both – to illustrate the laws of evolution as applied to human arts,' he wrote as early as 1884. Though, as with Schliemann, we still lack a definitive biography of Evans, it seems reasonable to link his own ideas about historical change, progress and decline with those of his time. This biological view of human evolution, for instance, may have tempted Evans to date the Linear B tablets earlier than we now know they are. In his eyes Linear B had to be 'a considerable advance in the Art of Writing', as he wrote in 1909, and later, in 1921, 'the highest development of the Minoan system of writing', and yet again 'a graphic expression of the tendency which produced the beautiful "Palace Style" of Art'. Therefore the tablets could hardly be of the last period of the palace, which Evans thought a time of decline. Accordingly he tried to justify a fifteenth-century dating for the tablets by reinterpreting their find circumstances as recorded in his field notes: this is what has caused the massive discrepancies between the *Palace of Minos* and the original day books and reports, discrepancies which have caused bitter scholarly argument and even led to accusations of fraud in the popular press. In fact Linear B was the language of foreign, Greek, conquerors and none of the caches of tablets can be certainly, or even convincingly, dated before the last phase of the palace, the one which ended *c*.1200 BC in the conflagration of which Evans found evidence in his first days in the dig in 1900.

Of course Evans was dealing with a very complex site whose history extended back to Neolithic times. Like Schliemann he was a pioneer, and pioneers inevitably make mistakes. The bulk of Evans' work, including his remarkable comparative chronology for the Bronze-Age Aegean, has triumphantly stood the test of time. But it is interesting with hindsight to see how Evans read his evidence as it came out of the soil in the spring of 1900, and how later his desire to impose an all-embracing system on it persuaded him to modify his ideas with dramatic effect on subsequent ideas about the Late Bronze Age in Crete.

THE MAINLANDERS

Why were we so timid at Mycenae ten years ago when we came to draw conclusions from your discoveries in the beehive tombs? It seems to me we were too much frightened by what we found and that we have rather badly misdated [the Treasury of] Atreus. You know, this old traditional view that we have all swallowed without question and that the 'Cretans' are always proclaiming is certainly all wrong – I mean the view that Late Helladic III [1400–1200] was a period of decadence … [it] was the climax of Mycenaean greatness in wealth, power and splendour; and the greatest height was reached in the thirteenth century.

CARL BLEGEN in a letter to Alan Wace, 29 March 1931

Evans' view dominated his field for half a century, helped by his failure to publish the Linear B tablets in full. But of course from Schliemann's time onwards, a mass of important work was done all over the Aegean world through which a coherent picture of Mycenaean civilisation gradually emerged. All along there were many scholars who felt that Evans' picture of the Bronze Age was wrong and that Mycenaean civilisation was Greek. As early as the 1890s the Greek archaeologist Tsountas, who had succeeded Schliemann at Mycenae, was putting forward this view; it was shared among others by the English Homerist Walter Leaf. In the period between the excavation at Knossos and the beginning of the Second World War more work was done on a number of important mainland sites – Orchomenos, Tiryns, Gla, Thebes, Asine, Midea and Athens, to name only the most important ones – and in some, fragmentary Linear B inscriptions were found, suggesting that the language might not necessarily be Cretan. During this period the mainland chronology was established by detailed attention to stratigraphy and pottery styles. The landmarks were the digs of the British archaeologist Alan Wace at Mycenae in 1922–3 and the American Carl Blegen at Korakou, Zygouries and Prosymna.

Wace and Blegen are important figures in our story, and both believed from the start that Mycenaean civilisation was Greek. Their archaeological arguments saw no cultural break, no intrusion of new people, between the Middle Bronze Age and the Dark-Age Greek world: hence the Greeks must already have been present at least as far back as the early second millennium

BC. These ideas were supported by other discoveries. Linguists working on the structure, origins and relationships of the Indo-European languages arrived at much the same date for the coming of the Greeks. Similarly, Nilsson's studies in Greek mythology and religion showed, for instance, that all the great classical Greek myths were tied to Mycenaean centres: the Atreids at Mycenae, Oedipus at Thebes, Jason at Iolkos, Herakles at Tiryns, and many more including obscure sites like Lerna, Nemea, Troizen, Sicyon, Midea and so on. If Greek mythology was so anchored in prehistoric times, then must not those times have been Greek? This view was held so strongly by archaeologists like Wace and Blegen (who, unlike Evans, were experts in mainland sites) that in the 1920s they were confidently putting the arrival of the Greeks in Greece at around 1900 BC. This thesis was underlined in an article signed by them both which was published in 1939 before Blegen's sensational finds at Pylos; this piece remains a *tour de force* in its use of the totality of the evidence, in which Mycenaean influence was traced all over the Aegean in the fourteenth and thirteenth centuries BC and the Mycenaean conquest of Crete was argued with firm assurance. This epoch-making article was, however, tucked away in a German periodical, such was Evans' influence over British publications; indeed there are still some who resist Wace and Blegen's conclusions.

So a broad picture of the internal chronology, and a model for the mainland Mycenaean society, were assembled without recourse to the controversial evidence from Knossos. The natural step for Blegen, after his successes on mainland sites, was to turn back to the place which had started the whole search: Troy itself. So many questions needed answers; so much had been destroyed or inadequately described by Schliemann that he had left almost as many mysteries as facts. Dörpfeld had done an admirable job of untangling the main architectural sequence of the site, but the study of Mycenaean pottery had been in its early days then, and Dörpfeld had not been able to offer precise dating for the Late-Bronze-Age sequences. In fact the pottery of the whole of the

Late Bronze Age (what we call Troys VI and VIIa and b) had been lumped together for the purposes of classification – no more precision had been possible in the 1890s, and Dörpfeld had left the approximate end of Bronze-Age Troy at around 1000 BC. Blegen was determined to return to Troy to make a sober and scientific re-excavation of parts of the site, including some areas left untouched by Schliemann and Dörpfeld. But sober and scientific as he undoubtedly was, at the back of his mind clearly lay another question. With so much more sophisticated stratigraphical techniques at his disposal than were available to Schliemann and Dörpfeld, might it be possible to determine at which level in Hisarlik Homer's Troy had existed? It will not perhaps be a great surprise to the reader to discover that, not for the first time in the search for Troy, the archaeologists found what they hoped to find.

Blegen's dig at Troy lasted seven seasons, from 1932 to 1938. It was one of the most skilful excavations carried out anywhere in the world up to that time, and remains a landmark in archaeology: for the third time Hisarlik became, as it were, a testing ground for archaeological technique. It is documented in the publication *Troy*, vols I–IV, and by a vast set of photographs now in the University of Cincinnati along with a considerable quantity of film – perhaps the first time that an Aegean Bronze-Age dig was thus documented (one reel preserves Dörpfeld's visit to the site in 1935). The significance of the dig to the history of science had nothing to do with the Trojan War, of course, but with the growth of our knowledge of the development of civilisation in north-west Anatolia in the Bronze Age: its true importance lay in the earlier levels, Troys I and II. Blegen was able to establish about fifty lesser strata within the nine major 'cities' superimposed on Hisarlik, taking the history of occupation on the site back into the fourth millennium BC (we would now date the foundation of Troy I to about 3600 BC). But inevitably the curiosity of the archaeologists was at its sharpest when they re-examined strata of Troy VI, which Dörpfeld had claimed as Homer's Troy. Blegen soon became convinced that the destruction here could not have been by the hand of man, as Dörpfeld had thought. In one place the foundation of the wall had actually shifted; elsewhere whole internal walls had fallen over and still lay heaped, covered by later deposits. There seemed no way out of this – even Dörpfeld himself, who looked at the piled rubble on site, had to agree. Troy VI, the city of the great walls, had been destroyed by an earthquake, not by Agamemnon's army. But in other places, where he could examine untouched strata above the ruins of Troy VI, Blegen made a truly dramatic discovery.

THE SIEGE OF TROY DISCOVERED?

We believe that Troy VIIa has yielded actual evidence showing that the town was subjected to siege, capture, and destruction by hostile forces at some time in the general period assigned by Greek tradition to the Trojan War, and that it may safely be identified as the Troy of Priam and of Homer.

CARL BLEGEN, *Troy*, Vol. IV, 1958

Blegen's attention focused on the successor to Troy VI, which he called VIIa. After the earthquake the inhabitants had patched up the place: they were the same people, and there had been no change of population. The main circuit of the walls still stood, although the superstructure had been damaged. But a dramatic change had come over the city. The wide streets now contained a network of shanties crammed together, with storage jars sunk into their floors – some honeycombed with as many as twenty or thirty in a space covering only a few square feet. Where before there had been elegant free-standing buildings, only around a couple of dozen in the entire citadel, now there were gloomy little bungalows partitioned off, one-roomed, barely furnished 'multiple tenancies', squashed up against the walls in what had been the spacious circular terraces and wide walks. The implications of this in terms of the social history of Troy were not fully examined by Blegen: he came to a simple conclusion, that a much larger population had had to be *temporarily* sheltered inside the walls. Normally taciturn archaeologists were prepared to talk of an atmosphere of retrenchment and fear, of – dare we say it – a siege mentality. Some of the finds had a contemporary resonance. Right inside the main gate Blegen found what he thought was a bakery adjoining a public saloon or shop which he called the 'snack bar', and where he thought bread and wine had been dispensed to harassed Homeric heroes as they staggered back from the front line with battle shock. Blegen inferred a war economy like the soup kitchens during the Blitz of London, the images of his own day. Other signs betokened growing isolation, as if the city had been cut off: there were no imported luxuries, and few (if any) sherds from imported pots – mainly poor local imitations of Mycenaean wares.

Whatever the townspeople were frightened of seemed to have destroyed them, or so Blegen thought. Everywhere their city was marked by the ravages of fire, buried in masses of burned mudbrick, charred wood and debris: 'The effect,' said Blegen, 'was one of utter desolation.' There was little doubt that it had come from the hand of man. In the doorway of a house were found parts of a human skeleton covered in burnt timbers, stones and debris from the houses which had collapsed on the victims; in places the heaped ashes and wreckage were 5 feet deep. In the street outside the snack bar was part of a skull; remnants of another skull were found further to the west. In the burned rubbish covering a house outside the eastern citadel wall was the jawbone of a human skull, the rest of the skull crushed by a stone. An arrowhead found west of the main street, Blegen thought, 'might have been discharged by an invading Achaean'.

The destruction by fire, the traces of bodies, the arrowhead – put them together with the overcrowded conditions, the soup kitchen, the storage jars, and there you have it: a threatened community desperately laying in supplies to withstand a siege, and then the evidence of their final destruction. Was this the archaeological proof – so long sought – that the Trojan War had actually taken place? All now depended on the date. It was obvious that it was roughly right, but was it before or after the fall of the great palaces on the mainland in around 1200? Clearly Agamemnon would not have sailed to sack Troy *after* Mycenae had been sacked and started its decline. In particular, and scholars have often forgotten this, Troy VIIa had to be destroyed before the end of Pylos, which Blegen started excavating in 1939 – *after* the dig at Troy, but before its publication: clearly old King Nestor could not depart for Troy from a palace already in ashes and which, as the archaeologists had immediately seen in 1939, was never reoccupied. Consciously or subconsciously, this must have been in Blegen's mind as he attempted to show that the Trojan War really existed in archaeological fact.

From the Mycenaean pottery present in the ruins of Troy VI and VIIa Blegen concluded that the city was sacked very soon after the earthquake which he thought had damaged Troy VI: 'no more than half a century or perhaps even a single generation,' he said in his final report, and in 'the middle rather than a late stage of the [thirteenth] century.' Later he was tempted to suggest a date not later than 1240 BC and even to push it back to nearer 1270, near enough the traditional date of the Trojan War, and right in 'the period when the Mycenaean palaces on the Greek mainland seem to have been highly prosperous and wealthy and most likely to have been able to join together in an ambitious overseas military expedition'. Everything seemed to fit.

Here then, in the extreme northwestern corner of Asia Minor – exactly where Greek tradition, folk memory and the epic poems place the site of Ilios – we have the physical remains of a fortified stronghold, obviously the capital of a region. As shown by persuasive archaeological evidence, it was besieged and captured by enemies and destroyed by fire, no doubt after being thoroughly pillaged, just as Hellenic poetry and folk-tale describe the destruction of King Priam's Troy…. It is settlement VIIa, then, that must be recognised as *the actual Troy*, the ill-fated stronghold, the siege and capture of which caught the fancy and imagination of contemporary troubadours and bards who transmitted orally to their successors their songs about the heroes who fought in the war…. It can no longer be doubted, when one surveys the state of our knowledge today, that there really was *an actual historical Trojan War* in which a coalition of Achaeans, or Mycenaeans, under a king whose overlordship was recognised, fought against the people of Troy and their allies. (My italics.)

Troy and the Trojans (1963)

Of course it all boils down to what archaeology can or cannot prove. Blegen's arguments are essentially no different from those used by Dörpfeld and Leaf (see pp. 98–9), and like them Blegen went so far as to assert that his finds demonstrated that 'a good many of the individual heroes who are mentioned in the poems were drawn from real personalities'. The response to Blegen's thesis was inevitably a grateful, even joyful, one among the majority of classical scholars. As one put it, 'The Sack of Troy is a historical fact, the Siege a probability.' And indeed here at last was clear evidence of a sacking. The few dissenters were dismissed as sourpusses when they pointed out that one arrowhead does not make a war (it was perhaps not even Greek); that sunken pithoi were found throughout the Middle- and Late-Bronze-Age layers on Hisarlik (they can still be seen today in Anatolia); that 'snack bars' are found by the gates of other ancient sites (Pompeii, for instance); and that Blegen's pottery dating was questionable. And an even more critical question was *never* asked as Blegen looked at VIIa and found Homer – was the fall of Troy VI *really* due to an earthquake at all? For the moment, though, the definitive nature of Blegen's report, and the lack of any further major area of Hisarlik to dig, made it seem unlikely that we would ever be better informed.

THE PALACE OF NESTOR AT PYLOS

The travellers now came to Pylos, the stately citadel of Neleus, where they found the people on the sea-beach, sacrificing jet-black bulls to Poseidon, Lord of the Earth.

HOMER, *Odyssey*

Despite the publicity surrounding the 'finding' of the Trojan War, Blegen's dig at Troy was of more significance to Anatolian archaeologists than to Aegean scholarship. If it had seemed to confirm the truth of Homer's tale, it still could not solve the really important questions of Aegean archaeology which were still unanswered: how had mainland civilisation developed? What was the relation of Minoan to Mycenaean civilisation? Most important, when had the Greeks first arrived in the Balkans? *Were* the Mycenaeans Greeks, as Wace and Blegen had proposed, and as Schliemann had believed before them? The scholarly controversy between the supporters and the opponents of Evans' Minoan theories was so bitter that there was no prospect of agreement without a new corpus of material to go on, evidence to which no doubt attached.

Accordingly Blegen determined to find an untouched mainland palace from the Bronze Age which could be excavated using modern techniques. As with Schliemann, Homer was the guide. But which Homeric palace was the best bet? Tiryns had been excavated before scientific archaeological techniques had been developed. The palace at Mycenae had been largely destroyed, though what was left had been elucidated by Tsountas and Wace. The Menelaion site had not excited great hopes for the palace of Helen and Menelaos. All traces of the palaces at Orchomenos and Argos seemed to have been destroyed by later building. Iolkos lay under a modern town. Only one of Homer's great mainland palaces suggested itself: the palace of old King Nestor at 'sandy Pylos', the seat of one of Agamemnon's chief allies who had led 'eighty black ships' to Troy. Pylos, however, presented a major difficulty which had defeated all previous searchers: no one knew precisely where Bronze-Age Pylos had stood – only that it was in the general area of Messenia in the south-western Peloponnese. Unlike Mycenae and Knossos, there was no site pointed out. Tradition had unaccountably lost all memory of the great palace of Nestor, if it had existed: so much so that its location was a famous conundrum even in antiquity when a proverb ran, 'There is a Pylos before a Pylos, and another one before that.' In fact several places had borne the name, and no one was sure whether modern Pylos, by the wonderful natural harbour of Navarino, where the Turks were defeated by an allied fleet in 1823, was even roughly right. Schliemann's collaborator Wilhelm Dörpfeld had put the considerable weight of his name behind a much more northerly location. Blegen was not convinced, and had clues to back up his hope of finding an undisturbed Mycenaean palace. In 1912 and 1926 the Greek archaeologist Kourouniotis had discovered two tholos tombs in the hilly country north of Navarino – both had been robbed in antiquity but still contained Mycenaean pottery; in the neighbourhood were signs of more graves. Blegen, who had first searched the area in the 1920s, believed the tombs were royal ones and that a palace must have stood nearby in which the kings of the region had lived.

In 1939 he and Kourouniotis combed the area north-east of the bay with the help of local residents who knew where ancient remains existed, or had been found within living memory. Over ten days eight sites were discovered which on the basis of surface pottery seemed to be Mycenaean, but the key site turned out to be perhaps the obvious one, the one where, as Blegen later said, 'if you were a Mycenaean king, you would build a palace.' The place is 6 miles from the sandy beaches of Navarino Bay, but it commands a magnificent view over the whole of the bay and all the ranges of hills which surround it, with a spectacular vista along the whole backbone of the Aigaleon range towards the north and north-east. Here, on the most dominating position of all, a hill called Ano Englianos, ancient remains had been disturbed in the 1890s when the road to Chora had been built. In an olive grove on the steep-sided hill, amazingly, two masses of hard, concrete-like debris stuck out of the ground, exactly like those found by Kalokairinos at Knossos: calcined stumps of wall fused by the action of rainwater on fire-powdered gypsum.

And so that spring, as the world was poised to go to war, Blegen began his dig among the olive trees on Ano Englianos. He wrote:

Top: The plain of Troy – the 'tomb of Ajax' and the mouth of the
Scamander, with Imbros behind, in the eighteenth century. 'The noblest
situation for the head of a great Empire,' wrote Lady Wortley Montague
in 1718, admiring 'the exact geography of Homer'.
Above: A medieval representation of the Trojan horse.

Below: Heinrich Schliemann, the excavator of Troy – a charlatan and teller of tall stories, but also the father of archaeology.
Left: Sophie Schliemann wearing the 'Jewels of Helen'.

Left: Schliemann's 'great ramp' of Troy II in 1893. The 'Jewels of Helen' were probably found just outside the wall (centre, left) in a stone-lined cist grave dug into the ruins from above.

Above: The Lion Gate at Mycenae in the 1880s. Standing to the left of the gate is Dörpfeld; to the right Sophie Schliemann (?) sits on a boulder.

Top: The walls of Troy VI c.1300 BC. This is probably the city remembered by Greek tradition.
Above: Orchomenos – the ceiling of the tomb chamber.
Opposite: Goldwork from Mycenaean Greece – the famous mask from the shaft graves at Mycenae (top) and the Vaphio Cup (bottom).

Opposite top: An aerial view of Tiryns today.
Opposite bottom: Tiryns c.1886 during Schliemann's excavations.
Below: Schliemann sits with Dörpfeld's hand on his shoulder. Frank Calvert, who led him to the site of Troy, stands on the right. This was Schliemann's last campaign.
Bottom: Hisarlik from the north in 1894. Dörpfeld's dig had uncovered the east bastion; the hill was now masked by huge spoil heaps.
Overleaf: The great eastern bastion of Troy VI.

The first trench was laid out early on April 4, and by mid morning even the rosiest expectations had been surpassed: substantial stone walls, more than one metre thick, had been exposed to view; fragments of plaster retaining vestiges of painted decoration had been recovered; a cement-like lime floor had been reached; and five clay tablets bearing inscribed signs of the Linear B script had come virtually undamaged, though lime-coated, out of the soil, the first of their kind to be found in mainland Greece. It was at once obvious that a palatial building occupied the hill.

In a chamber at the end of that first trench Blegen came across the archive room with 600 tablets and fragments in the same language as Evans had found at Knossos. In the following month (the dig ended on 10 May) exploration showed that the palace at Ano Englianos was of a size comparable to the known mainland palaces and the presence of the archive suggested strongly that it had been the centre of its region, and very likely the centre of a kingdom of Messenia. Blegen himself had no doubt, publishing his finds under the title *The Palace of King Nestor at Pylos* (though he later asserted that he had not gone to Messenia with 'any preconceived idea about whose palace it might turn out to be, if actually found').

In its material culture the palace was in every way similar to those found at Mycenae and Tiryns, and to the last palace at Knossos. There was the same megaron (royal hall) as at Tiryns and Mycenae, its central hearth still in place with its painted decoration; there were storerooms full of the crockery of a Bronze-Age palace, thousands of drinking cups, jars and containers; magazines containing the wealth of the palace, oil, wine and grain; its frescoes bore scenes of chariots, warriors in boar's-tusk helmets fighting roughly clad mountain people; there were griffins depicted in the royal apartments exactly as at Knossos; there was even a painting of a bard playing the lyre. In all respects the palaces seemed to belong to one world, and the presence of the Linear B showed that they did, though it would only be after the Second World War that tablets were found at

Mycenae, and in the 1980s at Tiryns. In 1939 the question immediately arose: was Pylos a Cretan colony, ruled by a Minoan expatriate aristocracy, as Evans' theories might have indicated – foreign nabobs who used the Cretan Linear script for their bureaucracy, like the British in India? Did the Pylians use Cretan scribes? Or was Pylos typical of mainland civilisation, using the language of the mainland, and hence was Knossos in its last phase ruled by mainlanders? These ideas were already current in the 1920s and 1930s, as we have seen, and Pylos was to prove decisive against Evans' view. Here, unlike Knossos, there could be no argument about the chronology: with improved knowledge of pottery styles, it could be shown that Pylos had been destroyed in around 1200 BC or a few years later: 200 years after Evans' date for the destruction at Knossos. There could no longer be much doubt that Knossos had finally been part of the Mycenaean world, and modern research has shown it to be possible that the Knossos archive also dates from around 1200 BC, contrary to Evans' view. These problems were greatly clarified when in 1952 the unknown script of Linear B was deciphered, an event which has been called, with some exaggeration, the 'Everest of archaeology'.

But before we turn to the decipherment there is one aspect of the dating of the fall of Pylos which is of crucial importance in our search for Troy. It is worth re-emphasising that all Aegean dating depends on pottery styles. When Blegen wrote, the change between LH III B and III C pottery was thought to be around 1200 BC or a little earlier; as no III C pottery was found in the debris at Pylos, Blegen concluded that the palace had fallen in around 1200. But also on Blegen's mind was the Trojan story, and the reader will recall that Blegen concluded that Troy VIIa – his Homeric Troy – also fell before III C pottery came in. But had Troy VIIa really fallen before Pylos? If not, there was clearly a problem in accepting the Homeric tale as fact, for Blegen's Trojan War would have taken place when the Pylos of old King Nestor was already a ruin! As knowledge of the pottery styles accumulated in the post-war period, doubts started to emerge that there had after all been III C pottery in Troy VIIa, and that it had fallen *after* the destruction of some of the mainland Greek palaces in around 1200 BC. But those doubts took a long time to materialise: Troy VIIa was still generally accepted as the Homeric Troy until the late 1970s, and the belief remains widespread.

In the meantime the most important of all discoveries in Aegean archaeology was about to take place: the decipherment of the Linear B script, which had been known to exist since Minos Kalokairinos had dug at Knossos in 1878, was available in quantity in tablets from Evans' digs of 1900–10, and was now known from inscriptions from Thebes, Elefsis, Tiryns, Orchomenos and Pylos. Less than four months after Blegen's first campaign at Pylos had ended, the Second World War broke out, to be prolonged in Greece by a more terrible aftermath, a bitter civil war in which 400,000 Greeks died, and in which a British army ended up fighting on Greek soil on the side of Greeks against Greeks. It was not until 1952 that archaeological work could be resumed at Pylos, and by then the world had changed. In that same year Evans' beloved Knossos was handed over to the Greek government (Evans himself had died in 1941). The war had postponed the publication of the Pylos tablets – most of Evans' Knossos tablets were still unpublished – but as soon as they were made available, in 1951, the efforts of the decipherers were crowned with success.

THE DECIPHERMENT OF LINEAR B

During the last few weeks, I have come to the conclusion that the Knossos and Pylos tablets must, after all, be written in Greek – a difficult and archaic Greek, seeing that it is 500 years older than Homer and written in a rather abbreviated form, but Greek nevertheless.

MICHAEL VENTRIS, on the BBC Third Programme, reprinted in the *Listener*, 10 July 1952

Michael Ventris, the young man who cracked the Linear B code, was an amateur in the world of professional Greek scholarship, an architect who had been fascinated by the Linear B mystery since as a fourteen-year-old schoolboy he had heard a lecture by Sir Arthur Evans at Burlington House in 1936. He was not yet thirty when he made that famous radio broadcast, thirty-four when he died in a car crash on the A1 in 1956. We need not deal here with how the decipherment was achieved: this exciting story can be read in the compelling and affectionate tribute by Ventris' collaborator John Chadwick, *The Decipherment of Linear B*, and in their great joint work, *Documents in Mycenaean Greek*.

That Linear B was Greek went against the previously held opinion of most linguists, and though some archaeologists had already put forward the idea that Greek speakers came into Greece as early as 1900 BC, such was the force of Evans' Minoan theory that even Ventris had thought the idea out of the question, 'based on a deliberate disregard for historical plausibility'. Now there was proof of the proposition Schliemann had cherished eighty years before: the world of the Bronze-Age palaces *was* a Greek one. Perhaps the most surprising thing about the tablets was that the world they revealed was not 'heroic' at all, but bureaucratic to the most extraordinary degree. Here were lists of flocks down to the last ewe or ram; the names of individual shepherds and tax inspectors; the minutest enumerations of equipment and war gear; individual thrones and chariots listed with their accoutrements and defects, including even broken or useless bits of equipment – chariot bodies or wheels, say, faithfully noted as 'useless' or 'burnt at the end'. Here even individual oxen are named: 'Blacky' and 'Spot'. But here too was an apparently feudal social order with (as most scholars agree) the king at the top – the *wanax*, the same word as Homer uses for Agamemnon, 'king of men'; here were the lesser chiefs, the soldiers with their elaborate war gear, their body armour, greaves, shields, helmets, spears, swords, bows and arrows; here were lists of troop dispositions bearing more than a passing resemblance to Homer's catalogue of the ships which the Greeks took to Troy. Here, in sum, was an aristocratic, hierarchical and militarist class armed to the teeth, with massive expenditure on specialised war gear and palace ornament. The tablets also offered voluminous evidence (still being assessed today by economic and linguistic experts) for the staples which sustained the palaces: the wheat, wine, olives, flax and timber which were carefully noted down to the last litre or bale by the palace scribes. Lastly, at the other end of the social scale, there were the hundreds of slave women and their children who worked these estates, distinguished by names like 'captives', again the same word used by Homer.

The possibilities opened up by the decipherment were immense, and are still being explored. Though hard evidence about social order and religious belief was lacking – so much was inevitably allusive in these laconic notations – the evidence for the economies and local organisation of these Bronze-Age kingdoms was rich, and as more places are identified doubtless more evidence will be provided. Some general conclusions about the tablets and the Mycenaean kingdoms will be presented in Chapter 5. First, though, it will be obvious that the decipherment had the most dramatic effect on the study of Homer. Now it was known that the inhabitants of the Bronze-Age palaces at the time of the Trojan War actually spoke Greek, the language of Homer. Here in some cases were the same words, the same grammatical constructions (like the archaic ending *oio*); proof of lost features of early Greek which scholars had already deduced (for instance the loss of *w*, the digamma, as in *W*ilios = Ilios, Troy). The Linear B tablets now put the history of the Greek language back at least 500 years and opened up a new perspective on Homer. Could the Bronze-Age elements in Homer – the descriptions of artefacts like the boar's-tusk helmet, for example – now be paralleled by linguistic evidence to *prove* that the Homeric tale in essence went back to the Bronze Age? Had Ajax's great body shield, for instance, been handed down from the *Mycenaean* epic? Could Homer's 'silverstudded swords' have their parallel in the two swords 'with gold studs on either side of the hilt' from the

Pylos tablets? How were scholars to explain the appearance of so many Homeric personal names – including Hector and Achilles – as ordinary people's names in the tablets? Could Homer's catalogue of ships be derived from an actual Bronze-Age list like those on the Pylos tablets, or at least from a Mycenaean epic on the Trojan expedition? In short, was it possible that the story of Troy had already been sung by Mycenaean bards in the royal halls of Pylos, Mycenae and Tiryns, sung by bards like the lyre player painted on the Pylos fresco? What *was* 'Homer', and where had his tale of Troy come from? All these questions will be examined in Chapter 4.

FOUR

HOMER: THE SINGER OF TALES

How could Homer have known about these things?
When all this happened he was a camel in Bactria!

LUCIAN, *The Dream*

They [the Greeks] were late in learning the alphabet and found the
lesson difficult ... it is a highly controversial and disputed question
whether even those who took part in the Trojan campaign made use
of letters, and the true and prevalent view is rather that they were
ignorant of the present-day mode of writing. Throughout the whole
range of Greek literature no disputed work is found more ancient
than the poetry of Homer. His date, however, is clearly later than the
Trojan War; and even he, they say, did not leave his poems in writing.
At first transmitted by memory the scattered songs were not united
until later; to which circumstance the numerous inconsistencies of
the work are attributable.

JOSEPHUS, *Against Apion*

THE ILIAD AND THE ODYSSEY are by common consent the
beginning of European literature. It is an extraordinary paradox –
unique in culture – that the beginnings should be unexcelled
masterpieces; not inchoate 'primitive' works, but great poems of
enormous length and sophistication. We can safely assume that
there had been earlier and cruder Greek epic poetry before
Homer, but we know nothing of it. Instead, here, 'leaping out of
the head of Zeus fully armed' are representations of a heroic age
so vividly and powerfully realised that, ever since, their audience
has been unable to resist the idea that they are in some way 'true'.
In the classical world it was generally accepted that their author
was a poet of genius called Homer, of whom virtually nothing

was known: even the name suggests a pseudonym (*homeros* = hostage). In the ancient world it was also accepted that Homer composed without the aid of writing – that is, he was an oral poet.

Recently detailed studies of oral epic poetry have been made in different parts of the world – Serbia, where it survived in a debased form until recently; Ireland, where the last (prose) epic performer lived long enough to be recorded, in the 1940s; Albania and Armenia, where shreds of the bardic tradition still hang; Zaïre, where until recently the full-blown thing itself could still be witnessed. All these have taught us a great deal about how great poems – and exceedingly long ones – can be orally composed and transmitted without the aid of writing. The characteristics of such works – notably the so-called formulas, or repeat phrases – show that the Homeric poems are, as Josephus and the ancients thought, characteristically oral poems. But in what sense were they composed? Was there one act of composition, or a gradual accretion of a poetic tradition? Did Homer exist? When were the poems written down, and what relation does the written text we have bear to that first written text, let alone to the orally composed poem(s) which may have preceded it? These are the problems which for the last two centuries have been at the centre of what scholars call the 'Homeric Question'.

Though we assume that 'Homer' was orally composed, we only know his poems through writing – through written texts. In the last century our knowledge of the text has increased with the discovery of over 600 papyrus fragments from Egypt which preserve parts of the Homeric text, but essentially they have not meant any real change in what we call Homer. In the case of the *Iliad* this means a manuscript tradition which starts in the tenth century AD in Constantinople: our two best and earliest manuscripts were produced at that time (the bulk of 200 surviving MSS of Homer are from the fourteenth and fifteenth centuries AD).

Though Greek studies had largely died out in the Latin west during the Dark Ages, 'Homer' continued to be studied in Byzantium where it remained part of the school curriculum despite its pagan ethos. In the great period of the AD 860s a new revised edition of Homer was prepared by Byzantine scholars in the imperial university, and subsequent work on the manuscript traditions led to the famous book, now in St Mark's in Venice, known as Venetus A, the most authoritative edition of the *Iliad*. As always, the bulk of the early and rare texts did not survive because of war: in this respect the sack of Constantinople in 1204 must have been a great disaster, if not on a par with the loss of the library at Alexandria by fire in the first century BC. Even before the final sack of Constantinople, in 1453, the tradition was taken up in the west by Italian humanists who brought back a large number of manuscripts from the Byzantine Empire in the last century of its existence. After 1453 manuscripts were taken from surviving Greek monastic libraries; today such places are virtually denuded of classical texts, but their plundering has ensured the survival of Greek literature.

The tale of Troy, as we saw earlier, never lost its interest, being part of the intellectual currency of the Latin west. Homer's text itself was already attracting attention in the mid-fourteenth century when the Italian poet Petrarch took Greek lessons, though he did not acquire enough to read a copy of Homer given him as a present by a Byzantine ambassador. In the 1360s the Italian scholar Pliato, a friend of Boccaccio, attempted translations of part of Homer into Latin, and by the end of the century you could attend lectures on Homer in Italy.

The idea of establishing a text scientifically took longer to come about, and it was not until the new art of printing was being practised that we find a spate of editions, first of Latin classics and then of Greek, in the last decades of the fifteenth century. In their way these were the most important element in the west's rediscovery of Greece, which earlier in this book we viewed from the point of view of the travellers, the *physical* rediscovery. The first printed text of Homer appeared in Florence in 1488, its editor a Greek. However it was in Venice – which was to be the centre not only of the printing trade as such, but of the Greek publishing trade for three centuries – that the great printed edition of Homer was brought out in 1504 by the Aldine press, founded by Aldus Manutius with the express idea of printing Greek texts; the editorial work was again done by a Greek, the Cretan scholar Musurus. The dissemination of the printed text (seven major European editions were brought out in the sixteenth century) opened up modern critical discussion of the text, and as scholars compared Homer with other classical Greek literature it quickly became obvious that it could not be analysed on the same basis. He was evidently not a writer at all, but an oral composer, and ancient authority could be found to corroborate this idea.

The passage from Josephus quoted above was used by early modern scholars who concluded that, no matter how old the manuscripts, it would be impossible to hope for a sound text of an author who had composed orally perhaps centuries before he was 'collected' and put down in writing. Early scholars generally followed the tradition found first in the Roman writer Cicero that Homer had only been written down in *c.*550 BC at the command of the Athenian tyrant Pisistratus. The first modern attempt to set Homer in his culture was that of the philosopher Vico, who maintained that Homer was really a collective name for the work of successive generations of poets who made up the oral tradition. The *Iliad*, then, would be a 'collective' work only set down in writing by the Pisistratids in the sixth century; there were, in short, many Homers. Vico's brilliant theory anticipated much of modern research, but at the time he had no influence. Instead it was the Anglo-Irish traveller Robert Wood, whom we met in the search for Troy, who was the first to argue critically for Homer's orality in his *Essay on the Original Genius of Homer* of 1769. Among the languages into which Wood's book was translated was German, and in Germany it had its profoundest influence. Indeed it was instrumental in provoking what is widely regarded as the greatest of all books on Homer, F. A. Wolf's *Prolegomena*. Wolf wrote in 1795, with the advantage of the recent (1788) publication of the greatest of all manuscripts of the *Iliad*, the Venetus A, which, though of the tenth century AD, is packed with the marginal notes of centuries of commentators, going back to the Alexandrian criticism of the third century BC. Wolf was convinced that Homer had been illiterate, that he had composed around 950 BC, and that his poems were transmitted by memory until, around 550 BC, they were committed to writing by Pisistratus. He was, however, also prepared to believe in a real Homer, a single poet of genius who 'began the weaving of the web' and, he wrote in his *Preface to the* Iliad,

carried the threads down to a certain point.... Perhaps it will never be possible to show – even with probability – the precise points at which new threads in the weave begin: but if I am not mistaken we can say that Homer was responsible for a major part of the songs, the remainder the Homeridae who followed the lines laid down by him.

After Wolf, there was a tendency to 'disintegrate' the text of Homer into a mass of interpolations and shorter oral poems grafted on to a primitive 'original *Iliad*' by later poets and editors. Some, though, still emphasised the 'single poet' idea: Goethe, for instance, wrote a short treatise on the unity of the Homeric poems, a view, incidentally, strongly held at the present time. But Wolf stated all the problems with a clarity and tact which have not been bettered, and it would be misleading to suggest that an answer has yet been reached.

In the two centuries since Wolf wrote, three major discoveries have been made which have had a fundamental influence on the Homeric question. Two we have already met. The first was the rise of scientific archaeology, and the opportunity it offered to discover a 'real' Bronze Age underneath the Homeric poems. This we have seen as the driving force of Schliemann's obsession with Homer and Troy. And indeed this bore rapid fruits in the discovery that Homer did indeed describe artefacts from the Bronze Age: at Mycenae Schliemann himself was soon looking at representations of boar's-tusk helmets and tower shields, and handling silver-studded swords: a 'real' connection seemed to be demonstrated. Soon enough the palace at Tiryns presented an image of a Bronze-Age royal establishment which again bore clear similarities to the Homeric megaron (see p. 87). Archaeology was also suggesting that the places Homer mentioned as being important in the Bronze Age were indeed so, even if insignificant afterwards. The decisive discovery was Dörpfeld's unearthing of the Mycenaean-period citadel on Hisarlik, since this suggested for the first time that the central tale of the *Iliad* was indeed based on a real Bronze-Age place and real events. Archaeology has continued to build on these impressions over the last century, impressions both tantalisingly evocative of Homer and at other points utterly divergent. But the assumption of a strong connection remains, and given a degree of critical scepticism seems justified.

The second discovery was largely the work of Milman Parry and his follower Albert Lord, who were able to prove that oral transmission lies behind Homer's text, thus supporting the argument of Josephus, and of scholars up to Wolf, that this text was composed without writing. The way in which oral poets work, the nature of formulaic composition, has been examined in many cultures and field workers have recorded comparable material in a number of countries, as mentioned at the beginning of this chapter. The lines of this are clear, and some of the important publications are listed in the bibliography.

The third and most recent revolution in Homeric scholarship was the discovery that the Linear B tablets were in Greek, and that therefore there was a cultural and linguistic continuity between Homer and the Bronze Age. Parry's discoveries about oral techniques could now be applied to the transmission of the epic through the Dark Ages up to the time when writing began again in Greece (the first monumental inscriptions appear a little before 700 BC). Moreover it was now possible to look at the continuity of the language in detail, to study dialect change and to see, for instance, how many of Homer's words appear in Linear B Greek, how many actual phrases there are in which Homer is describing Bronze-Age artefacts with Mycenaean words, or where the subject is accurately described even though the older language has dropped out. Much work needs to be done on this: for instance, no work has yet been done on Mycenaean Greek words existing in inferior texts of Homer which were dropped out of the main tradition by later editors, though they may actually have greater authority. The decipherment of Linear B has opened up possibilities for Homeric studies which are only just starting to be explored.

WHEN WAS THE *ILIAD* COMPOSED?

The general opinion today about the *Iliad* (and the *Odyssey* too) is that they were composed not orally, but by a poet building on oral tradition though using writing. In the eyes of many people, the introduction of writing into Greece was in some way tied up with Homer's genius: it has even been suggested that the Greek alphabet was actually devised to write down the Homeric poems in *c.*700 BC. There are obvious objections to this idea. First, the writing of these two immense poems in a predominantly oral culture at the very moment of the introduction of writing goes against all we know of such processes in history; this is not how the introduction of 'communications technology' works in relation to creative art, whether in the transition from preliterate to literate culture, from writing culture to print, or (to point to our own time) from print to electronic systems. It is difficult to imagine that such a mammoth and expensive task as recording (on papyrus or parchment?) such lengthy poems could have been undertaken when society – and, more important, the poet's audience – was still to all intents and purposes illiterate. This idea is based on the idea that Homer's originality was such that he *foresaw* the importance of writing. In fact, as we know now, the poem's language and style point to oral composition. There is nothing in either poem, however long and sophisticated they are, which exceeds what we now know of oral composition. Homer then could have composed orally, but his work may have been recorded in writing considerably later.

On this scenario the earliest time of recording would be around 650 BC, when writing was developed in Greece. But the oral epic tradition was still thriving in the fifth century BC, so oral 'composition' of the *Iliad* and the *Odyssey* as late as the sixth century BC is not impossible. In fact, as we have seen, there existed in antiquity a tradition that the Homeric poems had been collected and given their final form in Athens during the reign of Pisistratus, one of the last of the Athenian tyrants, in the sixth century. The history of the texts could go something like this.

Once upon a time there was a famous oral poet whose name was Homer. He came from the world of the Ionian Greek colonies, perhaps from Chios or Smyrna, and it is thought that he may have composed around 730 BC. For some reason, perhaps because he was the best, he came to be regarded as the embodiment of oral epic poetry as such, and the most famous later group of singers considered themselves to be his descendants; these were the so-called Homeridae, the 'sons of Homer', on Chios. Homer lived perhaps in the eighth century BC, by which time the tale of Troy was evidently widely told in Aegean courts, for we find potentates naming themselves after its heroes: Hector of Chios, Agamemnon of Kyme. Perhaps their courts were where Homer found his patrons and sang his songs, along with the festivals of the Ionian cities, especially the Panionion at Mykale. Such was Homer's impact that later generations came to consider much of the early epic poetry as his, and much of it may have been handed down, taking care to preserve the words 'as Homer sang them'. Then, during the expansion of sixth-century Athens, a tyrant with political ambitions wished to turn the local festival to the goddess Athena into one with a more 'national' appeal. A magnificent temple of Athena was built on the acropolis (predecessor of the surviving Parthenon), public festivals were promoted, and among other activities recitals of epic and historical poems were arranged to glorify the Athenian state. At this time, as he sought the leadership of Greece for Athens, he conceived the idea of securing for Athens what were unanimously viewed as the most magnificent of the traditional Greek epics, especially the *Iliad*, which told of the first undertaking by a united Hellas. He therefore paid for the best of the Homeridae to come to Athens to dictate Homer as 'truly', as fully and as beautifully as possible to an Athenian scribe.

The *Iliad* text which lies behind the one we know could have been recorded from a bard so late on, then; but even if this specific scenario be rejected we should probably look after 650 BC. Such collection and writing down of the ancient songs usually takes its impetus from the outside, and often comes at times when writing is beginning to be more widely used. An obvious parallel is Charlemagne's collection and recording of the old oral vernacular epics of the Frankish and Germanic peoples following his reforms in writing and literacy in eighth-century-AD Europe. Today, in the early twenty-first century, as oral traditions are all but dead in industrialised countries, we ourselves are attempting to do something similar. Homer then, we may guess, was recorded by a 'collector', if posthumously.

We began with the premise of Josephus that these poems were created when writing was unknown in Greece. As mentioned earlier, when modern studies of Homer began, Robert Wood and F. A. Wolf agreed that Homer had not known writing, and Wolf concluded that Homer's original was irretrievably lost. The oral-formulaic views of Milman Parry and his school, by analogy with Yugoslav bards, were in many ways a return to Wolf's point of view. In recent years we have had to combine the 'oral' view with the idea that it was Homer's originality to see the way his great work could be preserved by writing, in other words that Homer composed at an important cultural moment, just as writing was introduced into Greece: thus the 'great man' theory of literary creation found its advocates. Today, our interpretation presents a synthesis of all these views: poems perhaps 'composed' only in the seventh or sixth century BC – specifically to be written down – but poems which carefully preserved more ancient strata handed down in the oral poetic traditions of Ionia. We may therefore say that, because of the oral nature of the poems, we have the 'originals' fairly closely; that is, the poems recorded in 650–550 BC. What relation they have to Homer, if he existed, is no longer so easy to prove, but it seems likely that the Homeridae of the sixth century BC could give a reasonably close account of stories already formulated in the eighth century BC. But like all oral poets they selected, omitted and innovated to suit the occasion and the patron, singing their poems in the form most pleasing to the audience at hand. Later editors certainly played their part in altering the text after the sixth century BC; the most influential period was the third century BC, when the Alexandrian school of critics tried to establish a definitive text. An interesting case is their alteration made at the start of Book Six where a line 'in the ancient books' about fighting 'between the river Scamander and the *stomalimne*' was changed to 'between the waters of Xanthos and Simois' by Aristarchos because it did not fit the topography of the Troad in his own day. Some passages were condemned simply for their 'low tone'; many other words have evidently dropped out of the transmission because they were no longer understood, though this must have gone on long before the poems were committed to writing.

WAS THERE MYCENAEAN EPIC POETRY?

From what tradition of poetry did Homer ultimately derive? Was there oral epic in Mycenaean times which has come down, however dimly, in Homeric epic? Was the tale of Troy itself already sung in Mycenaean citadels before their world collapsed? The Linear B tablets, of course, are the very antithesis of poetry in their bureaucratic notations. But there were certainly singers of songs or tales, for one of the Pylos frescoes showed a lyre player or bard, and fragments of a lyre were found in a tholos tomb at Menidi. It is, on the face of it, likely that there was actual epic poetry celebrating the deeds of the Mycenaean kings which came down to us in Homer, and this is assumed now by many scholars. Certainly themes like those in the *Iliad* and other Greek myths are commonly found in the poetry of many contemporary Bronze-Age peoples, especially in Ugarit, the great trading city in northern Syria, where the epic of *Krt* is another tale of abduction of a royal woman and the siege of a city.

But how are we to judge the Bronze-Age substratum in

Homer? First there are descriptions of actual Mycenaean objects in Homer. The tower-shaped body shield usually associated with Ajax and represented on the Thera frescoes was already obsolete by the thirteenth century BC. The figure-of-eight shield occurs on thirteenth-century frescoes from Mycenae, Tiryns and probably Knossos. The 'silver-studded sword' is known from sixteenth- and fifteenth-century finds. The leg greaves indicated in Homer's epithet about the 'well-greaved Achaians' likewise have been found in Bronze-Age tombs and not in the succeeding Iron Age. The boar's-tusk helmet, perhaps the most famous of all (carefully described in *Iliad*, X, 261) has been found on numerous representations, with a full example from Knossos; Homer even notes how the tusks are laid in rows with the curves alternating. Nestor's cup, decorated with doves (*Iliad*, XI, 632 ff) and with two handles, sounds something like the cup found by Schliemann in Shaft Grave IV at Mycenae. The technique of metalwork inlay described in the making of Achilles' shield is exemplified in the shaft grave daggers (on which the tower shields are well pictured). There is also the question of Homer's references to a thorax, or suit of body armour, made of bronze plates: such a suit has now been found at Dendra. Add to these examples the almost universal assumption in Homer that bronze is the metal for swords and tools, and you have an impressive collection of detail in the military sphere which suggests that Homer is preserving descriptions from long before his time, though our knowledge of the intervening Dark Age is too imperfect for us to say with absolute certainty that some of these artefacts could not have been used after the collapse of Mycenaean power. The only sure way of showing that the Homeric tradition had roots in the heroic poetry of the Mycenaean Age would be by demonstrating survivals of specifically Mycenaean poetic language in Homer. Unfortunately this is difficult to do. The language of Homer is a mixture of many dialects and periods, predominantly Ionic (reflecting Homer's background in the Smyrna region and that of his successors, the Chiot Homeridae?), but it also contains a number of words in the more ancient Arcado-Cypriot dialect, spoken in the isolated areas of Arcadia and Cyprus, both of which go back to the Mycenaean period. Such words then can indicate a survival of more ancient forms; so too can some of the rarer Linear B words. Unfortunately in all of Homer only one phrase looks to be certainly Mycenaean, namely the *phasganon arguroelon*, 'silver-studded sword', with its variant, *ksiphos arguroelon*. *Phasganon* and *ksiphos* ('sword') are Mycenaean words, as is *arguros* ('silver') and perhaps *alos* ('stud'). Such swords have not so far been found between the later Mycenaean period and around 700 BC, which suggests that the epithet became attached to swords in the Bronze Age. But such a poor harvest suggests that direct verbal survivals coming down to the Ionian bards were very rare indeed.

It will also be clear that there are areas where Homer diverges completely from what we know of the Bronze Age. Most obviously, Homer has no idea of the complex bureaucratic world of the palaces with their accounting and rationings, their penny-pinching control over every sheep: evidently this world passed right out of the tradition, leaving instead the nostalgic 'heroic' Golden Age idealised retrospectively in the eighth century BC by the immigrant society of Ionia. An interesting sidelight on this is Homer's idea of the use of chariots. In the Bronze Age they were actually used for fighting – at least they were among the Hittites and Egyptians, and both Linear B and Hittite tablets suggest that the Greeks used them in this way too, as we shall see. In the *Iliad*, however, chariots are only used for transport, apart from odd phrases which suggest a dim memory of the real state of affairs, as in Nestor's orders to the Pylian troops: arraying chariots and cavalry in front, infantry behind: 'When a man from his own car encounters the enemy chariots, let him stab with his spear.... So the men before your time sacked tower and city' (*Iliad*, IV, 308). So the poetic tradition only vaguely remembered the details of true 'heroic' warfare, and obviously very little Mycenaean poetry about warfare and palace life passed into later epic tradition.

146

Consequently the epic tradition itself is unlikely to have formed around the remains of already existing Mycenaean epics on the tale of Troy, as has been assumed – *even if* the tale of Troy was a theme for Bronze-Age poets. It was in the Dark Age which followed the Mycenaean world that the creative part of the pre-Homeric epic tradition began to work. This has been confirmed by much modern work on Homer; it was popular singers of the Dark Age who spun their nostalgic tales about the great days of the Mycenaean past, and we can point to parallel developments in epic tradition in many cultures, Celtic, Germanic and African.

Such conclusions may be depressing for those who would wish to see the Mycenaean world faithfully reflected in the Homeric stories, but of course they do not rule out the idea that the basic story of the siege of Troy – and even some of the characters – still goes back to the Bronze Age, for an epic tradition can still accurately preserve events without ever using Mycenaean language. What about the basic tale, then?

THE CATALOGUE OF SHIPS

As Schliemann was the first to demonstrate, the places mentioned by Homer as having been the chief centre of his story were indeed the chief places in Mycenaean Greece. Mycenae *was* the greatest citadel and the most powerful; Tiryns, Pylos and Orchomenos were of a similar rank. Where Linear B archives give names, they confirm many of the Homeric names – Pylos, Knossos, Amnisos, Phaestos and Cydonia, to name only the best known; that Mycenae was called by its Homeric and classical name is shown by an Egyptian inscription of the fourteenth century BC. This was perhaps only to be expected, especially once it was discovered that Linear B was Greek and that there was thus linguistic continuity between Homer and the Late Bronze Age. But in the Second Book of the *Iliad* there is a remarkable list of 164 places said to have sent troops to Troy, the so-called catalogue of ships:

They who held Argos and Tiryns of the huge walls,
Hermione and Asine lying down the deep gulf,
Troizen and Eionai and Epidauros of the vineyards,
They who held Aigina and Mases, sons of the Achaians,
Of these the leader was Diomedes of the great war cry....
Translated by R. Lattimore

The catalogue was originally constructed independently of the *Iliad*; indeed it is generally accepted that it is earlier than the *Iliad*, and was created separately as a list of names though its language is as purely Homeric as the rest of the poem. This independence is shown not merely by the differences and discrepancies between it and the *Iliad* proper, but by its placing, for it was not designed to occupy its place in the *Iliad*, purporting to be a record of the assembly of the Greek forces at the start of the war. At what stage it was placed in the *Iliad* has been argued fruitlessly for a long time. Nevertheless many critics have seen it as embodying Mycenaean tradition in a purer form than the *Iliad* as a whole. Indeed some have gone so far as to accept it for what it claims to be, the actual muster list of the Greek forces which sacked the historical Troy. This theory indeed has gained some support from a number of Linear B tablets from Pylos (see p. 133), which record military dispositions and troop numbers. The late Denys Page, in one of the most stimulating studies on this subject, boldly concluded not only that the catalogue was substantially from the Mycenaean period, but that it was an actual order of battle and its connection with an overseas expedition 'must be historically true'. He thought the list was preserved independently of the poetical tradition which culminated in the *Iliad* and was incorporated at a late stage, because it differs so much from the *Iliad* over points of fact. Lastly, Page thought the list of peoples and places 'not much altered', though the numbers might be a late invention. This dramatic conclusion, so seductive in its appeal – that we possess an authentic record of the Greek army which went to Troy – must be treated with caution. Is it true to say that this list – even if it is from the Bronze Age – 'must be' a battle order? Why do early societies construct such lists? What *is* the catalogue?

WHAT'S IN A LIST?

First let us make a general point. While we may be rightly sceptical of the idea that the catalogue may go back to a *written* list on Linear B tablets, it is nevertheless the *kind* of list which appears time and again on those tablets: lists of names, lists of produce, lists of military gear and armed forces (scholars have even claimed to have found an authentic Mycenaean 'ship catalogue' in the Pylos tablets). Linear B was not flexible enough for the Greek language; it was a highly conventionalised and purely syllabic system of writing which could cope with administrative notations but not with complicated historical and literary composition. We can see the same principle in the development of Mesopotamian cuneiform writing: three-quarters of all extant inscriptions (there are around 150,000 of them) are administrative documents – in essence, lists. Even the Ugaritic tablets (fourteenth to thirteenth centuries BC), though they include literary texts, are mainly (two-thirds of the 500) lists, including lists of people and geographical names. Indeed in Egyptian texts contemporary with the palaces of Mycenae and Ugarit we find scribal manuals where the whole structure of the cosmos can be broken down into enormous lists to be learned as part of a scribe's training, including the ninety-six towns of Egypt, expressions for mankind, and names of foreign people and places 'drawing up Keftiu names and of the foreign places in the islands'. Schoolboys of the XVIII dynasty also had to list the names and typical produce of countries, using 'as many foreign words and names as possible'. Such lists, if we had them complete with descriptive epithets, would form a counterpart to the Homeric catalogues, as a thirteenth-century papyrus suggests: 'Have you been to the land of the Hittites? Do you know what Khedem is like? Have you trodden the road to Meger with its many cypresses ... Byblos, Beirut, Sidon ... Nezen by the river,

Tyre of the port, richer in fish than sand.' The Egyptian ambassadors of the fourteenth century BC who recorded with phonetic accuracy lists of Syrian, Near Eastern and Aegean cities, including Amnisos, Knossos and Mycenae (see p. 201), were only performing in a small way a feat educated people did all the time. (The practice, incidentally, did not stop in the Bronze Age: Dorothy Sayers' Lord Peter Wimsey could 'deliver himself with fair accuracy, of a page or so of Homer's Catalogue of the Ships' when he wanted to declaim something solemn and impressive, and at least one elderly civil servant would recite it as a cure for insomnia, according to *The Times* of 12 November 1964!)

Such lists, then, have been seen by anthropologists as characteristic of societies making a transition from illiteracy to literacy (Homer's age), or when literacy is only a limited and cumbersome medium and the preserve of a very small number of people (as was the case with the Late Mycenaean bureaucracy). Egyptian and other parallels could suggest that lists like the catalogue were more likely to have been learned as 'interesting lists' rather than to have begun life on clay tablets before being transferred to the oral tradition (if such a thing is even conceivable).

The fact is that as yet we know too little about the nature and extent of literacy in Mycenaean kingdoms – and next to nothing about the poetry which was recited by Mycenaean bards in their royal halls – to be able to suggest how and why the catalogue first came into being. We also need to be wary of the tendency on the part of societies to invent tradition: just because it may be roughly contemporary does not necessarily mean it is 'true'. With that in mind, let us look at what the list has to tell us.

A number of clues suggest that the catalogue reflects Mycenaean Greece. Most important is that several places are named, and can be securely located, which were inhabited in Mycenaean times but not subsequently lived in until after the eighth century BC, when the catalogue is assumed to have reached its present form. Eutresis in Boeotia is the best example, abandoned around 1200 BC and not resettled until 600 years later; others include Krisa, the spectacular site overlooking the gorge below

Delphi, Pylos and Dorion (Malthi in the Soulima valley) in Messenia, and Hyrie (Dramesi) in Boeotia. It was at Hyrie that a ship stele was discovered which Blegen thought was a monument to an overseas expedition, such as that against Troy. That the catalogue preserves *any* such places suggests that it goes back at least to Mycenaean traditions of the twelfth century BC. Perhaps even more significant is the fact that none of the identifiable places named in the catalogue can be shown *not* to have been inhabited in Mycenaean times; of the eighty or ninety so far located, three-quarters have shown signs of Mycenaean occupation. Moreover, *all* those excavated have revealed Mycenaean occupation, and of these about a third have failed to produce evidence of subsequent Iron-Age occupation. These facts can be said to *prove* a Mycenaean origin for at least part of the catalogue (though of course they do not necessarily prove that it has anything to do with the Trojan War). The only argument against it would be if we could show that some places in it did not exist then, and, as we have seen, this is not so. Let us look at one example in more detail.

'WINDY ENISPE'

It is difficult to find these places today, and you would be no better off if you did, because no one lives there.
STRABO, *Geography*

My example from the catalogue is chosen to illustrate an important point: that many of the catalogue sites could not be located by the Greeks themselves in classical times. Homer might have known about Mycenae and Tiryns from visible remains and folk-tales, but how did he come to select numerous other places for which the geographers in historical times looked high and low before giving up in disgust: 'cannot be found anywhere', 'does not exist', 'disappeared'? How did Homer even know that such places existed? How did he know their names? How did he know that Messe had pigeons or that Enispe was windy? In particular, how did he know about places which, as we have seen,

151

were abandoned at the end of the Mycenaean era and were never lived in again?

By common consent among catalogue buffs the most hopeless case for modern identification was the triad of obscure little places in Arcadia: 'Ripe, Stratie and windy Enispe'. Even Lazenby and Hope-Simpson, the doyens of footsloggers-after-Homer, admitted defeat without a fight, not even knowing whether to steer their legendary battered Morris towards western or central Arcadia!

However, a Greek archaeologist, C. T. Syriopoulos, following up unpublished clues unearthed in a road cutting in 1939, has located a prehistoric site in north-western Arcadia near Dimitra in Gortynia, which was intensively inhabited from Neolithic times to the twelfth century BC, when it was deserted for ever. The site is on a rocky hill on the southern slopes of Mount Aphrodision (it is accessible from the Tripolis–Olympia road) and dominates one of the crossings of the river Ladon. The Ladon flows down into the Alpheios and its steep wooded valley is one of the loveliest and most untouched areas of the Peloponnese. West of the habitation site on the commanding peak of Agios Elias are fortification walls which may be of the thirteenth century BC. The pottery is 'provincial', which is what we would expect of an apparent backwater. Pausanias says that 'some people think Enispe, Stratie and Ripe were once inhabited islands in the Ladon', to which he replies, 'anyone who believes that should realise it is nonsense: the Ladon could never make an island the size of a ferry boat!' But if the word for island (*nesos*) is interpreted (as it can be) as a piece of land made between a river and its tributary, then Dimitra could indeed be called an island in the Ladon, between the main river and two tributaries. And if this is accepted, then neighbouring Stratie could also be an 'island' in the Ladon, the place called Stratos by the second-century-BC historian Polybius, which might plausibly be placed (on Polybius' evidence) at a place called Stavri, three hours' walk from Dimitra along the course of the Ladon to the south-west. As for 'windy' Enispe, the name could hardly be more appropriate: the Dimitra site is buffeted by strong winds which scour up the valley of the Ladon and its tributary the Kako-Lagadi: the present-day threshing floor on top of the prehistoric site – using the constant wind for grain-winnowing – underlines the point. And if the fortifications on Agios Elias are indeed Bronze Age, and were the refuge of the inhabitants of thirteenth- to twelfth-century-BC Enispe, then so much the better for wind!

If the identification of these sites is right, and if Pausanias' informants were correct, then the third lost site, Ripe, should be at the confluence of another tributary of the Ladon. Indeed there is a site further down the Ladon, an hour and a half's journey on foot from Stratie at a place called Agios Georgios, on another 'island' of the Ladon, where tombs of the later Mycenaean period are alleged to exist.

Homer's account, then, describes in a plausible order the three main settlements of this mountainous area of north-west Arcadia, and they fall into place intelligibly in the sequence and direction of his list of all the Arcadian sites. An enigma which defeated no less than Strabo and Pausanias may be solved.

The cumulative effect of the discoveries of modern archaeology is to show that for all its strangeness, and accepting its later accretions, the catalogue goes back to a genuine list from the Bronze Age. Homer says there were pigeons at Messe and Thisbe, wind at Enispe, coast at Helos (and horses and wind at Troy, for that matter), because it was true. How else could Eutresis, uninhabited since around 1200 BC, appear in the list?

However, when we turn to the political arrangements of the kingdoms described by Homer, the groupings of all the obscure places, we encounter grave difficulties in making the catalogue fit what we know of thirteenth-century-BC Greece. Here our only real control is information from the palace archives. The Linear B tablets give us detailed records of two Mycenaean kingdoms named in the catalogues, Knossos and Pylos, which can be compared with Homer's catalogue. The Knossos problem is a thorny one, as we have seen, but if the revised dating of the tablets is accepted, then the archive dates to around 1200 BC, roughly the same time as the catalogue purports to be. However, only three of Homer's seven Cretan towns are named in the tablets (Knossos, Lyktos and Phaestos), though the tablets agree with Homer that Idomeneus' kingdom was restricted to the central area, and many places named in the tablets still await elucidation (another town in the catalogue, Milatos, has now produced important Late-Bronze-Age remains). Pylos presents even more difficulty, for though Homer and the tablets both give Messenia nine towns (an interesting coincidence in itself), only Pylos and Kyparissia are present in both lists, though Homer's Amphigeneia and Helos may also be identifiable on other fragments among the Pylos tablets. But the remaining seven names of the chief Pylian towns on the tablets cannot be squared with Homer, and thus a leading authority on Linear B now believes Homer to be 'almost worthless' in any attempt to reconstruct the geography of Mycenaean Greece. Homer does, however, seem to be speaking of real places in his lists, and though the discrepancy with the tablets is disturbing, it is worth asking whether the political divisions in the catalogue – bizarre as they are in some cases – reflect a real situation which once pertained, *but at another time.* For instance could Homer's Pylian kingdom reflect a situation *after* the destruction of Pylos? If, say, a bard were reconstructing a list of famous places in the twelfth century BC, he would surely have known that Pylos had been the centre of Messenia, even though it was destroyed before his day? There may even have been some Dorian petty dynast who claimed to be Nestor's inheritor, rather like the Celts in the sub-Roman twilight in Britain. In any case, Pylian refugees who had emigrated to Athens would have kept alive the memory of 'sandy Pylos'. Elsewhere there was still a recognisably Mycenaean life in kingdoms like Mycenae, Tiryns and Athens in the twelfth century BC; in Lakonia, too, some sort of occupation continued on the Menelaion, and there was evidently a kind of continuity at certain sites like Amyklai: indeed Homer's list of places in Lakonia fits very well with the archaeology.

The catalogue is full of strange political divisions. It ignores the *Iliad* by giving the chief heroes, Achilles and Odysseus, insignificant kingdoms; it relegates Ajax to tiny Salamis; it divides the plain of Argos, with Agamemnon – that is, Mycenae – ruling only the northern plain and the Isthmus area, and Diomedes of Tiryns in control of the lower plain, Argos and Asine. Perversely, most experts have thought that these divisions are so unlikely that they must reflect a real situation which once obtained in Greece; but trying to make them work for the thirteenth-century heyday has proved difficult. Nevertheless, as the evidence of the sites themselves strongly suggests that the core of the list of sites itself comes from the Bronze Age, it seems at least conceivable that some of the political divisions in it could be Bronze Age. The answer may be that the kingdoms reflect the century or so *after* the heyday of Mycenae; that originally, stripped of its later accretions, the catalogue is actually the creation of the twelfth or eleventh centuries BC, after the decay of Mycenaean civilisation, when some of the kingdoms had declined and when some palaces had been destroyed, but when Mycenaean civilisation hung on in some places. For example, in the case of Mycenae the catalogue suggests a time when a larger state comprising the north-west of the Peloponnese had split into two: for Mycenae and Tiryns the catalogue is inexplicable as a document from the thirteenth century (LH III B), when Mycenae was the centre of the Argolid with a network of roads from it (see Chapter 5), but it *is* plausible as relating to the situation after 1200 when, if anything, Tiryns grew in power and population (see p. 232). Again – as we shall see – the evidence for Orchomenos suggests the same, confined to one small corner of Lake Copais (p. 174). Here too the catalogue's emphasis on the Boeotians – dominating it, but playing no role in the story – is explained: in fact tradition in Thucydides' day had it that they did not arrive in Boeotia until sixty years *after* the Trojan War. The catalogue then betrays traces of the Mycenaean decline, and originally must date from the (late?) twelfth century BC. That it refers to places destroyed around 1200 BC is no argument against this: oral traditions of the Mycenaean world were presumably still strong enough in the succeeding three or four generations for their names and even their distinguishing epithets to be remembered. We may suspect that the catalogue was composed in the declining years of the late Mycenaean world for the edification of the petty dynasts who ruled in the shoes of the Atreids in an ever-diminishing Mycenae. That it had anything to do with a possible Trojan War is unprovable; even if it came from the Mycenaean world this is no guarantee that it is not simply a list of 'interesting places' associated with the war in an 'invention of tradition' of a kind which often happens in the aftermath of golden ages: sub-heroic audiences are the most avid consumers of such fictions. The catalogue, then, with its visions of a united Greece in its last great overseas venture, harks back to the 'good old days' when Achaia was great and had strong and glorious kings – 'leaders of men' and 'kings of many islands' who knew what to do when foreigners came and plundered their treasures or carried off their women.

That said, did the bards, who originally conceived the idea of recording in song the names and deeds of the heroes who took part in the 'Trojan War', actually know something about the leaders and forces of a real war, or did they concoct the great list of places from Mycenaean Greece? Did they invent heroes from the stock names, like Ajax, whose tower shield perhaps betrays him as a hero of an earlier stratum of epic? Or Achilles, with his sea goddess mother and his magical attributes? Also, if there *was* Mycenaean epic poetry, then the tale of Troy would not have been the first siege to be the subject of song. We find a siege portrayed on the sixteenth-century 'siege rhyton' (vase) found by Schliemann; an attack on a town was depicted on a wall-painting in the megaron at Mycenae; the story of the expedition against Thebes may already have been the subject of story and song, and a suitable model. Are there, in fact, any specific elements in the tale of Troy which suggest that the epic which has come down to us accurately remembered details and incidents of a real Bronze-Age event?

HOMER'S STORY

I take it that certain central facts in Homer's story must be correct if we are to accept even the basic *likelihood* of the tale of Troy. If we cannot yet prove that a city called Troy was sacked by Greeks, we can at least show that in other significant details Homeric tradition was right. For instance, Hittite and Egyptian evidence suggests that Homer was correct in names he called the peoples: Achaians and Danaans, in the case of the Greeks, and Dardanians in the case of the Trojans. But was Troy actually called Troy?

As we have seen, nothing has ever been found on the site of Hisarlik which indicates its name in the Bronze Age. Even if diplomatic tablets did exist there, they were destroyed long ago. Linear B could give us a Trojan woman (*Toroja*) but we cannot be certain. In a Hittite document of *c.*1420 BC the western Anatolian state of Wilusa or (Wilusiya) appears next to a place called Taruisa, which – tantalisingly – appears only this once in the Hittite archive. If we could postulate an alternative form, Taruiya, for this name then we might have similar forms to Homer's Troia and Wilios in north-western Anatolia at the right time. However the present state of research into Hittite geography means that this seductive hypothesis cannot be pressed too far. The knotty problems surrounding the possible appearance of Greeks in Hittite sources are discussed in Chapter 6, but we can at least say that, as our evidence for Late-Bronze-Age geography grows, Homer has not yet been proved wrong and in some new instances we can corroborate his story. But it is to Hisarlik itself that we must go to have any hope of answering the question, did the story centre on Hisarlik–Troy from the Late Bronze Age: *was* Hisarlik always the focus of the Greek epic of Troy?

'SACRED ILIOS': HOMER ON THE TOPOGRAPHY OF TROY

How long had Troy featured in the tale? In other words, was the story always about a city which stood near the Dardanelles in the region since called the Troad? We need to ask this question, for it has often been claimed that the bards grafted the Trojan location on to an older model, for instance a poem about the Mycenaean sack of Thebes, or even an Achaian attack on Egypt such as that mentioned in the *Odyssey*. In a sense it does not matter what date we assign to Homer, whether the tale was composed in Ionia in 730 BC or was written down from a Chiot bard in around 550 BC. Whichever date we choose, we are concerned with the period of the Aeolian Greek colony founded on Hisarlik in the eighth century BC. We have seen evidence in the tale of the Lokrian maidens in Chapter 1 that this place was already associated with the tale of a Greek expedition to Troy before around 700. Even if we assume, as many do, that a bard called Homer actually visited the Aeolian colony of Ilion soon after its foundation in *c.*750 BC, we have to explain why obscure little Ilion became the centrepiece for the Greek national epic. It is a question which those who flatly deny the historicity of the Trojan War have found difficult to answer. What we cannot know for certain is whether, around 730 BC, architectural features of Bronze-Age Hisarlik (Troy VI–VII) were still visible. But if an epic tale which goes back to the end of the Bronze Age told of an attack on a real citadel of that time, should there not be surviving traces in Homer's description?

As we saw in Chapter 1, the earliest travellers to the Troad were convinced that the poet had sung from personal observation – that he had actually been there. From Cyriac of Ancona to Alexander Kinglake visitors had seen, for instance, that it is indeed possible to see Samothrace from the top of Hisarlik, peeping over the heights of Imbros 50 miles away: 'So Homer appointed it, and it was,' as Kinglake said. There was certainly no disputing the general lie of the land – the islands, the Dardanelles, Mount Ida and so on – but other aspects of Homeric topography caused (and still cause) controversy; for instance the double spring of hot and cold water below the western wall – perhaps the most precise topographical feature that Homer mentions – could not be found and led as acute an investigator as Lechevalier astray, to the 'Forty Eyes' springs at Bunarbashi. Schliemann did in fact find remains of a spring, 200 yards from the west wall at Hisarlik, which had been blocked long ago by an earthquake, though it seems likely that the poet merged the Bunarbashi springs with the Hisarlik one for poetic effect. The problem is not so much Homer's 'accuracy' as a topographer, which is strictly a nonsensical idea, but the powerful effect his largely generic descriptions have had on everyone who reads him – but then that is what good poets do! On any reading of the evidence it would be expecting too much to expect all these epithets and details to cohere on the ground, but is it possible that, as Bronze-Age elements have certainly survived elsewhere in the poem, something has been preserved of Troy itself?

The general epithets Homer uses for Troy are of course not inapposite for the citadel on Hisarlik – 'well-built, beetling, steep, horse breeding', and so on – but none is linguistically early; horse breeding, for instance, has attracted the attention of archaeologists because their finds of numerous horse bones suggest that horse breeding was a feature of the Bronze-Age Trojan plain (as it was later); but the phrase itself is not of Mycenaean date, though the memory is conceivably early. Well-built walls, strong towers and wide streets – which impressed Dörpfeld so much in Troy VI – are certainly applicable to Late-Bronze-Age Hisarlik more than to any other fortress in the Aegean, but they are applied to other places by Homer. 'Windy' is interesting; it is used of only one other place, Enispe, as we have already seen, and it is certainly applicable to Hisarlik, as anyone knows who has stood on it and felt the north wind which sweeps all year long round what was once a higher promontory. But such a description does not mean we have touched the Bronze Age. The description of Ilios as 'holy' is notable and raises a special linguistic problem: the word used comes from Aeolia, the north-western Aegean, and not Ionia, and may well be from an early linguistic stratum of the story, though probably not of the Mycenaean Age; nevertheless the finds of cult idols around the gates of Troy VI on Hisarlik, including six at the southern gate alone, could suggest that the place was remembered as having been uniquely sacred.

It is a pity that Homer is not more precise about the

relationship of the citadel to the sea for new discoveries show that in the Bronze Age Hisarlik was actually a sea-girt headland. At the time of Troy II the ramp found by Schliemann went down to a narrow plain and the sea, a wide bay which was entered between two headlands. By the time of Troy VI the sea was probably a mile from the hill. Troy, then, was a major port at the mouth of the Dardanelles which, like Miletus and Ephesus, eventually silted up and lost its *raison d'être*. This crucial discovery makes sense of the whole history of Troy–Hisarlik in a way impossible before (though the existence of the bay was assumed by ancient writers and by early modern writers such as Wood). Homer's topographical indications, however, do not in this case describe what he must have seen, though two phrases *may* reflect it, where he has the eddying Scamander coming down to the 'broad bay of the sea' and when he describes a ship turning aside from the main channel of the Hellespont to come 'within Ilios'. We cannot, it would seem, say that Homer's topography is more like the Late Bronze Age than his own time, though some geomorphologists who have studied the new evidence think that it might be.

The poetic diction surrounding Troy and Ilios is not, of course, restricted to noun-epithet phrases like 'windy Troy' and so on. It contains certain archaic features which are not closely datable, such as the strange preposition *proti* and the regular observance of the digamma (the 'W', which does not exist in later Greek) in *W*ilios, the original form of Ilios. The broad impression gained by linguistics from this kind of material is that the story and its phraseology have been gradually refined and reduced to achieve extraordinary flexibility and utility with a very small vocabulary – an important proof that the tale of Troy had been told many times before it reached the form it takes in the *Iliad*. But what linguists cannot say is whether those many tellings spanned one, ten or twenty generations of epic singers.

To summarise: it is thought that narrative poetry of some kind existed in the Mycenaean Age and that some fragments of it exist in Homer, but very few in number; a very large part of Homeric formulaic vocabulary is more recent. But of course fragments of the hypothetical Mycenaean saga may exist in the Homeric epic quite independently of vocabulary and diction. The most striking example is the famous boar's-tusk helmet, manifestly a Mycenaean object though there is nothing in the diction of Homer's description which is ancient in itself. This reminds us that archaic diction can drop out of a text transmitted in this way even when an accurate description remains. In this light let us finally look at three points in Homer's physical description of Troy which can be considered as going back to the Bronze Age and which a singer of Homer's day may perhaps not have known. In none is there any linguistic feature which *must* be old; in all there are rare authentic details which could derive from an actual siege description of Bronze-Age Hisarlik.

1. The 'batter' or 'angle' of the walls of Troy: 'three times Patroclus climbed up the angle of the lofty wall' (*Iliad*, XVI, 702). Is this a description of the characteristic feature of the architecture of Troy VI? Blegen notes in his report that there were sections where the blocks were not close-fitting which his workmen could easily scale in just this fashion. (Only the top courses of the walls of Troy VI were visible in the eighth century BC, 'so weathered that they could hardly be recognised as the once splendid masonry', said Dörpfeld.)

2. 'The great tower of Ilios' (*Iliad*, VI, 386). This was a beautifully built tower flanking the main gate of Troy, and there is an implication that it could be a place of propitiation – Andromache goes there instead of to the temple of Athena. The south gate of Troy VI was certainly the main gate of the Late-Bronze-Age city, the 'Scaean Gate' if any (now that we know the plain was a bay it makes sense that the main gate faced inland, and there is no archaeological evidence for a major gate facing the bay). The south gate of Troy VI vas flanked by a great tower of finely jointed limestone blocks; moreover it was built round a major altar, and outside were six pedestals (for cult idols?) and a cult house for burnt sacrifices. All in all there seems a case that the 'great tower of Ilios' preserves a memory of Troy VI.

3. Perhaps the most precise memory of all is the stretch of wall

that was *epidromos* 'by the fig tree where the city is openest to attack and where the wall may be mounted' (*Iliad*, VI, 434). This tradition of a weak wall, apparently on the west, received extraordinary archaeological confirmation when Dörpfeld, as we saw in Chapter 2, found that the circuit wall had been modernised except in one short stretch of inferior construction on the western side. Again, this suggests an authentic detail from Troy VI.

It seems fair to conclude that the tale of Troy antedates the *Iliad* by at *least* the length of time needed for Ionian oral singers to create the extensive and elaborate but refined and economised range of epithets and formulas for Ilios, Troy and the Trojans. There is good reason to think, as Martin Nilsson did in his classic study *Homer and Mycenae* (1933), that the expedition against Troy is the fundamental fact and central point of the myth and must go back to the Bronze Age. Non-Homeric, mainland, versions of the saga existed too, suggesting that the story antedated at least part of the migration period. These pointers carry the theme well before the Aeolian Greek settlement of the Troad and the refounding of Greek Ilion, whose earliest possible date is *c*.750 BC. Only the strange story of the Lokrian maidens (see p. 31) suggests any Greek connection with, or interest in, the Troad in the Dark Ages, and there seems no historical or archaeological peg to explain the creation of a tale of Troy between the end of the Bronze Age and the eighth century BC. This is one of the arguments which in my opinion defeat the attempts of some scholars to deny any connection between the story and the site of Hisarlik. A deserted, ruined and overgrown site in a sparsely populated area of northwest Anatolia, with no visible links with Greece, surely cannot have been selected as the setting for the Greek national epic unless it had at some time in the past been the focus of warlike deeds memorable enough to have been celebrated in song. The simplest explanation is that the tale of Troy owed its central place in later epic tradition to the fact that it was the *last* such exploit before the disintegration of the Mycenaean world – bards in all cultures must have in their repertoire the most up-to-date songs as well as the traditional ones, and Troy was the last.

FIVE

AGAMEMNON'S EMPIRE

… Powerful Agamemnon
Stood up holding the sceptre Hephaistos had wrought him carefully.
Hephaistos gave it to Zeus the king, the son of Kronos,
And Zeus in turn gave it to the courier Argeiphontes,
And lord Hermes gave it to Pelops, driver of horses,
And Pelops again gave it to Atreus, the shepherd of the people.
Atreus dying left it to Thyestes of the rich flocks,
And Thyestes left it in turn to Agamemnon to carry
And to be lord of many islands and over all Argos.

HOMER, *Iliad*, II, 101–8 (translated by R. Lattimore)

IN HOMER'S VERSION of the tale of Troy, despite the anachronisms, one basic fact is clear and consistent in his picture of Greece – that Agamemnon of Mycenae was the most powerful king in Greece, and that he wielded some sort of loose overlordship over the other independent kings of mainland Greece, of Crete, and some of the islands. In Homer's eyes, then, mainland Greece and the islands are one world, in which it is quite feasible for local rulers to acknowledge the leadership of a 'high king', at least in time of war. If we are to accept Homer's tale, this situation is basic to it. We might note at the outset that such overlordships are a common feature of this kind of society in many historical epochs, for instance in the European Dark Ages, and are frequently encountered in Bronze-Age kingship in the Near East, so Homer's picture of Greece is in itself by no means impossible or implausible. But is it correct? Is it really conceivable that an Achaian Greek coalition under a Mycenaean overlord could have attacked north-western Asia Minor and sacked a city there? In the previous four chapters I have tried to trace the background to, and the assumptions behind, the search for Troy and the Trojan War. It is now time to start piecing together an interpretation.

First I want to make a general observation on the trail-blazing efforts of Schliemann, Tsountas, Evans, Wace, Blegen and the rest. Archaeology *has* been able to show that the most prosperous and populous age of the mainland Greek states, the 'palace' or 'empire' period when Mycenaean expansion in the Aegean was at its height, was the fourteenth and early thirteenth centuries BC, in other words in the period leading up to the time to which ancient tradition unanimously placed the 'imperial' venture of the Trojan expedition. The first great buildings of Cyclopean walls at Mycenae, Tiryns and Gla are no earlier than the fourteenth century BC; the really massive final achievement — walls, gates, the immense tholos tombs at Mycenae and Orchomenos — is mid-thirteenth century. The time and the scale of the achievement are right.

Mycenae was undoubtedly the greatest palace-fortress in Greece. Tiryns may have been subsidiary to it, though recent finds of Linear B tablets there have suggested a measure of independence. Pylos, Iolkos, Thebes and Orchomenos were clearly also major regional 'capitals' with richly adorned palaces. Lakonia (Sparta) has not yet produced for certain the palace site which Schliemann sought, but two possible major centres are known, at Vaphio and the Menelaion, and the latter is of very large extent, reoccupied in the mid-thirteenth century. So in Sparta too — the other great Homeric palace of the mainland — we may well have a major dynastic centre to match that in the epic; conceivably we may even have reoccupation of an old Lakonian royal site by the newcomer, the foreign, Atreid King Menelaos whom legend says married into the Spartan royal family and became their king at this time. The other key site in Lakonia is the cult (and palace?) site at Amyklai, again mentioned by Homer (it is where Paris first meets Helen); here recent research has indicated some kind of continuity of worship into classical times. All these places were closely linked in their culture, so far as we can judge by the archaeological remains. Mycenae, Pylos and the Menelaion are indistinguishable in their pottery; the frescoes of Mycenae, Tiryns and Pylos speak of the same royal and noble civilisation, the same artistic traditions and tastes; the Linear B archives now known also from Thebes and Tiryns show that the main kingdoms all shared the same organisation and bureaucratic method; their stone and stucco ornament is so similar in design and execution that it has suggested to many (including Arthur Evans) that the same artists and sculptors may have travelled from kingdom to kingdom (just as Homer asserts in the *Odyssey*, though the same was true of his own time). The great tholos tombs at Orchomenos and Mycenae are so close in measurement and technique that they have been attributed to the same architect. This swift, impressionistic survey shows that there is a powerful argument for the homogeneity of Mycenaean culture, and, over 100 years on from Schliemann's dig at Tiryns, I can only emphasise how correct this extraordinary 'amateur' was in his basic hunch: this was indeed one world, it shared a common culture and (we now know) a common language; hence it seems entirely justifiable to speculate that the rulers of this world had a sense of their 'Greekness' and had a common word to describe themselves, perhaps something like Homer's *Achaiwoi*, 'Achaians'.

A VISIT TO MYCENAE AT THE TIME OF THE TROJAN WAR

Mycenae was built for war. In its origin, it must have been what the Turks call a *dervendji* – that is, a castle built at a juncture of mountain passes for the purpose of levying tribute or tax on all traffic that passes through; a stronghold of robber barons. It stands on a craggy hill underneath two triangular peaks, its back to the mountains, 'folded up into a menacing crouch', as Henry Miller put it. In front, southwards, the rich plain of Argos opens to the sea. To the north are mountains beyond which lie the plain of Corinth and Sicyon, areas which Homer says were in the kingdom of Agamemnon. Among these mountains stands Mycenae, massively walled, armed to the teeth. Tucked away up in the north-western corner of the plain, it is not near the sea and does not have good arable land within its immediate grasp. It is hard to see how such a place could thrive, or why it needed such great walls, until you walk round it and notice that it stands at the meeting-place of an ancient system of tracks leading north and south, linking the Argive and Corinthian plains, and the smaller plain of Berbati and the Kontoporeia pass. If the life of Mycenae began as a local chief's stronghold, it had risen to great wealth by the sixteenth century BC when Schliemann's shaft graves were constructed. From then on the place must have depended for its greatness upon industry and commerce with a wider world.

I begin with a general impression, admittedly subjective, but I think not misguided, which is that Mycenae in the thirteenth century BC has *imperial* characteristics, both in its architectural style and in the artistic and material links which connect it to other Mycenaean centres. Such ideas are naturally approached with some reluctance by professional archaeologists – they perhaps run beyond the strictly observable facts in the ground, but they are immediately striking to the political journalist in terms of parallels with other cultures, especially the Near Eastern 'empires' of the thirteenth century BC. Mycenae quite simply *looks like* an imperial city. Let me explain what I mean by imagining a visit to Agamemnon's capital at the height of its power and architectural development, say around 1250 BC. If we think of our visitor as an ambassador from one of the other great empires of the time, the Hittites or the Egyptians, it will serve to remind us that Mycenaean Greece had contacts with the great kingships of the Near East, and was influenced by their styles. They certainly had such contacts (as we shall see in Chapter 6): the record has been discovered recently of an Egyptian embassy to Greece, including Mycenae, around 1380 BC. We can even point to the kind of men who went on such high-level exchanges (see p. 198). Let us try to see Mycenae through the eyes of such a man as well as our own. If we do, I suggest its architecture and outward display shows it to be an imperial city in the same way as the Hittites' Hattusas, Dark-Age Aachen or Winchester – or even, in a distant way, late-nineteenth-century London for that matter.

That said, a word of warning about terminology is necessary. If we use the term 'empire' let us not understand by this the unitary kind of control and communications we see in modern empires like the British, or even the Roman. The analogies are with 'empires' like that of the Hittites (see p. 220): controlling a heartland which was ruled by the king, neighbouring which lay allied states bound by treaty or oath to the overlord, beyond which in turn existed the coercive arrangements made by an overlord towards his subject peoples: the payment of tribute, the exchange of gifts, the taking of hostages. In these outside lands power shelved into 'segmentary' rule through local men, and finally into subject relations guaranteed by a sophisticated kind of protection money.

By definition an emperor ruled other kings. Hittite treaties survive from this period showing the kind of obligations which subject kings owed their overlords. Frontiers were laid out and guaranteed, promises were made for mutual aid in offensive or defensive campaigns, extradition treaties and terms for the return of fugitives were drawn up. These kind of obligations existed in all early Indo-European kingships and can be closely paralleled in Anglo-Saxon, Celtic and continental Germanic kingship in the European Dark Ages. 'Empires' then advanced and receded rapidly, depending on the power and ability of the individual 'Great King' to guarantee them. Frequently on a king's accession the 'empire' had to be enforced anew by vigorous campaigning. The benefits for the lesser kingdoms were stability, protection from outside attack, and support of their own dynasty against rivals. Ideas like these are a plausible way of interpreting some of our evidence for Greece. The obligation which Homer alleges that the other kings owed Agamemnon *in war* makes great sense in terms of such obligations as we know they existed among the

Hittites – or the Anglo-Saxons for that matter. This, then, is the loose sense in which I use the term 'empire', but such was the power of Mycenae at this time that it may have exerted a cultural uniformity on the other kingdoms of southern Greece.

We are approaching Mycenae from the sea at Tiryns, up the paved Mycenaean road which runs northwards up the Chavos ravine. The road we are on is one of at least five paved roads which have so far been traced running from Mycenae; all of them have elaborate bridges and culverts. The main road from Prosymna, for instance, had at least five bridges and the impressive remains of one can still be seen today on the right of the modern road: though the arch is gone the massive southern end is preserved, over 12 feet high and 20 feet wide and built of finely laid courses of stone. This bridge spans the winter torrent which sweeps down from the citadel; it was over 14 feet wide in the middle, so chariots could pass each other, and what it looked like when complete can be seen from the surviving intact bridge at Kasarma, east of Tiryns. The road system is a clear indication of the centralised power of Mycenae; almost certainly it linked the city with the formerly independent city states of the Argive plain: Argos, Tiryns, Midea and Prosymna. The individual *territoria* of the cities were marked out with watchposts on their borders.

At the Chavos bridge the citadel comes into view with the palace on top, between the two mountains, one of which is capped by a watchtower and beacon post: perhaps news of our arrival by sea has been communicated by beacon to the citadel. At this point, the visitor of around 1250 BC would have passed on his left hand the first of the immense royal tombs of the Atreid dynasty: the so-called Treasury of Atreus. It was clearly intended as a great public monument, for inside its low-walled forecourt, at the end of the long entrance, you faced a façade over 30 feet high framing tremendous wooden doors, 17½ feet high, decorated with bronze; the façade itself was decorated by half columns in green marble with finely cut zigzag decorations; above it, framed by smaller half columns, was an elaborate linear decoration of red and green marble. If we had been privileged enough to be allowed to look inside this spectacular monument, we would have seen its lower courses lined with bronze plates, the last of which were removed by Lord Aberdeen in 1803. The most recent of these great tombs, the so-called tomb of Clytemnestra (c.AD 1250), was equally impressive with blue and white marble on its façade, the relieving triangle perhaps containing the triangular bull relief found by Lord Elgin: bulls were an emblem of kingship and it is not impossible that this is the tomb of Agamemnon himself. Had these magnificent monuments survived in a better condition (the half columns were still on the Atreus façade as late as 1801) our mental impression of the 'typology' of Mycenaean kingship – which tends to be governed by the impressive but crude 'Cyclopean' walls – would be very different. These were undeniably the most sophisticated monuments from prehistoric Europe.

We now approach the citadel itself. The road led under the enormous Cyclopean bastion which still stands 26 feet high on top of the rock outcrop, and may originally have been nearer 36 feet. The main gate is set back in a narrow entrance with another bastion on the right hand. The gateway itself is surmounted by a muscular relief of lions on either side of a column bearing the entablature of a building – the palace itself. Made of hard, blackish limestone, it is 10 feet high and a little wider. The heads of the lions are missing today, but were probably of a softer material such as steatite and would have looked out frontally to greet the approaching visitor with flashing eyes of metal or precious stone. The whole relief symbolises the palace guarded by lions, the house of Atreus itself: an emblem of Mycenae and the dynasty of Agamemnon. The altar on which the column rests signifies divine blessing on the house's right to rule. In effect, then, the Lion Gate sculpture is a coat of arms: the lions, like the bull, are the oldest symbols of kingship in the Near East.

When the wooden gates were opened you went through to see a ramp rising ahead (the steps at the bottom are modern). To your right was a great circle of upright, flat stones. This area, the visitor would have been informed, was the circle of the ancestral graves. It was only in the thirteenth century BC that this circle, originally outside the citadel walls, was brought inside with a new wall and supporting terrace. At the same time the graves were refurbished and inscribed gravestones erected, so that the area, so conspicuous inside the main gate, became an object of show and cult (there is an interesting parallel in 'archaeological' work on the restoration of royal graves in Egypt in the mid-thirteenth century BC). Whether these dead kings – the shaft grave people found by Schliemann – were of the same dynasty as the Atreids we do not know; perhaps they were what legend calls the Perseids, the family of the city's founder, Perseus. Whoever they were, the later kings of the Atreid line clearly wished to use their graves to show their own sense of history and pedigree, perhaps also their association with the older dynasty. The Bronze-Age visitor would probably make a sacrifice here before passing on up the ramp.

As we go up the ramp we remember that below it, in debris fallen from further up the hill, Schliemann found fragments of red porphyry friezes suggesting that higher up, on our left hand, palace buildings had been decorated with elaborate stone reliefs cut with spirals, rosettes and palmettes. At the top of the ramp you reached the royal apartments themselves with their wonderful view over the Argive plain. While the chambers were not comparable in size or grandeur to an Egyptian or Babylonian royal palace, they compare favourably with the Hittite palace in the 'great fort' at Hattusas: a large outer room with stucco and gypsum floors, its portico columned and painted; the throne-room itself decorated with shield frescoes and depictions of warfare and a siege scene showing a hero falling from the battlements of a town. Here the Mycenaean king would receive ambassadors, who would be feasted to the strains of lyre players and bards reciting the great deeds of the king and his ancestors, surrounded by the Mycenaean nobility resplendent in 'royal cloaks' with ornate war gear.

Of course the observant visitor could have found out much more about Mycenae's contacts had he nosed about a little. He would have discovered Asian slave women seized on piratical raids working in the textile industry in the lower town. In the (merchants'?) houses he would have seen spices – 'ginger grass' from Syria, cumin from Egypt, sesame from Mesopotamia, cyperus seed from Cyprus; he may have seen dyed stuffs and condiments from Canaan. As at Pylos or Knossos, he might have met natives of Egypt, Cyprus and Anatolia. But it is the outward show we are concerned with here. Kings, I suspect, do not differ much in their basic attitudes to their royalty whether they be Hittites or Anglo-Saxons; on these grounds it is difficult not to see this architectural achievement as in some way 'imperial', with its vast expenditure on superfluous ornament, on royal cult, on royal tombs with public decoration, on the reliefs, columns and gates with heraldic devices, elaborate defences, bridges and road systems. This is not small-scale kingship, not the kingship of a small city state; its wealth is inexplicable as merely the product of the domination of its immediate neighbours. An interesting indication of this is provided by the red and green marble used in the Treasury of Atreus. It is now known that the red marble, *rosso antico*, comes from quarries at Kyprianon in the south of the Mani in the Peloponnese; the green marble seems to have come from the same place, a group of five quarries 3 miles or so from the sea, where a little Mycenaean port existed above the modern village of Spira. These quarries were used from the fifteenth century BC until the Renaissance, and the Atreus decorations show that the king of Mycenae was able to bring tons of the stone from the Mani to the Argolid, a sea journey of over 125 miles, followed by 10 miles overland up the plain.

The source of the white marble used in the Treasury of Atreus has not been ascertained – there is no quarry for good-quality white marble in Lakonia – but it is likely that it comes from the Pentelic quarries 12 miles north-east of Athens, which seem to be the source of the white marble used for the Treasury of Minyas at Orchomenos; the grey in the latter is from Levadhia.

Another interesting example of this aspect of Mycenaean authority and technology also comes from Lakonia. Here, in the hills above the Evrótas valley near Krokeai, are the overgrown quarries which are the only source of the strange mottled porphyry known as 'Spartan stone' which ranges from dark green flecked with yellow to a reddish colour. This stone was widely sought after for luxury items in the Late Bronze Age, and was massively exploited in the Roman period when there was an imperial monopoly with a *dispensator* living on site – it is very likely that a similar arrangement existed in the Mycenaean period. In classical times the stone was particularly used for decorating holy places, as Pausanias noted, and was highly valued in the Renaissance: the visitor to the Vatican, for instance, may notice that the cobbles around the obelisk in St Peter's Square are made of alternate green Spartan stone and *rosso antico* from Spira.

All mainland finds of this stone on Mycenaean sites – and they are mainly from Mycenae itself – date from the fourteenth and thirteenth centuries BC. In the sculptor's shop at Knossos Evans found an unworked pile of Spartan stone, ready for use. The context of the find led him to think that this area was rebuilt in the final phase of the palace, in which case, on the revised dating of the palace, it should be from the thirteenth century BC, and certainly dates from after the Greek conquest of Crete. Here, then, is a remarkable piece of evidence which shows that at the height of the Mycenaean world a Greek dynast at Knossos was able to have stone quarried in Lakonia and shipped to Crete for use in the royal workshops in Knossos. The port from which the stone was exported was Agios Stephanos, where numerous fragments have been recovered, along with signs of other industrial activity; now overgrown, silted up and abandoned, the place was still being used by small-time Frankish merchants in the thirteenth century AD: memories – or geographical necessity – run deep in Mediterranean history.

There is no mention of mining in the Linear B tablets, so we must conjecture, but it seems plausible to think that just as a Hittite king might control trade and exercise a monopoly on foreign traders, just as Mycenaean and Hittite kings might have a monopoly on the importing of copper, so they might have controlled the mining of precious stone, and a Mycenaean quarry manager may have lived near Spira. Finds of stone from the Mani in Mycenae and Knossos, and smaller items elsewhere, may be seen as a good example of the Greek kingdoms' ability to organise themselves; it tells us about their wealth, their connections, their stability at their height, and perhaps is an indicator of the (loose) unity of their world. It may not be extravagant to compare such detail with, for example, the expensive stone used by Roman builders to build and adorn the temple at Colchester – red and green marble from those same Spira quarries, alabaster and black marble from Asia Minor and North Africa. Once again, this is not local kingship.

A PREHISTORIC ARMS RACE?

What was the relation between Mycenae and the other palaces? Historians have been perplexed by the presence of several great fortresses in the same area, as in the plain of Argos. Were Mycenae, Tiryns, Argos and Midea under the same king or independent rulers? Why were such massive fortifications built so close to each other? It seems hard to believe they were wholly independent of each other in such a small area. We must remember that these were unsettled times, constantly threatened by outside attack, and prime agricultural land with its dense population would need a string of fortresses to protect it; Mycenae, so far from the sea, could hardly do that. The rulers of the Argolid may have had royal residences in each place, perhaps lived in by members of the royal family, kings' brothers, sons and royal mothers, as, say, in the Saudi royal family today. It is even possible that, as now, the different places had separate functions: Tiryns the port, Argos the main market of the plain, Nauplion the posh seaside town and so on. But with its large population and its elaborate drainage system – revealed by recent discovery of a dam near Tiryns – the plain needed to be heavily defended.

It would appear, then, that mainland Greece was divided between a number of powerful 'city states' – larger than later classical ones – which might dominate their lesser neighbours and which might acknowledge the leadership of the most powerful in time of war. Much of their military technology may have been intended as defence against each other. In central Greece legend says that Thebes and Orchomenos were deadly enemies, and we know now that Orchomenos defended itself and its elaborate drainage works at Lake Copais by a string of forts and watchtowers around the lake and along the border with Thebes, centring on the huge fort at Gla. Thebes too had a number of fortified towns, including Eutresis whose walls were hardly less extensive than those at Gla. Had the Mycenaean world perhaps broken up into mutally hostile groups by around 1300 BC, with Thebes and Orchomenos contending in central Greece, and Mycenae the leader in the Peloponnese? Certainly we can see from the Argolid and the Copais defences that warfare was of a rather sophisticated kind, on a level recalling city-state warfare in the Near East, with material prosperity and technological skill which allowed numerous massive and elaborate fortifications to be erected in a very brief span of time. In this kind of society it was presumably easy enough to reallocate the mass of the work-force to this work outside the sowing and harvest seasons, though we do not know how compliant they were (did this massive arms race – with its conspicuous expenditure – play its part in the subsequent collapse, one wonders?).

But if the period of the Mycenaean heyday was characterised by frequent internecine warfare, it was nevertheless one of common culture and political ideas. When we think of the exporting of building stone from Lakonia to Mycenae and Knossos; the exporting of stirrup jars from Crete to the mainland palaces of Thebes, Mycenae, Tiryns and Eleusis; the identical design and measurements of the 'treasuries' at Mycenae and Orchomenos; the identical bureaucracy, even down to mistakes in the 'form', at Pylos and Knossos – then we are entitled to assume that the rulers of this period moved in the same world, cultivated the same ideas, and employed the same artists, architects and painters. In this light it is plausible that these 'city states' could at one time or other have acknowledged the pre-eminence of a 'first among equals'. Such 'kings of the Achaiwoi' need not have been from the same kingdom, but tradition held that three generations of the Atreids at Mycenae wielded such power over southern Greece, and it remains a possibility. They cannot have literally 'ruled' Greece, of course, let alone *all* Greece, but we can imagine a chief king in the Argolid having leadership of much of the Peloponnese in time of war, and being bound to others by alliance or marriage: let us remember here that legend held that the king of Sparta was Agamemnon's brother, just as the kings of Pylos were of the same kin as the royal family of Iolkos. The aid of such a king might be sought by dynasties outside his immediate influence if they were confronted by powerful rivals, as, say, was the case between Orchomenos and Thebes – the legend says that Thebes sacked Orchomenos and ruined its dykes, and that forces from 'Argos' then burned Thebes.

It is, then, not impossible that a king of Mycenae could have called himself 'king of the Achaians'. Admittedly our knowledge of such relations in Greece is speculative. But in Anatolia and the Near East in the second millennium BC there is a mass of detail about the relations between vassals and lords, kings and overkings, particularly from Hittite treaties of the fourteenth and thirteenth centuries. These relationships were frequently expressed in terms of 'brotherhood' or 'sonship', and they were defined with legal obligations imposed on the vassal. If you were 'lord' of your 'brother' king, or 'father' to a 'son', then he had accepted a legal bond; 'brotherhood' seems to have had a different connotation: in that case – strikingly like the Homeric model – you might be a member of a confederation which accepted the Great King's leadership in foreign policy and war, but you were not as fully subject to him as his 'sons'. This might be a helpful model for Agamemnon's 'empire'. In the Hittite empire a distinction was made between 'associated' states, where obligations might be partially reciprocal – no tribute exacted, but foreign policy subordinate to the Great King and help given in time of war – and on the other hand purely vassal states who paid tribute and fought in the Great King's own ranks. 'Sons', then, were usually subordinate kings, 'brothers' often equals. Such ideas may help us imagine relations between Mycenae and, say, Pylos or Orchomenos. But if there was at times a 'Great King' of 'Achaia-land' (and we shall see in Chapter 6 that the Hittites thought there was), then by definition he was a king who ruled other kings.

HEROIC KINGSHIP?

What kind of kingship was it? What would the rule of Agamemnon have been like? Because of the paucity of hard facts in the Linear B tablets, historians have been tempted to return to Homer and call Late-Bronze-Age Greek kingship 'heroic'. What is meant by this?

Over the last century much work has been done by scholars on 'heroic' kingship in Dark-Age western Europe, both Celtic and Germanic, where abundant material survives in the form of annals, laws and homilies defining the role of the king in societies which in some respects bear a resemblance to that portrayed in Homer. Here too epic poems, such as *Beowulf*, formed the basis of the interpretation. Indeed the parallels between Anglo-Saxon and Homeric epic poetry inspired one of the earliest attempts to draw together these early European traditions of 'heroic' kingship, the classic *Heroic Age* of H.M. Chadwick (1911), a book which heavily influenced Homeric scholars in the English-speaking world. Chadwick was convinced that the ideals and the way of life portrayed in early Germanic epic had much in common with Homer, and that the later Norse, Celtic and Anglo-Saxon traditions were very similar. In some ways this was right: it was inevitable that broad social and material characteristics – even political ones too – should have coincided in similar militarist aristocratic societies where the king surrounded himself with warriors attracted by his generosity and success in war, where the warlike ideals of the royal clan and its military retinue found their expression in the trappings of war weaponry, fine war gear, good horses. But while there were similarities, these are the similarities found in oral epic in many cultures, whether it be *Beowulf*, the *Iliad* or the early Indian epics. The closeness, then, is a product of the epic, not necessarily of the societies; historians and anthropologists now tend to see these 'heroic' traits as literary creations, characteristic of periods of nostalgic decay. Nevertheless archaeology has often brought the 'heroic' age of the epic tantalisingly close. The discovery of the Sutton Hoo ship burial thirty years after Chadwick wrote had much the same effect on Anglo-Saxon studies as Schliemann's dig at Mycenae had on Homeric scholarship: here once again the world of epic poetry found its correlation in real artefacts (the boar's-crest helmet described in *Beowulf* and found at Sutton Hoo immediately springs to mind as a Homeric parallel). With a necessary caveat, we will stick to our use of the word 'heroic' as it applies to a society geared to war with aristocratic martial ideals, the world of the 'sackers of cities'.

THE RISE OF MYCENAE

A brief sketch of the rise of Mycenaean power would be as follows. Greek-speaking peoples are thought to have entered what is now Greece soon after 1900 BC, though some scholars think they may have been present since Neolithic times (a minority think their arrival was much later, but this seems unlikely). At this time the great age of the Cretan palaces was beginning, a civilisation modelled on the Egyptian–Syrian; also at this time the Hurrian civilisation (which preceded the Hittite) was developing in Anatolia, strongly influenced by the Mesopotamian–Old Assyrian culture with which it had close contacts down the Euphrates valley: Assyrian merchant colonies of considerable size were already established in several places in

Anatolia by 1800 BC. In Greece between 1700 and 1600 BC there seems to have been a sudden flowering of Mycenaean civilisation, strongly coloured by Cretan elements; this flowering is exemplified in the shaft graves found by Schliemann at Mycenae, dating from the sixteenth century BC. Before this time mainland civilisation does not appear to have been palace-based, though the 'House of Tiles' at Lerna (third millennium BC) looks like an early form of the mainland 'megaron'. It would seem a plausible guess that large mainland kingdoms like Mycenae grew from local chiefdoms centred on glorified farms by conquering and assimilating lesser local dynasties in the seventeenth and sixteenth centuries BC, though exactly *how* the shaft grave dynasty became so wealthy is as yet unknown, and neither do we know when Mycenae took over places like Berbati and Prosymna, which look like former independent local centres. Even more of a problem is the relation of Mycenae to the other big palace sites in the Argolid, namely Argos, Tiryns and Midea. Classical tradition may perhaps be used to help us here, though with the necessary caution. Ancient tradition said that Mycenae was founded by the Perseid dynasty and that the Atreids (Pelops, Atreus, Agamemnon) were outsiders. The same kind of story is told of the Cadmeans of Thebes. The origins of the Atreids are said to have been Anatolian, Lydian, where we know that there was a Greek presence from the fifteenth century BC, but fascinating as this story is, the present state of our knowledge does not allow us to say anything more about the alleged outside origin of some of the Late-Bronze-Age Greek dynasties. If the essential lines of the tradition are correct, though, the shaft grave dynasty found by Schliemann might be the Perseids, and hence the great wealth of those graves the wealth of that clan. The Atreids would be later (originally installed at Midea by the Perseids). Their power would cover the late fourteenth and the thirteenth centuries BC, and this fits well, for what it is worth, with the traditional attribution of the great tholos tombs of Mycenae to their dynasty: the so-called treasuries of Atreus and Clytemnestra could actually be those of Atreus and his son

Agamemnon. Again, the legends are insistent that the rise of Mycenae to pre-eminence in the mainland only took place late, under the Atreids. In this context the earlier local extension of Mycenaean power across the Argive plain to places like Nemea, Lerna, and even Tiryns itself, may be reflected in legend: the Labours of Hercules (Herakles) of Tiryns were performed for Eurystheus, the last Perseid king of Mycenae; after Eurystheus' death fighting the children of Herakles, the people of Mycenae are said to have chosen his brother-in-law Atreus to rule over them, for he was best able to protect them from their neighbouring enemies. Looking at the archaeology in relation to the legendary account, impressive as is the gold of the shaft grave people (sixteenth century BC), experts have not detected a Mycenaean presence outside the Argolid at that stage, and the general level of civilisation – the architecture, for example – was no higher than in the first centuries of the second millennium. In other words we can observe certain facts about the rise of the mainland kingdoms, and especially Mycenae, but we cannot as yet explain the extraordinary transformation of the fourteenth and thirteenth centuries, with the great building of what I have termed 'imperial' Mycenae. By then its power, as well as its influence and material culture, had surely extended well beyond the Argolid.

Direct evidence for their kingship can only be found in the archaeology. But the shaft graves, the architecture and later the Linear B tablets tell us much about noble and royal culture which can be paralleled elsewhere. Kings like Agamemnon expended an extraordinary amount of their income and wealth on royal graves and royal cult. They lavished great wealth and craftsmanship on weaponry and war gear. It may not be going too far to see the depictions of hunting and fighting on the beautiful inlaid daggers, on the frescoes and on the monumental standing stones, as revealing the typical preoccupations of the ruling class, whether we call it 'heroic' or not. This was a royal warrior élite with a wide gulf separating it from the common people. Now, like many other such kingships of which we have details – Celtic,

Germanic and Indian – the king doubtless needed to sustain his military following by generosity, that is, by gift-giving, food, hospitality and perhaps by grants of land (though the tablets leave us uncertain about land tenure). 'Agamemnon' would have had to feed his court and its officers, equip and reward his army – investing ample resources in time and treasure to the training of the military force which backed him, especially his horses and chariotry, the most expensive and time-consuming investment. To do all this, and to keep his army loyal, his friends happy and his enemies subdued, he needed to take land, slaves, women, treasure and booty. This required regular warfare, forays and piratical expeditions. From Thucydides onwards all commentators on the Trojan story have understood it in this light. Schliemann himself came to this conclusion at Mycenae in 1876:

The question naturally arises how the city obtained its gold at that remote period when there was no commerce as yet. It appears indeed that it cannot have obtained it in any other way than by powerful piratical expeditions to the Asiatic coast.

Of the commerce we will learn more in Chapter 7. Of the warfare we can assume it was the métier of all Bronze-Age kings. Regular summer hostings may have been the order of the day. The late-fourteenth-century-BC annals of the Hittite king Mursilis II mention ten campaigns in twenty-six years against the frontier Kaska peoples, leaving aside his major campaigns to the south in Syria, and westwards into Assuwa and Arzawa, where one campaign yielded 66,000 prisoners. Two Assyrian campaigns against the Hittites in the Euphrates gained 28,000 and 14,400 prisoners after the sack of scores of towns and villages. These are large figures, if we can trust them. But how big were 'national' armies of the period of the Trojan War? The biggest recorded army of the time is the Hittite force at Kadesh (1275–1274 BC), 2500 chariots and 37,000 infantry, but this was exceptional and included the retinues of sixteen allied states as well as the 'feudal' levies of the Hittite king, and mercenaries. Armies in the Aegean world must have been far smaller. Estimates for the populations of Mycenaean kingdoms are only approximate, but that of Pylos can hardly have been less than 50,000, and estimates for the possible populations of the Argolid states (by food production from cultivatable land) have suggested maxima of 180,000 for Mycenae, 70,000 for Midea, 90,000 for Tiryns and 60,000 for Argos. The idea that anything near 10 per cent of a pre-industrial society could be mobilised for war is probably far-fetched, so we may assume that an army of a few hundred heavily armed men was a large one. One group of damaged Pylos tablets mentions over 400 rowers and at least 700 men as defensive troops, but it would be surprising if the king could muster more than a couple of thousand well-armed and trained troops for an offensive expedition. A Greek marauder in Lycia in around 1420 BC presented a threat to a Hittite army with a force of 100 chariots and perhaps 1000 troops; a rich city like Ugarit could man 150 ships (with mercenaries?) for an offensive campaign – perhaps 7000 fighting men. This last figure is of the order we would expect for a Mycenaean campaign against Troy, if it took place. But equally a mere seven ships could be a deadly threat to Ugarit when its own fleet was absent. This is the scale of Bronze-Age warfare – comparable, say, to the warfare of the Viking Age in Europe where, for instance, the garrisons of thirty fortified centres in Wessex totalled 26,671 men, with the mobile royal army probably numbering a few thousand at most. It is likely, then, that in the thirteenth century BC a few hundred heavily armed 'bronze-clad' warriors with their servants, horses, carts, chariots, spares and support staff constituted an army for an expedition against a hostile state. Clearly the main kingdoms of the Peloponnese alone could have raised a force of several thousands. The citadel on Hisarlik, however – if it was Troy – can hardly have raised more than a few hundred warriors on its own. Is it possible that the Mycenaean 'empire' would have attacked such a small place – and why? Is there in fact any evidence that the Mycenaean kingdoms might have campaigned in western Anatolia?

'WOMEN OF ASIA' AND THE SACKERS OF CITIES

In the Linear B tablets there is one remarkable body of evidence which has not been exploited in the search for the Trojan War. At Pylos in particular groups of women are recorded doing menial tasks such as grinding corn, preparing flax and spinning. Their ration quotas suggest that they are to be numbered in hundreds. Many are distinguished by ethnic adjectives, presumably denoting the places they came from, and though some of these are still not understood, several of the women come from the eastern Aegean – Cnidus, Miletus, Lemnos, Zephyrus (i.e. Halicarnassos), Chios and *Aswija*. The last name occurs at Pylos, Knossos and Mycenae, and seems to denote the area originally known as Asia, that is, Lydia (Assuwa in Hittite). At Pylos there is even an enigmatic *To-ro-ja* ('The woman of Troy'?), 'servant of the god'. The Pylos tablets name 700 women, with their 400 girls and 300 boys, and another 300 men and boys who 'belong to them'. Some of the ethnic groups are sizeable: 'twenty-one women from Cnidus with their twelve girls and ten boys'. These descriptions often use the word *lawiaiai*, 'captives', which is the same word used by Homer to describe women seized by Achilles at Lyrnessos during a foray south of Troy (*Iliad*, XX, 193) and it is a remarkable fact that Homer also names a number of places in the eastern Aegean as the homes of women taken on Greek raids, including the islands of Lesbos, Skyros and Tenedos (*Iliad*, XVIII, 346).

These tablets are vivid evidence for the predatory nature of Mycenaean expansion in the eastern Aegean. The women must either have been captured on pirate raids, or bought from slave dealers in entrepôts such as Miletus. The fact that they are usually mentioned with their children but not with men implies the familiar raiding pattern of the sackers of cities, where the men are killed and the women carried off. The *Iliad* and the tablets complement each other here in a remarkable way, and it must be assumed that Homer is here again preserving a genuine Bronze-Age memory. Presumably the women would only have been called 'captives' for a short while before being assigned occupations, though they seem to have been kept together as ethnic groups, and as families (unlike, say, in the American Confederacy, where slave families were deliberately broken up). This would have had practical advantages for the slave owners – perhaps it made the captives work better – and there is an exact contemporary parallel in the Ugaritic tablets which mention 'the sons of the slave women of Kt' (i.e. Kition in Cyprus?). Here then, even without lonely *To-ro-ja*, we have the clearest possible context for the Trojan tale.

It did not need many ships full of armed raiders to threaten and sack a small city and enslave its people: six vessels sack Laomedon's Troy in the Herakles legend. Small groups of people, chieftains and their war bands, appear at many places in the thirteenth-century Near Eastern texts. As often as we read of armies plundering, we find small bands of adventurers trying to carve out a new home somewhere in the Eastern Mediterranean and Aegean. The title they most coveted, if we can trust Homer, was 'sacker of cities'. In the Homeric epics, and still in Aeschylus, it was a leader's greatest claim to glory. Agamemnon, Achilles, Nestor ('in my youth I was one') and even Athena herself bear the title of 'sacker of cities' in Homer.

We should not overdo the search for 'modern' motives for this. In the *Iliad* the sacker of cities does not destroy to increase his political power, to combat inflation, to open up trade routes to the Black Sea or to the tin mines of Europe; he does not destroy to appropriate the mackerel and tunny harvests. He sacks cities to get booty, treasure, horses, cattle, gold, silver, fine armour and weapons – and women. We must not forget the women (after all, the legend insists that the seizure of a woman was the cause of the Trojan War). Time and again Homer tells of the fight for 'the city and its women'. When Achilles tells Odysseus of the twenty-three cities he has sacked he mentions only 'treasure and women' as his gain. This is what makes him proud, and gives him fame after his death. And the more beautiful the women, the better. In this they are remarkably close to the great African 'high-kings' of the Zande, recorded in the anthropological work of E.E. Evans-Pritchard – the victorious chief takes the most beautiful women for himself and gives the others with their children to his retinue ('These *akanga vura*, "slaves of war", were not regarded very differently from ordinary wives....': could that offer a clue to the real 'Helen'?).

Such, then, were the goals of 'heroic' kingship. If economic necessity can partly explain such attacks – to replenish the slave labour in the 'state industries' – nevertheless it was doubtless still true that the greater the booty captured, the larger the quantities of gold and silver, the finer the horses and the more beautiful the women, the greater the honour due to the conqueror. This was what ensured the victorious king a large following, and it guaranteed their loyalty. And the larger the warrior band, the more ambitious the military enterprise that could be undertaken next time. Perhaps the Trojan War was such an enterprise. In this light the Asian women who laboured in the flax fields around Pylos, receiving their monthly rations and bringing up their children as slaves with Greek names, are perhaps our most eloquent testimony to the thought world of Agamemnon and the sackers of cities. This was the reality of the 'Heroic Age', and in its essential spirit Homer's tale has got this right. Until recently, I might add, it was still possible to touch on a real continuity with these women. In the countryside above Pylos, one of the palace's regional centres was by the modern village of Koukounara (Ro-uso?). In this region the tablets mention women retting flax, and here until the 1950s this back-breaking task was still performed by the local women; now man-made fibres have broken this ancient tradition, but the river where the 'women of Asia' bent in servitude in 1200 BC is still called Linaria: 'flax river'.

MYCENAEANS IN ASIA MINOR

In our search for the Mycenaeans in Asia Minor we can go further. Important evidence has emerged recently of a Mycenaean presence on the coast of Asia Minor, not merely as raiders but as settlers. We have noted the presence of slaves from these parts in Mycenaean mainland palaces. Archaeological evidence enables us to corroborate this picture in a most interesting way. Twenty-five sites have now been identified on the Turkish coast, or its immediate hinterland, where finds of Mycenaean pottery have been made. This of course does not prove the presence of Greeks, though tombs at Colophon and Pitane may suggest this. But Mycenaeans were certainly present in the south-western part of Anatolia, south of the river Maeander. Here archaeological evidence suggests a large enclave whose main centres were Miletus, Iasos and somewhere near Müsgebi where a rich cemetery has been found. These places all looked westwards, towards islands already colonised by Mycenaeans, especially Rhodes, Kos, Samos and Chios. There is also evidence of Mycenaean contact inland from Iasos into the plain of Mylasa, at least as traders; the two main river routes into the interior – the upper Maeander and the lower Hermus – have provided some further slight evidence of the carrying of Mycenaean goods. This makes sense: the country around the lower Hermus provided the Mycenaeans with slaves; the upper Maeander route into the interior leads to Beycesultan, where a few Mycenaean finds were made at the Late-Bronze-Age palace which may have been one of the centres of the Hittite allied state of Mira, a state important enough to correspond with Egypt.

These finds should not be over-exaggerated, but the evidence will obviously grow. Pottery was found in 1983 to add to that already discovered at Masat Hüyük, in the Hittite heartland, and Bronze-Age sites in Caria and Lycia, whose existence was denied not long ago, have recently come to light. The evidence of this Greek enclave is significant: Miletus, Iasos and Müsgebi – Halicarnassos could have controlled a significant hinterland, and many scholars believe this is what Hittite tablets tell us, as we shall see in Chapter 6.

MILETUS: A BRONZE-AGE GREEK 'COLONY'
IN ASIA MINOR?

It is worth looking at Miletus in a little more detail, as the exciting finds made there in the early years of the century have been largely destroyed without being published. Similarly no general account exists in English of the recent discoveries of the 'Mycenaean' wall.

Of all the sites on the coast of Asia Minor Miletus is the most dramatic to today's visitor. Once the self-styled 'first foundation of Ionia', 'metropolis of Asia' and 'mother city of numerous cities in many parts of the world', Miletus now lies 4 miles from the sea, left high and dry by the silt-bearing stream of the river Maeander. Now the visitor can walk across the sandy scrub of its harbour mouths, past the stone lions of the Lion Harbour. The immense ruins of the classical city extend along what was once a sea-girt promontory roughly a mile in length by 1200 yards across at its widest, narrowing to about 200 yards at the northern tip. The promontory had three main projections, forming natural harbours which looked out to the Aegean. On the southernmost and lowest of these, opposite the great theatre, German excavators since the Second World War have discovered remarkable remains of the Late Bronze Age. It appears that Miletus was originally a Cretan settlement taken over by Mycenaeans in the fifteenth century BC. The subsequent settlement was destroyed by a severe fire in around 1320 BC, after which a large fortification was built encircling the whole hill. The length of the wall was over 1100 yards, enclosing 50,000 square yards (compare Mycenae at 38,500 square yards, Tiryns at 22,000 and Troy VI at 20,000, for example). In other words the place was big enough to be the capital of a kingdom. The wall had a remarkable feature, square bastions every 15 yards, for which there are parallels in Hittite, late Mycenaean and Cypriot architecture, and it may be that Miletus was a cultural link between the Anatolian and Aegean worlds. Of the internal layout of the city we know little, but there were pottery kilns, houses, and on the low summit of the hill some sort of residential complex centring on a court – possibly a 'palace'. These excavations have been discontinued, though it might have been hoped that tablets would be found. The pottery associated with these remains includes much Mycenaean work, and there seems little doubt that Greeks were present in the city. This impression is reinforced by the discovery in 1907 of a cemetery at Degirmentepe a mile to the south-west of the city. Here today's visitor can still see at least a dozen rock-cut Mycenaean tombs with the characteristic circular chamber and narrow entrance. Unfortunately their contents were destroyed during the Second World War in Berlin, but what pottery had been exhibited was of the thirteenth century BC; it is likely that more tombs, going back to the Minoan settlement, remain to be found.

The standing of the people who had these tombs made is perhaps indicated by the cemetery found to the south at Müsgebi (fourteenth and thirteenth centuries BC). Here in about fifty chamber tombs were found large numbers of stirrup jars, small and large bowls, drinking cups, a typical pilgrim flask, cups, spouted ewers – all made on the mainland of Greece – along with spindle whorls, necklaces, incense burners, bracelets, small pots for incense or unguents, and a collection of immaculate bronze blades – spearheads, curved blades, a dagger and hilt, and a short sword. These finds, which are now exhibited in Bodrum Museum, create an impression of a well-to-do expatriate class; such, we may assume, were also at least some of the Mycenaean element in Miletus, and they obviously included craftsmen and craftswomen.

While we may be rightly sceptical of calling Miletus a Mycenaean 'colony' as such, the evidence shows that, throughout the heyday of Mycenaean power on the mainland, this place was an important centre for Greek contact with Anatolia. From around 1300 BC Mycenaeans seem to have been an important element in its population. Their presence in a rich cemetery does not, however, prove that they were the rulers of Miletus. Nevertheless from around 1300 Miletus was administered by a powerful authority which could erect a massive wall over 1000 yards in length; they imported Mycenaean pottery and made local copies; they had contact with other Anatolian Greek settlements, such as Iasos; they traded with Ugarit in Syria and perhaps Cyprus and Troy; at least one Hittite import has been found (a pilgrim flask). It also seems likely that this place was the origin of the slave women called *Milatiai* in the Linear B tablets, whom we find working in the flax industry on mainland estates. In view of Miletus' size and the wealth of its tombs, it seems difficult to avoid the conclusion that this was the biggest and wealthiest centre of Mycenaean influence in Asia Minor, with a large population of mixed Minoan, Greek, Lycian and Anatolian origin. Whether it had direct political relation to any part of the Greek mainland cannot be answered from archaeological evidence alone. As we shall see in Chapter 6, it is the Hittite tablets which suggest that it did.

TROY AND MYCENAE

So there is now a significant and growing body of evidence to show that the Greeks of the fourteenth and thirteenth centuries BC were involved in armed forays on the shores of Asia Minor. Indeed it is fair to say that we now have a plausible context for the tale told by Homer and the Greek epic. But was there any connection between Troy itself and the mainland of Greece? Here the archaeological record again provides us with clues.

First let us remember the Homeric tradition: the epic says there were *two* sacks of Troy in the Heroic Age, the first the sack of the city of Laomedon by Herakles, the second the expedition of Agamemnon against Priam. Carl Blegen's dig in the 1930s established two destructions of Hisarlik in the Late Bronze Age: the beautifully walled city of Troy VI we now know fell in around 1300 BC, apparently to an earthquake; its successor, Troy VIIa, the city of shanties, it has recently been established was sacked in around 1200 BC, correcting Blegen's dating. What did the excavator find to link Troy with Mycenae? Here we must remember that Hisarlik is still the only site in north-west Anatolia which has been thoroughly excavated, so the emphasis we give the finds may be misleading, but the quantities of Mycenaean pottery were sufficiently large and of such quality as to suggest to Blegen *direct* relations between Troy and Mycenae.

Trojan imports from the Mycenaean world start in the sixteenth century BC (LH II A) and continue abundantly through the fourteenth century into the first half of the thirteenth (LH III B 1). They stop at the latest in *c.*1250 BC. Only one sherd is known from 1250–1200 (LH III B 2), though of course earlier pottery will still have been in use. The totals found by earlier excavators are uncertain, but Blegen estimated the surviving sherds from *c.*1400–1250 added up to about 700–800 pots, nearly three-quarters of all Mycenaean pottery imports to Troy. It should be remembered, though, that Mycenaean wares account for only 1 or 2 per cent of the entire pottery of Troy VI: it is a tiny proportion when set against the local wares, and presumably represents the import of luxury produce (perfumed oil?) or simply exotic pottery desired for its intrinsic snob value.

This pattern, strong influx from around 1400 to 1250, then a gap, with the re-establishment of contact in the twelfth century (LH III C), can be paralleled in the south-west, as at Miletus. We may fairly take this as a guide to our general picture of relations between Troy and Mycenae.

To the pottery evidence we can add other imports from the Mycenaean world. Blegen found that the last phase of Troy VI (*c.*1400–1300 BC) brought in luxury items of Mycenaean origin: ivory boxes with the characteristic patterns, perhaps a gaming-board among them, carnelian and ivory beads, decorated ostrich eggs, electrum or silver pins, a Cretan lamp. Other finds suggest wider contacts: cylinder seals, which may be from the Hittite world, 'white slip' pottery from Cyprus (perhaps containing opium) – some of the decorated bowls like the Mycenaean ones, were appreciated as exotic products; tripod stone bowls may also have come to Troy from Cyprus. We might note here that the shipwreck found off Cape Gelidonya (see p. 226) was on the sea route from Cyprus to Troy, as well as to Greece: Cypriot pottery was found in the wreck as well as on Crete, Thera, Melos, Keos, Rhodes and Kos – some perhaps sailing stations on the way to Troy.

What did the Trojans give in return? The presence of many spindle whorls, reported by all the diggers on Hisarlik, has suggested that they may have specialised in wool, spun yarn and textiles. This is made all the more plausible if we remember that the neighbours of Ilium in classical times, towns like Scepsis, were known as sheep towns. The Trojans also exported their own pottery, for their local Grey Minyan ware has been found in Syria (at Ugarit, for example), in Cyprus and in Palestine. Fish has also been put forward as a source of Troy's wealth, and this is even more likely now that we know of the existence of the great bay. In later times the seasonal migrations of mackerel and tunny through the Dardanelles brought fishing fleets from all over the Aegean, and this has even been put forward as a possible motive for the Trojan War: the molesting of a Mycenaean fishing fleet having led to a sort of Bronze-Age cod war! The archaeology of Hisarlik could support the idea; Schliemann found deep strata of fish-bones, which could include mackerel and tunny (Schliemann's 'shark bones'?).

A legendary element in Troy's wealth may also have some basis in fact. Homer singles out Troy for its fine horses, and its citizens as horse breeders. The archaeologists found that Troy VI was distinguished by the presence of quantities of horse bones, and we can also point to horse breeding in the Troad in classical times (in fact there was an Ottoman Turkish stud farm near Troy as late as the First World War). The herds of wild horses still roaming the north-western part of Lesbos may be a distant link with the 'horse culture' of the Troy region in the Late Bronze Age. So, though we have only the Homeric epithets as direct testimony, it seems likely that horse breeding was one source of Troy's fabled riches: curiously enough the sack of Laomedon's Troy is attributed to a dispute over horses!

The most important question about the Trojans, however, we cannot yet answer. Who were they? Though the site of Hisarlik was inhabited from around 3600 BC, it is generally agreed that Troy VI was built by newcomers who brought with them, among other things, the horse. Blegen put their arrival at around 1900 BC, the same time that Greek speakers were thought to have entered Greece. In fact Blegen and others were tempted, because of the pottery, to think that originally the Greeks and Trojans were of the same stock. Characteristic of Troy VI was the Grey Minyan, which closely resembled that found in Middle-Bronze-Age Greece (it was named by Schliemann, who first found it at 'Minyan' Orchomenos). The common ceramic element led many Aegean archaeologists to believe that Troy VI and Greece were overrun by invaders of the same stock (offering the intriguing possibility that they might still have been able to understand each other in the thirteenth century BC). However these assumptions are questionable. Anatolian specialists have pointed out that this type of pottery is much more widely spread in western Anatolia than Blegen thought, and probably has its roots back in the third millennium BC in north-west Anatolia. Similarly mainland Grey Minyan can now be seen to have antecedents back in the Early Bronze Age, before 2000 BC, when an increasing number of experts now think that Greek speakers were already in Greece. The language and identity of the Trojans remains a mystery.

THE TROJAN WAR: THE VIEW FROM
BRONZE AGE MYCENAE

We may safely assume that the Greeks and Trojans knew each other and traded directly. That a Greek king might have coveted Troy's wealth seems not unlikely. If we want an imaginary contemporary scenario based on the archaeological evidence, it is easy enough to paint. Let us imagine a king of Mycenae in the mid-thirteenth century BC. He has troubles at home, perhaps. There are as always jealous kinsmen, rivals within the royal house, chafing underlings. The factories in the Argolid are on half production. The defence budget is massive and rising – bronze, like oil today, never gets cheaper, and if there were economic problems it may have become more difficult to obtain (particularly with the growing threat of piracy in the Aegean). The king needs a foreign war. He needs loot and slaves to keep the army loyal. He needs raw materials and precious metals. We do not have to imagine one great 'imperial' expedition. We may conjecture a number of armed forays into the north-eastern Aegean extending over many years. Troy can hardly have been the only objective, rather it was merely one of many places attacked and sacked for treasure and slaves. The Linear B tablets give us a context for the seizing of slaves in Asia Minor – over thirty places mentioned in this connection remain unidentified. Homer, too, preserves a tradition that many other places in the north-east Aegean were attacked, including Lesbos, where interestingly enough the main Bronze-Age town, Thermi, was destroyed c.1300 BC, apparently by armed attack.

The Homeric story, then, fits very well with what we know of Mycenaean relations with the coast of Asia Minor. The attack on Troy would have been one of a series of aggressive forays in those parts. Its memory might have been preserved because it was one of the last successful expeditions of this kind, the dynasty at Mycenae being rent by internal feuds soon afterwards (there is a destruction level at Mycenae datable to c.1230 BC). Our story is plausible, but no more.

Indeed, that is about as far as we can go at the present with the archaeological and literary evidence. To take it any further, we would need contemporary testimony, first-hand documentary sources: an almost impossible expectation, one might have thought, for the Late Bronze Age Aegean. But astonishingly, it now looks as if such material does in fact exist.

Top: Arthur Evans in a 1907 painting by Sir William Richmond.
Above: The throne room at Knossos after the excavation in April 1900. Evans stands in front of the tent on the right.

Opposite top: Reconstructing the palace of Knossos in the 1920s.
Opposite bottom: Troy, the plain from the city, 1893. This gives a vivid
impression of the steep height of the citadel.
Top: Seagoing ships from the Thera frescoes (c.1500 BC). Though earlier than
the Trojan War period, these give an idea of the kind of boats that may have
been used in the heyday of the Mycenaean 'empire'.
Above: A Linear B tablet from Pylos. 'Thus the watchers are guarding the
coasts' – the beginning of the end for Nestor's dynasty, the victors of Troy?

Opposite top: The citadel of Mycenae.
Opposite bottom: A Mycenaean bridge below the citadel. At the head of the valley is mount Prophitis Ilias, the site of a beacon post and watchtower, where, according to the fifth-century poet Aeschylus, the news of the fall of Troy reached Mycenae by a chain of fires lit across the Aegean.
Above: The entrance to the Treasury of Athens, the giant bee-hive tomb of one of the rulers of Mycenae c.1300 BC.

Above: Midea, the third great fortress of the Argolid and comparable in size to Mycenae. The cult of Hippodamia, the mother of Atreus and grandmother of Agamemnon, was later observed at a tomb here.
Opposite top: Boghaz Köy, one of the four main forts within the circuit of the city wall at the Hittite capital of Hattusas.
Opposite bottom: The southern defences of Boghaz Köy in early November.

Above: Troy imagined – the latest digital reconstruction of the legendary city begins to look uncannily like the Troy of Homer.

SIX

A FORGOTTEN EMPIRE: THE HITTITES AND THE GREEKS

Cut out the mythical elements in the tale and you are left as a kernel with the expedition of a powerful King of Mycenae against this town in the Scamander plain near the Hellespont. This kernel must be historical, but it is unlikely that we shall be able to reconstruct the actual course of events when we lack contemporary historical records.

EDUARD MEYER, *Geschichte des Altertums* (1928)

IN THIS NEXT STAGE of our search we come to a very different kind of evidence from that available to us in the previous five chapters. Remarkable discoveries in central Turkey have led to the decipherment of the Hittite language and have revealed the hitherto unsuspected existence of a great empire which stretched from the Aegean to the Euphrates valley at precisely the time when tradition places the Trojan War. In the Hittite archives, for the first time in our quest, we have 'real' historical texts to interpret: diplomatic letters, treaties, annals and royal auto-biographies in which the characters of the kings and queens of the Hittites come to life in a most vivid way. Most exciting of all is the claim that Troy and the Trojan War are to be found in these files of the 'Hittite Foreign Office'; indeed it is even possible on the face of it that we have surviving letters written to Agamemnon himself, and a treaty with the real Alexander of Ilios, who in the legend was Paris, the son of Priam, who abducted Helen and brought about the sack of the city of Troy.

The emergence of the Hittites from almost complete obscurity has been one of the great achievements of archaeology and philology of the last 100 years. That achievement has not received its full acknowledgement in the English-speaking world, probably because the main work has been done in German, and the Hittite language was deciphered by Germans and a Czech. Nevertheless the achievement has been nothing less than the rediscovery of one of the great Bronze-Age civilisations, and with it the earliest Indo-European language so far known, the Hittite branch of the tree from which Celtic, Germanic, Sanskrit – and Greek – grew.

Though the classical Greeks seem to have been quite unaware of the existence of a Hittite empire in Asia Minor in the Heroic Age, the Hittites were not entirely lost. In the Old Testament they are frequently referred to, though with no real hint of their importance. Only in two places is there any suggestion that the Hittites are other than merely another of the tribes encountered by the Israelites in Palestine. Solomon takes Hittite wives and buys costly Egyptian horses as gifts for the Hittite king (2 Chronicles 1:17); elsewhere we read of how the king of the Israelites can bring against his enemies the kings of the Hittites and the kings of the Egyptians (2 Kings 7:6–7). In fact, these biblical accounts touched on an empire which had stretched to the Aegean, and which had been destroyed soon after 1200 BC, several hundred years before these parts of the Bible were written.

The archaeological evidence for the Hittites was widely scattered – so widely that it took time for it to be drawn together. John Burkhardt had noted the unknown script at Hamath in Syria in 1812. But it was in central Anatolia in the 1830s that the pieces started to come together.

THE DISCOVERY OF THE HITTITES

In the summer of 1834 a young Frenchman was riding northwards through the majestic tableland between Sungurlu and Yozgat in central Turkey. This is still a wild and bare countryside with long sills of eroded sandstone, cut by watercourses, and few trees. Charles Texier was searching for the early remains of central Anatolia, and in particular the ancient town of Tavium where invading Celts had been settled in Roman times. What he actually found was to lead to something of far greater significance to history.

At the village of Boghaz Köy he learned that there were ruins nearby, and so he set off southwards up a dirt track towards a bowl of rugged hills which stands over the village. There to his astonishment he found the low foundations of a vast building. As he walked on he came to fortification walls, and beyond them a line of crags surmounted by smaller fortresses, not dissimilar to the Cyclopean architecture becoming familiar to scholars in Greece. At the top of the hill, a mile from the first ruins he had reached, the ridge was crested by an immense surrounding wall of which nearly a mile in length was still standing. At one gate was the larger than life-size figure of a man (a king or a god?) carved in relief, helmeted and holding an axe, with a short sword thrust into his belt. At the other end of this great stretch of wall Texier found a second gate flanked by massive stone lions. These he sketched. A local guide now led him over the ravine northwards to a second site tucked away in a cleft of rock in the cliffs at Yazilikaya; here, to his further astonishment, Texier saw carved processions of gods like the figure on the city gate, and in an inner sanctum protected by winged demons was a set of twelve carved figures distinguished by strange hieroglyphs in an unknown language. Texier paced the city walls out at between 2 and 3 miles, as large as classical Athens in its heyday. In his initial flush of excitement he thought he had found his lost Tavium, but, he says, 'I later found myself compelled to abandon this opinion ... no edifice of any Roman era fitted this; the grandeur and peculiar nature of the ruins perplexed me extraordinarily.' Boghaz Köy also perplexed the Englishman William Hamilton, who visited the site soon after Texier (Hamilton had been with Lord Elgin at Athens and Mycenae thirty years before); he saw a second site a few miles to the north near Alaça Hüyük, where a sphinx gate still protruded from the earth in front of a city mound. Hamilton published his observations in 1842, Texier his between 1839 and 1849, but nothing came of these remarkable finds until the 1870s, by which time Heinrich Schliemann's excavations in Greece and Troy had opened up new possibilities for archaeological science. Then in 1878–81 British excavations at Carchemish on the Euphrates opened up a vast Late-Bronze-Age palace mound revealing huge mudbrick walls, a mass of sculpture and hieroglyphic inscriptions which resembled the material seen at Boghaz Köy. Fifteen hundred miles to the west, near to the Aegean coast at Izmir, a mysterious rock carving of an unknown king in the Karabel Pass again seemed to have a connection. The man who made that connection was Schliemann's correspondent A. H. Sayce, the Oxford Professor of Assyriology. In his *Reminiscences*, published in 1923, he wrote:

A sudden inspiration came to me … that not only was the art the same at Boghaz Keui, at Karabel, at Ivriz and at Carchemish, but that the figures at Boghaz Keui were accompanied by hieroglyphs similar to those of Ivriz. It was clear that in pre-Hellenic days a powerful empire must have existed in Asia Minor which extended from the Aegean to the Halys and southward into Syria, to Carchemish and Hamath, and possessed its own special artistic culture and its own special script. And so the story of the Hittite empire was introduced into the world….

Sayce now proceeded to elaborate his theory with another brilliant suggestion. For over half a century scholars had known of an Egyptian account (preserved on the temple walls at Karnak, Luxor and Abydos) of a great battle at Kadesh in the Orontes valley in Syria. In this battle, which we now know to have been fought in 1275 or 1274 BC, the Egyptian Pharaoh Ramses II was opposed by the 'Great King of Khatti', who 'had gathered to himself all lands as far as the ends of the sea' including 'sixteen nations' and 2500 chariots. Sayce proposed that the king of Khatti was none other than the emperor of his Hittite empire, an empire powerful enough to check the great warrior pharaoh himself, and to negotiate the famous treaty carved on the walls of the temple of Karnak. These ideas were dramatically confirmed in 1887 by the discovery of several hundred cuneiform tablets from the diplomatic archive of the Egyptian palace at Tell el Amarna. Here numerous letters from petty kings in Syria and Palestine showed the reality of the Hittite presence in those parts in the century before Kadesh; here too was a letter from one of the 'Great Kings of Hatti', Suppiluliumas I himself.

It was inevitable now that Boghaz Köy should be the focus of the search for the capital of this proposed Hittite empire. In 1881 Sayce pressed Schliemann to dig there; the following year Karl Humann made a plan of the city and took casts of reliefs from the chapel at Yazilikaya. In 1893 Ernest Chantre made trial excavations on the site and the first cuneiform tablets were found. The stage was set for a major excavation, and this came between 1906 and 1908 under the German, Hugo Winckler. The results went beyond all expectations. Although the dig was conducted appallingly in terms of the recording of archaeological data, it hit on the archive room in the royal citadel. A total of 10,000 clay tablets was discovered, mainly in Hittite but many in Akkadian, the international language of diplomacy, with others – chiefly literary texts – in older Hurrian and Sumerian languages. Eight languages were found on the tablets, testimony to the multinational character of the empire ruled from Boghaz Köy – for this surely, now, was indeed the 'capital' of that empire.

Perhaps the most incredible discovery was made at an early stage in the dig.

… a marvellously preserved tablet which immediately promised to be significant. One glance at it and all the achievement of my life faded into insignificance. Here it was – something I might have jokingly called a gift from the fairies. Here it was: *Ramses writing to Hattusilis* about their joint treaty … confirmation that the famous treaty which we knew from the version carved on the temple walls at Karnak might also be illuminated from the other side. Ramses is identified by his royal titles and pedigree exactly as in the Karnak text of the treaty; Hattusilis is described in the same way – the content is identical, word for word with parts of the Egyptian version [and] written in beautiful cuneiform and excellent Babylonian....As with the history of the people of Hatti, the name of this place was completely forgotten. But the people of Hatti evidently played an important role in the evolution of the ancient Western world, and though the name of this city, and the name of the people were totally lost for so long, their rediscovery now opens up possibilities we cannot yet begin to think of.

Winckler's expectation proved accurate. The Hittite language was deciphered during the First World War and after, and revealed in the Boghaz Köy tablets material of extraordinary interest, much of which displayed very sympathetic aspects of their life and thought. There were literary, legal and religious texts, administrative notes which tell us a great deal about Hittite kingship, and one really fascinating discovery – the revelation of the Hittites' significant role in the writing of history. But the finds which caused most interest were the diplomatic tablets from the filing system of the Hittite Foreign Office, for they showed the workings of the 'empire' in great detail. We have yet to work out the full implications of this vast amount of material – for instance it has not yet proved possible to agree on the geography of the empire, on the placing of the twenty or so major states within it, let alone the forty or fifty minor 'lands' – but it has given us insights into every aspect of Hittite life, such as, for instance, the relatively high status accorded to women in their society.

It was inevitable that scholars should have looked for the Greeks in the Hittite documents. Here were accounts of detailed relations with western Anatolian states, Arzawa, Mira, Hapalla and Wilusa, which we can place on the map approximately. These states were at their peak under the Hittites in the fourteenth and thirteenth centuries BC – the very time when, as we have seen, the Greeks were spreading across the Aegean and planting settlements in western Anatolia. Particularly as the Greeks were known to be trading in the Eastern Mediterranean, in Egypt,

Syria and Palestine, surely the Hittites must have known them? So there seemed a strong hope that word of the Greeks might have been found in the Boghaz Köy archive. Nevertheless the announcement was sensational when it came. In 1924 the Swiss Hittitologist Emil Forrer announced that in a mysterious country called Ahhiyawa he had found the land of the Greeks – 'Achaia-land'; that Troy itself was here, and even Paris himself – 'Alexandros of Ilios' – with the Greek king's brother Eteocles causing the Hittites trouble at Miletus. These, Forrer claimed, were part of 200 years of diplomatic relations between the Hittites and a mainland Achaian Greek power catalogued in the Hittite archive. These seductive identifications were loftily dismissed by Ferdinand Sommer in 1932 in *Die Ahhijava Urkunden* (*The Ahhiyawa Documents*), one of the great works of Near Eastern and Aegean philology. However, acute as Sommer's observations undoubtedly were, they have not settled the controversy – indeed it still rages as furiously as ever. In this chapter I shall argue that the Greeks *do* appear in the tablets, and that Troy – and even perhaps the Trojan War – does too. I shall argue this not merely on the internal content of the tablets themselves and what they tell us about the kingdom of Ahhiyawa (which has to be placed somewhere), but on the grounds of the wider context of international diplomacy in the Near East and Anatolian and Aegean worlds at the time of the Trojan War. It has been argued that there is no reason why the Greeks and Hittites should have had any contact, or even known who each other was, but, as we shall see, the evidence now strongly supports the idea that the Hittites were dealing with a 'Great King' of Mycenaean Greece.

INTERNATIONAL DIPLOMACY AT THE TIME OF THE TROJAN WAR

When we turn from the Linear B tablets to the diplomatic tablets of the Near East, we enter a different world. Here is corres-pondence between real people whose thoughts and actions come vividly to life. In Egypt, Palestine, Syria and the Hittite lands we can reconstruct historical events in great detail at the time of Mycenaean supremacy in the Aegean. Their kings engaged in diplomacy and the exchange of gifts for many reasons: for status and prestige; for special trading concessions (perhaps to settle their merchants in foreign countries, for example); for security reasons, to protect their frontiers, and so on. As trade was wide-reaching, relations between kings were inevitably frequent, and it is in this context we should remember the presence of Mycenaean goods in Syria, Palestine and Egypt and the finds of Egyptian material in Greece and Crete. The Hittite and Egyptian letters of the fourteenth and thirteenth centuries BC show that there was quite a diplomatic community, for the main kingdoms – that is, Hatti, Egypt, Mitanni and Babylon – were in contact not only with each other but with many intermediate-sized states, including some in western Anatolia (Mira and Arzawa), islands such as Cyprus, and a mass of Near Eastern city states such as Pella, Hazor, Damascus, Tyre, Sidon, Byblos, Jerusalem, Lachish, Shechem, Megiddo and Gezer, some of them, such as Ugarit and Alalakh, trading cities of great wealth and influence. All these cities maintained scribes and communicated with the chief kings of the day. Their letters were on subjects such as merchants, trading concessions, military support and marriage alliances; we find them requesting gifts, asking for doctors or craftsmen, or even simply sending friendly greetings.

The way such contacts worked in a practical way is revealed in a fascinating exchange between the Hittite Suppiluliumas and the widow of the famous Tutankhamun of Egypt, on the matter of her request for a Hittite prince to marry. The story is told by Suppiluliumas' son, Mursilis II. The Egyptian embassy, led by a nobleman called Hani, made its request before the Hittite court in an emotional appeal after Suppiluliumas had sent a top court official, Hattusaziti, to Egypt, as he did not believe their good faith. Mursilis takes up the tale:

Then my father asked to see the tablet of the treaty [with Egypt] in which there was told ... how the Storm God concluded a treaty between the countries of Egypt and Hatti, and how they were since then continuously friendly with one another. And when they had read the tablet aloud before everyone, my father then addressed them thus: 'Of old Hatti and Egypt were friendly with each other, and now this too has taken place on our behalf between them. Thus let Hatti and Egypt be friendly with each other continuously [in the future].'

The sequel of the story is well known: Prince Zannanza was sent to Egypt but murdered there by a rival court faction, provoking a major diplomatic crisis. This marvellously vivid scene in the Hittite court shows precisely how the archive worked, how treaties and correspondence could be rooted out of the 'filing system' and used to illustrate and guide contemporary diplomatic practice.

AN EGYPTIAN EMBASSY TO MYCENAE

How far were the Mycenaeans a part of this select club, even a fringe part? Until recently the idea was generally thought preposterous – indeed, as I have said, it is often confidently asserted that the Hittites had no reason even to know who the Greeks were. However, as always, new discoveries lead to changing perspectives. We can, for instance, put our picture of Mycenaean relations with Egypt on a different footing now that we have the recently discovered statue base from Kom-el-Heitan near Egyptian Thebes with its list of Aegean names. The list starts with two generic names, 'Keftiu' (which we now know certainly to be Crete) and 'Danaja', which shows that Homer was right in calling the mainlanders Danaans. Then follow Amnisos, Phaestos(?) and Cydonia in Crete, and from the mainland Mycenae ('Mukanu'), an unidentified place called 'Deghajas', Messenia, Nauplia, the island of Kythera and a 'Wilia' which Egyptologists have been tempted, surely wrongly, to identify with Ilios. The list ends back on Crete with Knossos, Amnisos, Lyktos and a name which looks like 'Seteia'.

There are many significant deductions to be made from this extraordinary record. First of all, it seems to describe a journey, and most likely a journey by ambassadors from Amenophis III to the Aegean world at a time when Crete, Messenia and the Argolid were recognisably a political entity. In the eyes of his panegyrists, the Pharaoh had pretensions to a nominal hegemony over the Eastern Mediterranean, and sent ambassadors to many of the 'barbarian' countries on the fringe of his world, among them the 'foreigners in their islands across the Great Green'. In fact such a journey is precisely what we would expect from Egyptian evidence. An inscription of year 42 of Thutmose III (around 1450 BC) mentions tribute sent from the Danaja, including a silver vase of 'Keftiu work' and four bronze vessels; another list from Karnak of Amenophis III mentions Danaja with Ugarit and Cyprus; fifteenth-century accounts of Keftiu embassies to Egypt provide antecedents. There are also numerous Egyptian pieces on mainland sites such as Mycenae, and in Crete after the Greek conquest. Scarabs of Amenophis III at Cydonia and Knossos, an alabaster vase of Thutmose III at Knossos and several late Mycenaean alabastrons (ritual containers) found in Egypt can all be ascribed to diplomatic activity more plausibly than to random commerce; the vase bearing Thutmose's cartouche is the kind of gift exchanged in such diplomatic contacts, as are recently discovered faience plaques at Mycenae bearing the name of the Pharaoh Amenophis III.

Here, then, is a fascinating discovery with great significance to students of the Aegean world. It allows us to say that in around 1380 BC Egyptian ambassadors sailed first to Crete, then to mainland Messenia, then, rounding Capes Tainaron and Malea, landed in the Argolid at Nauplion and visited the king at Mycenae; they then sailed southwards via Kythera and stopped at Knossos, departing from Amnisos via eastern Crete for home. Such a visit brings to life the picture we have seen in Egyptian schoolbooks of pupils learning 'Keftiu names' in their proper forms; it fills out our evidence for considerable Mycenaean trade with Egypt, including a mass of pottery found at Amarna which perhaps can be dated to around 1350 BC during the brief lifespan of that city; it also enables us to imagine a little more of the circumstances of the life of a man such as *ai-ku-pi-ti-jo*, 'the Egyptian', who appears in the Knossos tablets: such expatriates may well have existed in the Aegean world.

An equally exciting discovery was announced as recently as 1981. It concerns the dig made in 1963 in the Mycenaean palace of Thebes in central Greece, which was destroyed in around 1220 BC. Here among many treasures were found thirty-six engraved lapis lazuli cylinder seals and nine unengraved ones, clearly part of the royal treasury. Lapis lazuli, which is mined in north-eastern Afghanistan, was particularly prized for its luminous blue colour, and it often occurs as the subject of Bronze-Age correspondence. Two letters sent to the king of Ugarit in the thirteenth century BC show that kings themselves were anxious to get their hands on this desirable royal treasure:'The Hittite king is very interested in lapis lazuli,' writes an ambassador.'If you send some to him he will show you favours.' Other letters show that one *mina* weight of lapis (about 500 grams) was an acceptable royal gift to foster 'good relations'. As it happens, among the Theban seals is a group from Babylon which actually weighs one *mina*, and it has proved possible to date and place them with some accuracy. They were part of the repository of the temple of Marduk in Babylon until it was sacked by the Assyrians in *c.*1225 BC. After this it would appear that they were sent by the Assyrian king to the ruler of Thebes 'for good relations'. Now we know that it was at precisely this time that the Hittites were attempting to enforce a trade embargo on Assyria, and there is evidence that the Greeks were included in the prohibition (see p. 206). If this hypothesis is correct, then the Assyrian king used his Babylonian loot – the precious lapis – to try to forge an alliance with one of the peoples who, like himself, were hostile to the Hittites. This important example of the way Greek kingdoms – and not only Mycenae – might have been involved in diplomacy should be kept in mind.

So now that we know that the Greeks had relations with the kingdoms of the Near East, it seems entirely believable that they should appear in the Hittite Foreign Office archive. Indeed, as we can point to a Greek presence on the shores of Asia Minor, it would be surprising *not* to find them in any representative selection of Hittite diplomatic letters involving western Asiatic kingdoms like Arzawa and Mira, with whom the Greeks must have come into direct contact. The question is a simple one. Can we identify the Mycenaean mainlanders with the kingdom known to the Hittites as Ahhiyawa? Regarding the name, Homer calls the Greeks 'Achaiwoi', from which the name for Greece would probably be Achaiwia, and this form has been found in Linear B. The Hittite form is sufficiently similar to make coincidence unlikely. It is, on the face of it, hard to imagine where such a powerful kingdom might be if not in Greece, but modern scholars have put it in various places – in western Anatolia, in the Troad (centring on Troy itself) and even in Thrace. We can certainly say that part of Ahhiyawan territory was in Asia Minor, for a boundary text places it west of Mira, a kingdom in the middle Maeander valley. This Asian territory of Ahhiyawa was controlled by a coastal city called by the Hittites Milawata or Millawanda, and it seems virtually certain that this situation corresponds to the Greek enclave around Miletus (the early form of this name seems to have been Milatos, perhaps Milwatos in Bronze-Age Greek). In support of this idea a whole network of Hittite place names from the tablets can be located in the hinterland of Miletus, making it probable that Greek Miletus was the Ahhiyawan Millawanda of the Hittite texts. In this case Ahhiyawa itself – which the Hittites frequently describe as 'overseas' – must be mainland Greece, and though it is not impossible that a king, say of Thebes or Orchomenos, could have been pre-eminent in the fourteenth or thirteenth centuries BC, it is surely most probable that Mycenae was the seat of the king whom the Hittite Foreign Office viewed as a 'Great King' in accordance with contemporary diplomatic practice, a 'Great King' not only of mainland Greece but of many islands as Homer says. This dramatic conclusion puts our view of Late-Bronze-Age Greece in a wholly different light, for it means that we have a record of their dealings with the Hittites for the two centuries of their heyday. Let us now see what the letters have to tell us.

MYCENAEAN DIPLOMACY WITH THE HITTITES

In Hittite eyes the Mycenaean mainlanders were a powerful overseas state with a pre-eminent 'Great King'. They were noted seafarers whose ships traded with the Eastern Mediterranean. The Greeks frequently had friendly relations with the Hittites. They sent gifts to the Hittite king, which were then shared among his vassals; these gifts might include clothes, draperies and textiles, and also copper objects 'in the Achaian style'. Along with ambassadors, members of the royal families might visit each other's courts: the Greek king's brother, Eteocles, and a Hittite royal groom had 'ridden in the same chariot'; likewise a Hittite king might banish his disgraced wife to Greece. Their relations were evidently governed by the kind of treaty we find all over the Near East at this time: the Emperor Mursilis could invoke an extradition clause to send a ship and 'bring back' the prince of Arzawa from Greece; similarly the Greek lands around Miletus were marked by a frontier agreed by treaty. Lastly, a fascinating text of around 1300 BC tells how cult idols from Greece and 'Lazpas' were sent to the plague-stricken Hittite king's bedside in the hope that they might work a cure; just the same kind of thing happened between Near Eastern states (these idols presumably looked like those found recently at Mycenae and Tiryns, and that they should also have been sought from Lesbos – Lazpas – makes sense, for the great pre-Greek god of Lesbos, Smintheus, was a plague god – his name has been found in Linear B).

The gradual progress by which the Greeks rose to being a significant element in western Anatolia is recorded in the tablets, from the raids of a marauding royal freebooter with his 100 chariots in around 1420 BC to the situation revealed in the early thirteenth century when the Greeks ruled an area known as 'Achaia-land' in south-western Anatolia, with its main city at Miletus. The Hittites acknowledged Miletus as Greek territory, with a defined frontier, but they were prepared to act against it if need be. In around 1315 BC Mursilis' generals sacked it (this destruction level has been identified), after which massive fortifications were built. Hattusilis III entered the city over another dispute in *c.*1250 BC; a little later it seems to have passed under a pro-Hittite regent. It was from Miletus, as we shall see, that the Achaian king's brother tried to establish a kingdom for an ally with Hittite blessing: a fascinating parallel to Homer's tale of Achaian royal brothers fighting in Asia Minor at Troy.

The extent of Greek interference in the affairs of western Anatolia is shown in a number of tablets. Not long before 1300 BC the Greek king was powerful enough to attract important Asian states into his orbit, including the most powerful, Arzawa, whose king, Uhhazitis, made war on the Hittites in alliance with the Greeks; the Arzawan royal family fled to Greece after their defeat. An Achaian king was in dispute with the Hittites in around 1260 BC over another western Anatolian state, Wilusa. Also in Hattusilis' reign the 'king of Achaia-land' was somehow involved in an alliance with the neighbouring Seha River land against the 'Great King of Hatti'. A reference of either the fourteenth or the thirteenth century speaks of the Achaians in connection with events in Assuwa, probably to the south of the Troad (see map pp. 6–7 for a tentative placing of these countries). Greek activity in Asia Minor was therefore not merely confined to the slave raiding revealed in Chapter 5.

By the thirteenth century BC, the traditional time of the great expedition to Troy, the Greeks were a significant element in Hittite diplomacy. They were sufficiently important to be listed in a Hittite treaty with Amurru in Syria, banning their ships from trading with Assyria. They were even important enough to be mentioned, though erased, in a rough draft of a treaty listing the kings of equal rank to the Hittite one, namely those of Egypt, Babylon and Assyria. In *c.*1263 BC a deposed Hittite king might actually ask the Greek king for help before his exile in Syria. In a letter of *c.*1260 the Emperor Hattusilis could mention his troubles with Ahhiyawa in the west in the same breath as the sack of his city of Carchemish in the east by the Assyrians. The Hittite Foreign Office cannot have been pleased about being drawn into western Anatolia in force – their preferred way was diplomacy –

but there is no doubt of their increasing involvement there; as the great Hittitologist Goetze remarked, 'Hittite kings and the military must have had reason to fear the man of Ahhiyawa.'

To sum up, as the Hittites saw them the Greeks were one of the most powerful of their western neighbours, who, because of their control of the Aegean, were able to seduce states such as Arzawa into alliance at times when the Hittite kings were vulnerable; in this they seem to have been especially successful at moments of dynastic crisis, for instance when a new Hittite king came to the throne and needed to reassert his overlordship over his western subordinates. In this light, if we combine the archaeological evidence from Chapter 5, we can see how well our picture from 'imperial Mycenae' fits the material in the archive from Boghaz Köy. If our identification is correct – and there seems no other plausible location for such a major kingdom as the Ahhiyawa – then the kings of the Atreid dynasty at Mycenae (specifically Atreus and Agamemnon according to legend!) were viewed as 'Great Kings' by the Hittite Foreign Office under Hattusilis III (c.1265–1235 BC) and Tudhalias IV (c.1235–1210 BC); they could be described as 'equals' and listed among the 'kings equal in rank' to Hatti, Babylon and Egypt. Clearly, then, to the Hittites Ahhiyawa was a powerful kingdom with vassal states, the kind of kingdom recognised by Hittite diplomats. Yet in the twenty-two references to it in the Hittite tablets Ahhiyawa plays a fringe role in their history – inexplicably peripheral if we would place it, as some have, in Anatolia. The answer must be that its main centre lay overseas, with its enclave in the south-west around Miletus.

Of course it is possible the other Greek kings might have been described as the 'King of Achaia-land' by the Hittites at various times. Orchomenos, with its vast dyke system in Copais, was clearly powerful (and the name Eteocles occurs in its legendary genealogies); before its destruction in c.1220 BC Thebes was also very wealthy, and, as we have seen, conducted diplomacy as far away as Assyria. Even Iolkos, the city of Jason, which legend says sent the Argonautic expedition to the Black

Sea around this time, is a possibility. But archaeology and the epic tradition surely point to Mycenae. With that in mind we can now turn to the most crucial Hittite tablet from the period of the Trojan War.

THE 'TAWAGALAWAS LETTER':
EMPEROR HATTUSILIS WRITES TO
A GREEK 'GREAT KING'

This is the most famous Hittite letter bearing on Ahhiyawa, and one of the most fascinating documents from the ancient Near East in its detail and characterisation. Let us look at it not so much for the situation it reveals, but for the evidence it gives us for a Greek king's involvement in international diplomacy. The date is the first half of the thirteenth century BC, possibly towards 1260; the Hittite emperor is most likely to be Hattusilis III; in legendary chronology the Achaian king could therefore just possibly be Agamemnon himself, or his father Atreus. The situation is swiftly sketched. Based in Millawanda (Miletus) is the Achaian king's brother Tawagalawas (two occurrences of the patronymic Etewokleweios at Pylos show that this name could be a rendering of the Greek name we know as Eteocles). All is not going well for the Hittites in the west; their hold on the Arzawan states is growing shaky. There is disaffection among their allies, who are subject to increasing Greek interference. Most serious, a powerful renegade called Pijamaradus, probably a royal Arzawan, is raiding in Lycia with an army and a fleet, apparently in collusion with Tawagalawas and the Greeks. Millawanda (Miletus) is at the centre of these operations, and eventually Hattusilis enters the city, from which Tawagalawas and Pijamaradus have fled 'overseas'. The Hittite emperor is anxious not to provoke an international incident and, though demanding the extradition of Pijamaradus, he decides to send a royal kinsman as a hostage to guarantee his safe conduct: he even apologises for his bluff, 'soldierly' turn of phrase which had been interpreted as aggression! Evidently he does not wish to antagonise his correspondent.

Throughout the letter Hattusilis addresses the Achaian king as 'my brother', standard address among the chief kings of the day, as in the Tell el Amarna letters. The key lines – which have caused terrific argument – are the ones in which Hattusilis implies that the Achaian king is of equal rank; our problem is in judging the tone – is the tone ironic, even sarcastic, for example? Clearly it is more sophisticated than many have thought: 'If any one of my lords had spoken to me – or even one of my brothers – I would have listened to his word. But now my brother the Great King, my equal, has written to me, so shall I not listen to the word of my equal?' However if the intent is sarcastic this could mean 'I do not hear the words of an equal' (in other words 'You are, or pretend to be, a Great King, my equal, but I do not hear the language which should be used between equals'). Just the same problem can be found on any page of Hansard: *how* something is said can be as important as *what* is said.

It is surprising that, in trying to understand the Tawagalawas letter, its context has been ignored. How are we to judge its tone in isolation? In fact there are other Hittite letters of the period which help us to understand it; one of them is written by the same king, Hattusilis III. Hattusilis had deposed his nephew, who had even applied to Ahhiyawa for help. Throughout his career Hattusilis was touchy about his usurpation, and was easily provoked into arguments about his standing whenever he imagined himself offended. This is important in interpreting the psychology of the Tawagalawas letter, as we can see in a letter from Ramses II to Hattusilis in reply to an aggrieved letter from Hattusilis, in which the Hittite emperor expressed himself hurt by what he judged to be the overbearing tone of a previous letter from the Egyptian king: he thought Ramses was implying that he was inferior, and not a 'Great King': Ramses had to write to reassure his 'brother':

I have just heard all the words that you have written to me my brother, saying, 'Why did you my brother write to me as if I were a mere subject of yours' – I resent what you wrote to me my brother

... you have accomplished great things in all lands: you are indeed a Great King in the Hatti lands.... Why should *I* write to you as though to a subject? You must remember that I am your brother. You should speak a gladdening word [such as]: 'May you feel good every day' and instead you utter these incomprehensible words not fit to be a message. [Translation by Ken Kitchen]

We could hardly have a closer correlation with the Hittite's taking offence in the Tawagalawas letter: Hattusilis may have been a grumpy man at the best of times, but there is no mistaking the same mind behind both letters.

Just what is implied in the situation revealed in the letter to the king of Ahhiyawa is revealed in another Hittite letter of Hattusilis or his brother Muwatallis to the Assyrian king, a *nouveau riche* among Near Eastern monarchs, who had helped himself to land up the Euphrates valley which had been a dependency of the Hittites. The Assyrian then wrote claiming Great King status and proposing an alliance. In a rage the Hittite king replied to him:

You brag that ... you have vanquished my ally and become a Great King. But what is this you keep saying about 'brotherhood'? You and I were we born of the same mother? Far from it, even as my father and grandfather were not in the habit of writing about 'brotherhood' to the King of Assyria [your predecessor], so stop writing to me about brotherhood and Great Kingship. I have no wish for it. [Translation by Ken Kitchen]

Don't you brother me! Such examples could be multiplied. They make quite clear what is going on in the Ahhiyawa letters: between 1265 and 1240 BC, 'Achaia-land' was on a ranking in Hittite diplomacy *comparable* to Egypt and Babylon; even Assyria was not, though she soon would be. Hattusilis may have been annoyed, may well be resorting to flattery, but the Greeks were a major power in the Eastern Mediterranean, perhaps more influential and powerful than states better attested in the Hittite tablets such as Arzawa, Wilusa and Mira. And they were important in Hittite eyes because they represented a real 'political' and military threat to the fringe of their empire.

We have here a marvellous insight into the workings of diplomacy of the time, and it is thrilling to think that such letters may have been read out in the royal megaron at Mycenae. Such diplomatic sophistication is precisely what we would expect of the thirteenth-century Hittites, who by then were taking the lead in the formulation of treaties: they were the masters and the Achaians the *nouveaux riches*, perhaps blind to the niceties and minutiae of etiquette which were instantly comprehended by, say, the Egyptian Foreign Office. We can also see how a detailed look at the Tawagalawas letter confirms our impression that during the time of Hattusilis (*c*.1265–1235 BC) and Tudhalias IV (*c*.1235–1210 BC) the Achaians could be regarded as Great Kings roughly on a par (allowing for flattery) with the great Near Eastern kingdoms. This squares perfectly with archaeology, and with Greek tradition, which says that this period was the heyday of the Atreid dynasty.

LITERACY – ARCHAEOLOGY AND TEXTUAL EVIDENCE

This kind of diplomacy suggests that the Achaian king had Hittite scribes in his territory (though it is a mark of the Achaians' fringe standing in international diplomacy that they wrote in Hittite cuneiform, not Akkadian, the language of diplomacy between the 'superpowers'). This would certainly mean the presence of Hittite scribes at Mycenae and Miletus. In the latter case there is obviously no problem, but is there *any* evidence for Hittites in the world of mainland Greece? So far archaeological finds of Hittite material are scanty, though they do exist; but the Linear B archives are interesting in this respect as they have men with Hittite names, particularly at Knossos, but also at Pylos where we find a Pijamaso. All in all, we must assume that the Achaian king employed Hittite scribes in his Foreign Office, like western Anatolian rulers such as the king of Mira writing to Ramses II of Egypt. No fragments of diplomatic correspondence have ever been found at Mycenae, but then neither has any fragment of anything but petty inventories: it is clear that the royal archive of the Atreids has not survived.

Our evidence of Arzawan and Miran correspondence with Egypt suggests strongly that the western Anatolian kingdoms, along with those of the Achaians and Hittites, may have participated in diplomacy in the manner of Near Eastern countries and city states. In this case we may well ask whether Troy itself may have been able to be a member of this community. No evidence of tablets was found by any of the excavators of Hisarlik, but then the site was so badly damaged that none would be expected. Nevertheless the possibility should be borne in mind that a city as sophisticated in its military and domestic architecture as Troy VI, a city which traded with Cyprus and Syria, could have employed scribes who could write in Hittite to the Great King, and perhaps even to Mycenaean Greece, with which it also had trading relations. The literacy of the Late-Bronze-Age world is something almost totally forgotten by the Homeric epic, but that King Priam could have corresponded with Hattusilis III – or Agamemnon for that matter – is at least conceivable.

The ambassadors and experts who did the legwork (and headwork) in such negotiations were obviously close to the royal king. 'I am sending a groom,' writes Hattusilis to the Achaian king, 'who from my youth used to ride with me on my chariot, and who also rode with your brother Tawagalawas ... since he has a wife of the queen's family ... is he not as good as my brother-in-law?' Their words, of course, were especially valued because of the ambassadors' wide-ranging experience: 'This story was told me by Enlil-bel-nishe, the envoy of the king of Babylon,' writes Queen Pudukhepa of the Hittites to Ramses II of some court gossip. But kings themselves could also make visits. In 1244, after Hittite diplomacy had patched up a peace with Assyria, Babylon and Egypt, Prince Hishmi-Sharumma, the future Tudhalias IV, visited Egypt and may have stayed for several months. His visit seems to have paved the way for Hattusilis himself in around 1239–1235 BC. At first grumpy ('Why should I come? What would we do?') and troubled by an ailment of the feet, Hattusilis seems to have met Ramses in Egypt, a 'summit' between the two most powerful men in the ancient world. That the Achaian king's brother Tawagalawas should have visited the Hittite court is therefore no surprise: we might even say the same for a Trojan king's son visiting the king of Mycenaean Sparta!

Such is the background to the international diplomacy at the time of the Trojan War. The Hittites were far more concerned with the east, with the growing power of the upstart Assyrians in the Euphrates valley, with the maintenance of their overlordship of the rich cities of Syria, with normalising relations with Egypt at the frontier with Canaan, even with keeping the warlike Kaska tribes to their Black Sea border region. The last thing they wanted was disruption in the west too. They wanted a diplomatic *cordon sanitaire* of allied states in western Anatolia, bound to them by treaty. In all this their desire to achieve stability by diplomacy rather than by war is characteristic – and understandable. The growing influence of the Achaians in western Anatolia was a threat, and, as all Hittitologists have recognised, in the thirteenth century BC the Hittite kings were forced to play a more active role in the west. It is in this light that we should view Hittite evidence for armed intervention by Greeks in the lands of the Hittites' western allies. It is possible that here we have the real 'political' background of the Trojan War.

ARE TROY AND THE TROJAN WAR IN THE HITTITE TABLETS?

We have come to the conclusion that the Hittites knew the Mycenaean Greeks, Homer's Achaiwoi, as a powerful seafaring state called Ahhiyawa, and that the Greeks were involved on the coast of Asia Minor in military and diplomatic activity. Can we go further than that? If the Trojan War really took place, even loosely in the manner Homer describes, then it would fit very well with the general evidence of the Hittite archive; but is such a war actually mentioned in the Boghaz Köy tablets?

The question divides into two parts. First, was a place called Troy known to the Hittites? If it was, it occurs in only one document, and that has recently been redated by linguists. Previously dated to the thirteenth century BC, it is now thought to come from the time of Tudhalias I (*c.*1440–1410 BC), a strong king whose annals record the Hittite conquest of Arzawa in western Anatolia. The tablet tells of the subjugation of a neighbouring country called Assuwa, whose name most scholars agree is the archetype of the Greek word Asia, an area originally confined to Lydia and the lands south of the Troad. Assuwa to the Hittites meant a specific place, with a 'town of Assuwa', but in alliance with it were twenty-two other places which many experts think are listed from south to north, ending in the north-west corner of Asia Minor, the region of Troy itself. The last name in the list is written in Hittite 'Taru[u]isa', which is assumed to be the northernmost component of the alliance, and on superficial resemblance temptingly close to Homer's Troia. Could this be Troy? The identification of the name is unfortunately problematical. One point in its favour is that phonetic rules do not always apply in transferring from one language to another, but on the face of it it does not match, and the only way it would is if we posit an original form, Taruiya, and assume that the form given in Tudhalias' annals derives from that (parallels for such a dual form do in fact exist – for instance Karkisa and Karkiya are evidently the same place). But this is too speculative a leap for most scholars.

Much more intriguing, though, is the association of the name Taruisa with the preceding place on the list, Uilusiia, pronounced Wilusiya. Now it is on the face of it a really remarkable coincidence that these two names should occur together, even in a document of *c.*1420, in roughly the same place that the legends place Troy. One of the inexplicable things about Homer's story is that in it Troy has two distinct names, Troy (which often seems to mean the city) and Ilios (often the country). As we saw in Chapter 4, originally the name Ilios was pronounced with a digamma, that is, Wilios, and this is certainly acceptable as a rendition of the Hittite Wilusa or Wilusiya (both forms occur). Is it possible that in the thirteenth century Hisarlik-Troy was *within* the wider realms of the Hittite state of Wilusa?

Of Hittite Wilusa we know a good deal, though unfortunately not its precise location. It was an Arzawan state and therefore one of the group of western Anatolian states which included Arzawa and Mira; if the former lay around the Hermus and Cayster valleys, and the latter in the middle and upper Maeander valleys including Beycesultan, then Wilusa probably lay north and north-east of Arzawa. One of the important powers in the west, Willus therefore most likely included the area of Troy. Of its relations with the Hittites and its neighbours we know details from a treaty dating from the time of Muwatallis (1296–1272 BC), and this gives another clue, for by a coincidence the king of Wilusa named in the treaty is Alaksandus, a name which strikingly recalls Homer's prince Alexandros (Paris) of Wilios. Could they be the same man? Astonishingly enough, an independent tradition survived into classical times among the native, Luvian, speakers of South West Turkey that the lover of Helen had indeed been the ally of Muwatallis. It is possible then that Homer has here preserved the real name of one of the kings of Wilusa – *and that Wilusa was Troy*.

Interesting facts about the history of Wilusa emerge from the treaty. Since the subjugation of Arzawa in the seventeenth century BC, Wilusa had always been loyal to the Hittites. Though an Arzawan state (presumably by racial affinity), it was loyal to the kings of Hatti even when Arzawa fought against them. Throughout the reigns of Tudhalias I and II, the great Suppiluliumas, and Mursilis II, whenever Hittite armies invaded Arzawa they never had to attack Wilusa, but were loyally supported by this apparently isolated state. This suggests that Wilusa was situated on the northern fringe of the Arzawan states, far enough from their capital Apasas (Ephesus?) to maintain a policy of its own.

The terms of Alaksandus' treaty with the Hittites included the obligation owed by a subject king in time of war to bring his army, his infantry and chariots, to the Hittite king's hosting ('The following campaigns from Hattusas are obligatory on you ... the King of Egypt ... the King of Assyria'). Now, it has been suggested by Egyptologists that the *Drdny*, who are named as being present among Muwatallis' allies at the battle of Kadesh in Syria in 1275 or 1274 BC (the period of the Wilusa treaty), are none other than 'Dardanians', a Homeric name for the people of the Troad. So a young man who fought at Kadesh with Muwatallis' 2500 chariots and the 'troops of sixteen nations' could perhaps as an old man have defended 'sacred Wilios' against the Achaians! If the king of Wilusa was as important as the treaty suggests, then the people of the Troad could well have been among his minor states whose rulers were his vassals, just as he was of the Great King. In the preceding 150 years many of the smaller states which had made up the Assuwan confederacy had doubtless been incorporated into Arzawa or Wilusa, just as Midea, Prosymna or Berbati had been brought into the kingdom of Mycenae.

The possibility should therefore be considered that in the mid-thirteenth century BC Troy lay within 'greater Wilusa', and that Wilusa does indeed lie behind Homer's Wilios with its prince Alexandros. But exciting as such speculations are, they are at present no more than that, for until the hotly contested theories over Hittite geography are settled such ideas are incapable of proof either way. Nevertheless there seems a strong case for thinking that the kingdom of Wilusa may have included the Troad; thus Wilusa would be the prototype for Homer's Wilios. If this was so, then it is of great interest that Ahhiyawa and the Hittites may have fought over Wilusa in the mid-thirteenth century BC.

WAR BETWEEN GREEKS AND HITTITES OVER WILUSA?

If we accept the identification of Ahhiyawa with Achaian Greece we can go further in our reconstruction of mid-thirteenth-century diplomacy involving the kingdom of Wilusa, which may have included Troy. In the Tawagalawas letter (*c*.1260?) are two hints that the Hittites and Achaians had actually come to blows over Wilusa. In view of the 400-year history of Wilusan loyalty to Hatti, we must assume that this had been the result of Achaian interference. The references are in Hattusilis' letter to the Achaian king, in which he asks the Greek to write to the troublesome Pijamaradus: 'Tell him that the King of Hatti and I, that in the matter of Wilusa over which we were at enmity, he has persuaded me, changed my mind, and we have made friends. A … war is wrong for us.' Later lines may have told of 'the matter in question concerning the town of Wilusa over which we made war (and over which we have now come to a settlement)'. This would be important evidence for a major diplomatic and military crisis in western Anatolia, but unfortunately the tablet is too damaged to allow us to be sure.

The quarrel over Wilusa is also hinted at in a tantalising letter of this period addressed to a Hittite king by Manapa-Dattas, king of the Seha River land. (This place was in some way adjacent to Arzawa and Wilusa, and the Seha was presumably one of the main rivers flowing into the Aegean.) Here we learn that a Hittite army has come west, and that someone 'has gone back to attack the land of Wilusa'. The king of the Seha River land has been overcome by the powerful Greek ally Pijamaradus who has also attacked Lazpas (Lesbos). Unfortunately this tablet is too fragmentary to say any more, but it may be roughly the same time as the Achaian attack on Wilusa. Our last reference to the troubles of Wilusa shows that shortly after these events (*c*.1230) the deposed ruler of Wilusa, King Walmu, took refuge in a neighbouring state, hoping to be reinstated by Tudhalias IV – a royal family in exile. It is in another tablet from the same period as the attack on Wilusa that we discover that the king of the Achaians may have been in person on the shores of Asia Minor, just as the Greek tradition holds.

THE TROJAN WAR IN THE HITTITE TEXTS?

For the searcher after a historical basis in the Trojan legend our next evidence is perhaps the most tantalising of all. It comes in a tablet from Boghaz Köy which can now be firmly attributed to Hattusilis III (1265–1235 BC). It is the only Hittite text which may speak of the personal involvement of the Achaian/Ahhiyawan king on the mainland of Anatolia, possibly fighting on Asian soil. The tale is told by Emperor Hattusilis after a successful campaign in the west. My version is from Sommer's German translation: within square brackets are Sommer's likely conjectures, for the text is damaged; I have amplified the text where I thought it necessary to aid the sense:

The land of the Seha River again transgressed. [*The people of the Seha River land then said:*] 'His Majesty's grandfather did not conquer us with the sword. When he conquered the Arzawa lands [*the father of his Majesty*] he did not conquer us with the sword. We have [*no obligation?*] to him.' [*So the Seha River land*] made war. And the King of Ahhiyawa withdrew. Now when he withdrew, I, the Great King, advanced. [*Then my enemies retreated into mountainous country:*] I subdued the mountain peak Harana. Then 500 teams of horses I brought back to Hattusas.

On the usually accepted reading of this text there are two crucial deductions: first, that the king of Ahhiyawa was present in western Anatolia, and second, that he was lending aid in war to a rebel against the Hittite king. Unfortunately this is not certain: the key word, the one translated here as 'withdrew', is capable of several meanings, including 'take refuge with' or 'relied on' (i.e. he *relied on* the king of Ahhiyawa for support), and this may be the likeliest interpretation.

We can perhaps take the story of the war in the Seha River land a little further. It does after all tell us that, at about the time to which tradition dates the Trojan War, an Achaian king was directly or indirectly involved in a war on the coast of Asia Minor in a place which lay close to the Troad. If we accept the translation above, with the king of Achaia-land 'withdrawing' from the Seha River country, then the story bears a startling resemblance to Homer's tale, for, as we noted at the start of this search, Homer tells of a first, failed, expedition when the Achaians under Achilles landed in Teuthrania, which they mistook for Trojan territory. There, in the valley of the Caïcus (now Bakii Çay), they were repulsed by Telephus, king of Mysia, and beaten to their ships (*Odyssey*, XI, 519). This tradition of a 'shameful retreat' after the ravaging of Mysia is found in a number of later Greek sources including Pindar and Strabo, and if the Caïcus was indeed the Seha, then the coincidence is certainly worth noting. Unfortunately we do not know the location of the Seha, and the Hittite text does not give the name of the 'king of Achaia-land' who 'withdrew'.

We have gone as far as the Hittite tablets allow on the present evidence, but we can at least feel that this rich mine of diplomatic material has enabled us to get nearer to the real power struggle in western Anatolia in the thirteenth century. It also provides us with a real context for the *kind* of war portrayed by Homer. In the last fifty years the archaeology, the Hittite and Greek tablets – and the Greek legend – have started to converge. We now have clear evidence of Greek aggression and settlement on the Anatolian coast, and the Boghaz Köy archive, if we have interpreted it correctly, makes sense in this light. If we cannot prove that the Trojan War happened as Homer says, we can at least show that something like it *could have happened*: a military invasion of the Troad, attacks on cities to the south and in Mysia, Achilles' devastation on Lesbos – all would fit very well with the tangled story revealed in the Hittite correspondence. Even some of the same places seem to be named. If there is anything at all in the legend, it must be tested against the only reliable sources for the history of the thirteenth century BC in Asia Minor – archaeological finds, Linear B names, Hittite diplomacy – and it holds up surprisingly well.

THE TROJAN WAR: THE HITTITE VERSION?

That said, we should, of course, be wary of attempting to make direct equations between the primary evidence of the Hittite tablets and an epic poem composed over 500 years later. What the Hittite tablets show, however, is that the Achaians caused major problems to the Hittites in the thirteenth century BC and that they may have sent military expeditions to western Anatolia, possibly even led by the 'king of Achaia-land' himself. It does not seem to be pushing the evidence too far to suggest that the Homeric epic reflects this, even though it may compress decades of action into one 'heroic' event. Can we go further and present even a tentative model from Hittite sources for what might have happened? Frankly, this is not possible on the present state of research into the Ahhiyawa tablets, but, as in Chapter 5, I will add a speculative piece to an already speculative chapter. I suspect it should be read for entertainment only, but it is at least based on the Hittite tablets, accepting the identification of the Greeks with Ahhiyawa.

Hattusilis III and Tudhalias IV had to strain the resources of their empire to the utmost to maintain their power, faced by the perennial threat of Kaska peoples on their northern frontier; the rivalry with Egypt in Syria where rich commercial cities were under their overlordship; and the new military power of Assyria in the Euphrates valley. To the west each new Hittite king had to enforce allegiance over the group of powerful western Anatolian states led by Arzawa. All these opponents necessitated frequent campaigning in the thirteenth century – against the Kaska enemies, for instance, a dozen campaigns were fought in twenty years. No other empire of the time faced so much pressure on all sides, and it is no wonder that Hittite diplomacy became so refined in the thirteenth century. In all this the increasing interest of the Achaians in western Anatolia was a serious additional pressure. The Hittites were prepared to concede that the area around Miletus was Greek, and to agree on its frontier; but the states of Arzawa, Mira, Wilusa and the Seha River land were in the Hittite diplomatic orbit, and any interference there – 'destabilisation', as the Americans would call it these days – had to be countered. This is what happened. The Greeks were becoming increasingly ambitious. In the mid-thirteenth century BC the brother of the Achaian king was giving aid to the Hittites' most dangerous western enemy after a war, of which we know no details, between the Achaians and Hittites over the kingdom of Wilusa, whose king was still perhaps Alaksandus: 'We have come to terms,' announces Hattusilis, 'over the aforesaid matter of the town of Wilusa, over which we waged war.' Only a decade or two later the surviving Wilusan royal family were in exile in a neighbouring western Anatolian state.

This war took place in the north-west of Anatolia, where the Greeks had been taking slaves on the shores and islands, and where they had close trading links with one strong and wealthy fortress, the town on Hisarlik which we call Troy VI. That Hisarlik was called something like Troia or Wilios seems possible. The Anatolian name Taruisa needs to be accounted for in its similarity to Greek Troia and in its association with the Hittite Wilusa, possibly the archetype of Wilios. These vague resemblances do not look like mere chance; Achaiwoi/Ahhiyawa; Alaksandus/Alexandros; Wilusa/Wilios; Taruisa/Troia: each in isolation presents problems, but *four* resemblances is pressing coincidence too far. It would appear, then, that Achaian troops attacked part of Wilusa perhaps in the late 1260s. This incident may be the basis of the Homeric tale, which even remembered the name of the Trojan king. In this case the city which was attacked is more likely to have been Troy VI; but we have yet to explore the implications of our evidence, which tends to point to that city, rather than Blegen's VIIa, as the Homeric citadel.

This may not have been the only occasion on which an Achaian prince took an army to north-western Anatolia. At about the same time – possibly even on the same campaign – Hattusilis fought in the west, after Achaian interference with a western Anatolian state. One of the Arzawan countries, the Seha River land, maintained they did not owe the allegiance claimed by the Great King of Hatti, and made an alliance with the Great King of the Achaians, just as the Arzawans had done before them. In this case the Achaian king *may* have landed an army on Anatolian soil, but when Hattusilis moved his army west the Greek king abandoned his ally, possibly 'retreating shamefully', as later Greek tradition had it. Hattusilis' account indicates that the Seha River land was ravaged by his army, the king deposed, and a loyal vassal instated. It may have been on this campaign that Thermi, the main city of Lesbos and one of the biggest towns in the Aegean, was sacked and burned by hostile forces: here again the unequivocal evidence of archaeology can be compared both with the Hittite story of the attack on Lesbos (Lazpas) by the Greek ally Pijamaradus and with Homer's tale of the sack of Lesbos by Achilles. In this light, then, we should see the *Iliad* as containing a compressed picture of *many* Greek forays in Asia Minor: the Hittite tablets certainly seem to confirm this.

Taking the view from Hattusas, these were serious disturbances in the north-west frontier of an already threatened empire. We have tended to see the Mycenaean kings as brutal and rapacious, cunning buccaneers with an eye to profit, always ready to take advantage of weakness. Perhaps the nature of our evidence for their thought world encourages that view, but I suspect it is not so far off the mark: such *was* the world of the sackers of cities. But as regards grumpy old Hattusilis, the long-time soldier with his painful feet, or the more intellectual Tudhalias, it is easy to imagine them in their private temple at Yazilikaya, or standing in the royal reception hall or the archive room in the 'great fort' at Boghaz Köy, and to feel some sympathy for these hard-pressed and hard-working Bronze-Age emperors. Hattusilis, for instance, had been so *reasonable* towards the Achaian king:

My Brother once wrote to me saying, 'You have acted aggressively towards me.' But at that time, my Brother, I was young [new to the job?]; if at that time I wrote anything insulting it was not done deliberately.... Such an expression comes naturally to a soldier, a general....

With the snow swirling down outside at the end of the long central Anatolian winter, he had to plan new campaigns almost every year against his many enemies and must have spent long hours with the braziers burning low discussing with his diplomats the treaty obligations with Wilusa, or the past dealings with Ahhiyawa. On file in his Foreign Office archive were tablets covering over 200 years of diplomacy with the west. Their knowledge of the Aegean world may have been sketchy, their interest even less, but it was now an important part of their policy. Both Hattusilis and Tudhalias composed memoirs or 'autobiographies', and it is a great pity that they have only survived in fragments; if we had them in full, perhaps many of the questions could be answered. In the meantime, on all these matters, as on the alleged Anatolian context of the Trojan tale, we can only hope that future discoveries of further Hittite archives – perhaps in the as yet undiscovered southern capital of the Hittites – will throw fresh light on old mysteries. It is, however, at least pleasing to imagine that the real Paris, Helen's lover, may not have been the playboy and habitué of dance-halls described by Homer, 'women-crazy', sneered at by friend and foe alike, notable only for his physical beauty, but instead a grizzled, middle-aged man-of-war, veteran of twenty years of battles from Syria to the Aegean.

SEVEN

THE PEOPLES OF THE SEA

*Now in earlier times the world's history had consisted so to speak
of a series of unrelated episodes, the origins and results of which
being as widely separated as their localities, but from this point
onwards history becomes an organic whole: the affairs of Italy and
Africa are connected with those of Asia and of Greece, and all
events bear a relationship and contribute to a single end.*

POLYBIUS, *World History*

SO POLYBIUS, the late-second-century-BC historian of the wars
between Rome and Carthage, assessed the significance of the rise
of Rome. In fact, the more we discover about the Late-Bronze-
Age world the more we find that the unity of the eastern
Mediterranean had its roots much further back in time than
Polybius thought: roots in the sense of the cultural and
commercial relations between the Aegean world, western
Anatolia, Crete and the Near East in the Bronze Age. Men had
travelled on the sea since Neolithic times, populating islands and
exploiting their natural resources as far as their technology
allowed. By the end of the Bronze Age land and sea routes had
been established between these different areas which were to
persist for millennia. Hence, as most experts believe, Mycenaean
merchants were resident in Cyprus and in Ugarit in the
fourteenth and thirteenth centuries BC, and may have been
active elsewhere, as for instance at Tell Abu Hawam near Haifa,
and at Sarafend in south Lebanon where a remarkable tomb of
this period has been found. The importance of these routes
meant that as early as the Middle Bronze Age connections had
been established between the different regions of the eastern
Mediterranean, and by the Late Bronze Age their destinies were
to a certain extent bound up; indeed, though it has not yet been
proved, it is likely that the collapse of centralised power in many

places in the Aegean and Anatolia may have been brought about by a combination of similar and even related circumstances. Accordingly this last stage of our search will broaden out to look at the wider context of the destructions of Troy, and the end of the Mycenaean 'empire'.

TRADE ROUTES AND CONTACTS

Trade was on an organised footing in the Near East even before the Greeks came to the Aegean world, and its influence crept westwards. There were already Assyrian merchant communities at Kanesh in Anatolia in 1800 BC, living in their own quarter, over an acre in extent, bound by treaty, their caravan routes stretching across to the western sea. Perhaps 'the great city of Smyrna', as it was called by the Anglo-Saxon traveller Saewulf, who around AD 1100 sailed through the Aegean, is the Ti-Smurna mentioned in the tablets found at Kanesh. Kings controlled commerce early, for it was the best way of bringing in surplus income and luxury products. The tremendous detail of the Linear B archives at Knossos and Pylos shows that Mycenaean kings of the thirteenth century BC had precisely that control. Among their imports were ivory, cumin, coriander and Cypriot copper, products which came by sea; perhaps there were even tiny foreign communities at Mycenaean Knossos, with people like the 'Egyptian' and the 'Lykian' mentioned in the tablets, and Pijamunu and others whose names are Anatolian. Just such a population must have existed in the mixed-race city of Miletus which has been such an important part of our story.

If, as I have argued, the kingdom of Ahhiyawa in the Hittite tablets is part of mainland Greece, then we can add to this picture Greek ships sailing to Amurru in Syria with goods bound for Assyria in the Euphrates valley. We hear mention of textiles, and copper vessels in the 'Ahhiyawan style'; they may have exported olive oil to Egypt where the olive does not thrive; their pottery appears on Near Eastern sites so extensively that one wonders whether it had some sort of snob value – or is it simply a mark of Greek commercial expertise? Is the ubiquitous stirrup jar just the 'Coke' bottle of its day?

To Greece came slaves from Asia Minor (and Africa?). The Knossos tablets mention cyperus seed from Cyprus, sesame, cumin, gold, and purple dye from Syria – all known by their Semitic names. Copper was a major economic need (it came of course from Cyprus, whose very name indicates its origin) and for this reason throughout the Bronze Age – bronze is made by alloying tin with copper – Cyprus was of central importance in the Mediterranean, the main entrepôt between the Greek and Aegean world on the one hand, and Syria, Ugarit and the Near East on the other.

Remarkable evidence of such trade has been uncovered recently in the first of what are likely to prove numerous Bronze-Age wrecks on the dangerous southern shore of Turkey. Off Cape Gelidonya a thirteenth-century-BC shipwreck brought to light fragments of up to 100 copper ingots, each weighing about 50 lb, clearly the main cargo of a boat heading westwards into the Aegean from Cyprus. Among the wreckage was a large toolkit of picks, shovels, axes, blades, an anvil, two mortars, storage jars, whetstones and so on. Perhaps belonging to the merchant himself were a spit, a set of weights, bronze wire, a lamp, a reed basket, a personal razor and mirror, Egyptian scarabs and a Near Eastern cylinder seal which the owner possibly used as his personal seal: a marvellous insight into the life of one of the individual captains or traders who criss-crossed the Aegean in the Late Bronze Age. A ship found off Kars in south-west Turkey in 1982 was carrying around 100 Aegean pithoi – perhaps heading eastwards with a cargo of grain or oil. Such trade can be traced further back into the Bronze Age: the oldest yet found is a wreck of the sixteenth century BC found in 1975 at Seytan Deresi near Bodrum (Halicarnassos); again the vessel was loaded with large pithoi, testimony to a trade which flourished for at least 3000 years, despite the rise and fall of civilisations, and the ever-present threat of piracy.

That such commerce could be organised on a 'state' level has already been suggested by the exporting of building stones from the Mani to Mycenae and Knossos, and indeed in the thirteenth century BC we find large-scale grain exports from Ugarit to Hittite country 'because of the famine there'. Presumably such transactions were organised at government level through diplomacy. Hence a trade embargo could appear in a treaty between Egypt and the Hittites, or a letter between the Hittites and Ahhiyawa. Likewise it seems reasonable to assume that the flood of Mycenaean pottery into the Eastern Mediterranean in the fourteenth and thirteenth centuries – with its remarkable uniformity of style – came from factories in the Argolid directly controlled by the king of Mycenae.

The path by which the Mycenaeans had come to dominate Aegean trade seems broadly clear. After the Old Assyrian trade network across Anatolia disintegrated, the Minoans of Crete seem first to have grown in commercial enterprise in the Aegean between the eighteenth and fifteenth centuries BC. This is what Thucydides alleged in his account of Minos' domination of the Cyclades, and archaeology is proving him right. British excavations at Phylakopi on Melos showed a Minoan 'colony' there, and another was found at Kythera. American digs on Keos have revealed a fortified town with strong Cretan connections at Ayia Irini in the sixteenth century BC. In the Cyclades, Amorgos, Thera, Siphnos and Delos have produced evidence of Minoan trading connections and even, as on Delos and Keos, the exporting of Minoan textile techniques. By the sixteenth century BC the Cretan influence is extremely marked on mainland Mycenaean pottery and especially in the craftsmanship of such Mycenaean masterpieces as the shaft grave daggers and cups. Westwards the Minoans reached southern Italy and Sicily (where one ancient authority alleges that Minos died on an expedition) and eastwards they planted settlements in Rhodes, Kos, Samos and even on the coast of Asia Minor at Iasos and Miletus: the last named gave Minoan traders access to the hinterland of Anatolia. Further afield Minoan merchants dealt with Syria and Egypt, and their ambassadors are portrayed in Egyptian wall-paintings: Keftiu

(Cretan) ships were evidently a common sight in Near Eastern ports, and the Minoans were the middlemen in the trade westwards. A high degree of commercial organisation is implied in some of our sources. Texts from Mari on the Euphrates show Cretans as permanent residents at Ugarit – with their interpreters – to buy Elamite tin which the king of Ugarit supplied from caravans crossing into Syria from the Euphrates valley: a typical train numbered twenty-nine donkeys and forty-four 'bronze men'. It was natural that the kings should wish to control these crucial raw materials and hence they organised the trade in a strikingly modern way. The Hittites, for instance, maintained officials at Ugarit to conduct their business, and a 'house of documents', a kind of bank, was set up by Ugarit at Hattusas. In Ugarit, finely built chamber tombs have been excavated, suggesting that the Minoan settlers there were people of wealth and sophistication, at ease in a multiracial and multilingual city. The Mycenaeans had already started to encroach into this world before they destroyed the power of the Minoans and occupied Knossos in around 1420 BC. In the previous century or so their own wares reached Melos and Naxos in quantity, and a certain amount went to Keos and Delos; further out, Minoan ware was still dominant. But after the sack of Knossos Mycenaean pottery is found right across the Cyclades. At Phylakopi, at Iasos, Miletus and many other places, Mycenaean traders step into Cretan shoes, and in Minoan settlements on islands like Kos and Rhodes Greek settlers seem to take the place of Minoan ones, at least as the ruling or commercial élites. By the thirteenth century BC (LH III B) Mycenaean pottery is all over the Aegean and found in quantities throughout Syria, Palestine and Egypt; new discoveries of it have even been made in the heartland of the Hittites.

The quantities of Mycenaean pottery from the fourteenth and thirteenth centuries BC found at Near Eastern sites at least enable us to say that the trade was important to the rulers of the Argolid and their neighbours: over sixty sites have produced such material in Syria, Lebanon and Palestine, about a quarter of them in notable quantity. Over twenty more sites are presently known in Egypt, as far south as Luxor and Thebes and including a major deposit at Tell el Amarna, which the excavator Flinders Petrie variously estimated at 200–300 and 800 pots: the smaller figure is more likely. Whatever was in these consignments – perfume and oil remain two possibilities – it is evident that we are dealing with no small-scale or casual trade over the Aegean and Eastern Mediterranean as a whole, but with a commerce central to the economy of the Late-Bronze-Age palaces. As we would have guessed from the meticulous detail of the Linear B archives, the palaces were geared to efficient production.

It will be obvious, then, for all the self-contained look of the kingdoms of the Argolid and Messenia, for all the smallness of their immediate heartlands, they depended greatly on outside contacts for their raw materials and luxury products. The conspicuous consumption of the great palaces and their estates in their heyday relied on overseas trade, and with their fragile economies they needed their world to remain relatively static in order to preserve their social and political order. They needed a continued supply of bronze, that is, of copper from Cyprus and of tin, in order to make the weapons with which they equipped their fighting forces. They needed a continued supply of slaves from Asia Minor, from Miletus, Cnidus, Halicarnassos (Zephyrus), Chios and Lemnos, to work their estates, not only producing for their own consumption, but making a surplus – textiles, oil or whatever for export. Another source of slaves may have been from the more backward mountain peoples who inhabited the fringe of their world within Greece. They needed to make constant armed raids overseas or into neighbouring territories in order to seize not only slaves but also treasure and booty with which to reward their armed followers, on whose strong arm their power rested. This is a condition of all early kingships. They needed, in short, a stable Aegean and Eastern Mediterranean world in order for their trade routes to exist, and for their markets to be accessible.

Our indications are that the fourteenth and most of the thirteenth centuries were indeed static periods for the mainland palaces of Greece, in which they rose to great wealth and architectural splendour. But this was also a period of massive defensive military building – clearly a world which needed to be constantly on its guard.

THE PEAK AND FALL OF THE MYCENAEAN WORLD

How does our (at present) fragmentary knowledge of trade in the late Bronze Age fit with what we know of the Mycenaean world? As we have seen, Mycenae reached 'capital' status in the fourteenth century; from then on it may have been the chief power in Greece, and may have been known to the Hittites as the kingdom of Ahhiyawa. The peak of its extent and architectural development was in the thirteenth century (LH III B). But before the end of III B, that is, before 1200, the major centres were destroyed by fire; these included Mycenae, Tiryns, Pylos, Thebes, Orchomenos, Araxos, Krisa and Menelaion – virtually all the major dynastic centres, the most famous palaces in Greek legend. Among the main ones only the Athens citadel seems to have escaped. Until recently it was conventional to associate this with what the ancient writers called the invasion of the Dorians, which Greek tradition held to have been the arrival of Greeks. This, however, seems to have no archaeological basis and it is now believed that the Dorians were already within Greece, and that they were Greek-speaking people (the lower classes?) who succeeded their masters after the fall of the palaces. The problem of what happened over this period is one of the most contentious in Aegean history, and the difficulties in providing an answer involve most of the classic problems of historical explanation which have engaged historians from Thucydides to Ibn Khaldun, Gibbon and Fernand Braudel. What 'happened' around 1200? Are all the destructions of the same time? Are they of the same cause? Or many different causes – possibly varying according to local conditions? Are they all man-made or was there some sort of natural catastrophe? Is external invasion involved, or internal feuding? Inter-dynastic strife or class war, peasants rising against lords? Simply to reel off possible arguments is to show how complex the problems are, and the reader should appreciate that no satisfactory explanations have yet been brought forward by the experts. Perhaps the error is to think that there can be one all-embracing solution.

Part of the problem lies in our evidence: the fact that no major Mycenaean palace except Pylos has been fully excavated with modern techniques. Some, such as Mycenae and Tiryns, were dug by Schliemann, while others, such as Orchomenos and Iolkos, have been touched piecemeal and their pottery remains unpublished. But Schliemann himself realised that the destructions at Mycenae and Tiryns were contemporary and had great significance not just for the Argolid but for Greece as a whole. It is Schliemann's successors at Tiryns who are coming up with some startling new answers to these questions.

Although, as at Mycenae, there was a lesser destruction in the citadel at Tiryns in the later thirteenth century BC (perhaps by a small earthquake), it is at about 1200 that the major one is placed, at the end of LH III B. The present excavators of Tiryns, working on the untouched 'lower citadel', think that this destruction was an earthquake of exceptional severity, and that it also caused the destruction at Mycenae (whose excavator agrees with this). At Tiryns all the great buildings collapsed, and the survivors rebuilt only with tiny temporary dwellings, before they reorganised themselves in the twelfth century BC with a well-planned town with insulae and north–south streets. To the surprise of the excavators this town contained a very much larger population, as if swelled by refugees from outside (architecturally the nearest analogies suggested were the new Greek colonies on Cyprus). From the 1190s to c.1150 this town thrived; then the population probably started to decline (though not so drastically as would be seen after 1100), pottery output fell, and poorer decoration appears. At a guess the population fell by half in this area. A similar decrease of population in Messenia and Lakonia has been observed after the end of the thirteenth century. Evidently, because the Argolid was on the sea and had good trade routes with the Levant and Italy, its economy survived longer than that of the western Peloponnese. For well over a century after 1200 the people here still thought of themselves as belonging to that earlier world – still Mycenaeans, as we would say: clear continuity was found, for instance, in the position of the cult rooms which were on the same spot until 1050 BC. In none of this detail do the Dorians have any role to play: archaeologically they are not even there. Here at least, then, the destructions do not appear to be the result of war. The evidence from Tiryns is recent, and needs to be properly evaluated. It suggests, though, that Mycenaean society – at least in its powerhouse in the Argolid – was experiencing quite complex change. Elsewhere, though, the evidence – both documentary and archaeological – seems to indicate that the 'foul din of war', as Hesiod put it, may have played its part in the process of decline.

The mid-thirteenth century BC, the Age of Agamemnon, was a militarist one. Archaeology tells us so clearly. At Mycenae and Tiryns immense fortifications were built, and elaborate precautions taken to ensure the water-supply by tunnelling into the rock under the citadel walls. At Athens, too, where remains of a massive Mycenaean defence wall from this period still survive on the Acropolis entrance, another deep cistern was dug, which was in use for only a few decades around 1200. Elsewhere on the Greek mainland huge forts were built in isolated places which can only have been intended as outer defence works, coastal or promontory forts serving as frontier works at a time when a hostile outer world began with the sea. At Araxos on the north-western tip of the Peloponnese great walls survive from this period, on a precipitous crag over the sea with wonderful vistas over the sea westwards. Perhaps this was 'Myrsinos the outermost' in Homer's catalogue of the ships which went to Troy. Again, on a wild and desolate promontory in the Mani in the far south of the Peloponnese, another Cyclopean fortress stood on 100-foot-high cliffs haunted by seabirds where the later Frankish castle of Maina stood, perhaps a front line of defence for the kingdom of Lakonia, Homer's 'Messe of the many pigeons'. In the north-east of the Peloponnese, at the isthmus of Corinth, a wall seems to have been commenced blocking the whole isthmus against attack from the north. The cumulative effect of this kind of evidence from the Peloponnese suggests a society expecting attack from the sea, and indeed this is plausible: Egyptian texts from as early as *c.*1300 BC show that sea raiders were troublesome in the Eastern Mediterranean and could mount dangerous concerted attacks which threatened well-organised kingdoms. Proof of this kind of interpretation has been sought in the tablets found in the palace of Pylos, from which some scholars think preparations for seaborne attack can be deduced. These dramatic documents afford us a fascinating insight into the world of a major palace on the eve of its destruction.

The last tablets at Pylos, for instance, speak of rowers being drawn from five places to go to Pleuron on the coast. A second list, incomplete, numbers 443 rowers: originally crews for at least fifteen ships. A much larger list, almost a Mycenaean catalogue of ships, speaks of 700 men as defensive troops: gaps on the tablet suggest that when complete around 1000 men were marked down, the equivalent of a force of thirty ships. If we reckon the possible size of the king's standing army as a couple of thousand or so, these represent sizeable forces, at least comparable to the ninety ships which Nestor took to Troy according to the *Iliad*. Pylos does not appear to have had any fortifications at this time: the king lived in his beautifully decorated palace high above the bay of sandy Pylos confident in his military might, or so it would appear. Now, however, we seem to see an organisation watching over the long coastline of the Peloponnese. One of the most important tablets is entitled 'Thus the watchers are guarding the coasts'. It reads rather like Home Guard instructions in England during the Second World War. Local feudal barons such as Ekhelawon and Wedaneu sent forty and twenty men respectively:

Command of Maleus at *Owitono* ... fifty men of *Owitona* to go to Oikhalia ... command of Nedwatas ... twenty men of Kyparissia, at *Aruwote*, ten Kyparissia men at *Aithalewes* ... command of Tros at

Ro-o-wa: Ka-da-si-jo a shareholder, performing feudal service …
110 men from Oikhalia to *A-ra-tu-wa*.

What happened then is something of a mystery. It is certain that immediately after the tablets were written the palace was burned down in a great fire and completely destroyed. No human remains were found, so perhaps there was no fight for the palace. If the disaster was by human agency we must assume that the king's treasures were looted and the women and children enslaved: the fate of Troy was now that of Pylos. The date was early in the year, as there had been no sheep-shearing or vintage: probably it was in the 'sailing month', Plowistio (March), when navigation resumes. The last act of the king of Pylos was to order sacrifices, perhaps human: 'Perform the rituals at the shrine of Zeus, and bring the gifts: to Zeus one gold bowl, one man, to Hera one gold bowl, one woman.' The tablet on which this was written was found unfinished, hastily scribbled and ill-written, perhaps executed immediately before the palace fell. Pylos was never lived in again by men or women.

It is a dramatic tale – if we have read it right. But we cannot be sure that these documents speak of a special emergency, a last-ditch defence, or even that the catastrophe was man-made. And even if it was, was the fate of Pylos the fate of the rest of the Mycenaean world? Many other places were destroyed at this time, as we have seen. Some, like Pylos, the Menelaion, Krisa, Zygouries, Midea and Eutresis, were never rebuilt. Some, like Mycenae, Tiryns and Araxos, were rebuilt and survived until later destructions in the twelfth century. Some escaped altogether, such as Athens and, surprisingly, Asine, on the coast near Tiryns. How are we to interpret such evidence? Historians are now moving away from the view that one catastrophe enveloped the Greek mainland, inundated by invaders: now it is thought that a whole variety of local conditions and multiple causes contributed to a decline which in some places was rapid, and accelerated by disasters like that at Pylos, but in others comprised a slow decline which lasted over a century and even experienced upturns in economy and population as at Tiryns. However, there was one external element which may have been significant, whether as cause or effect of the gradual worsening of the mainland economy towards the end of the thirteenth century; a new element which may have shaken the wealthy and static world of the mainland princes, and which may have necessitated the kind of military precautions we have seen all over southern Greece. These were the invaders who have often been seen as harbingers of the violent end of the Aegean Bronze Age: the Sea Peoples.

THE SEA PEOPLES: WHO WERE THEY?

The modern term 'Sea Peoples' is derived directly from the term used by the ancient Egyptians themselves to describe the people who threatened them in two major attacks in *c.*1210 BC and *c.*1180 BC. In fact the Sea Peoples are known in Egyptian sources from considerably earlier, but the two well-known references describe major assaults on Egypt. In *c.*1210 the Pharaoh Merenptah tells of his victory in the western desert over Libyans who had brought with them as allies 'Sherden-people, Sheklesh-people, Aqaiwasha-people of the foreign lands of the Sea ... Aqaiwasha the foreigners of the Sea'. Though the Aqaiwasha are the ones specified as 'Sea Peoples' it is clear that there are others who are regarded in the same way, and they appear in other Egyptian texts and inscriptions. In a list of the northern enemies of Ramses III (*c.*1180 BC) a Sherden chief is called 'Sherden of the Sea'; with him are 'the chief of the Tjekeryu-foes' and 'Tursha of the Sea' and the 'chief of the Pulisati (Philistine) foes'. Another inscription of Ramses III commemorating his successes against Libyan enemies in the west and Nubians in the south mentions as northern enemies 'peoples of the sea', literally 'the foreign lands, the isles who sailed over against his lands', and they included Philistines and 'Tursha from the midst of the Sea' (in all these references it must be understood that the Philistines have not yet settled in their biblical homeland: they are among the migrants from the north, the isles where biblical tradition insists their original home was Kaphtor, that is, Crete). Finally, in the Harris papyrus in the British Museum, Ramses III says: 'I overthrew all who transgressed the boundaries of Egypt, coming from their lands. I slew the Danuna from their isles, the Tjekkeru and Philistines … the Sherden and Weshesh of the Sea were made as if non-existent.'

Whoever these mysterious invaders were, the Egyptians had known them for a while. Some time around 1290 BC Ramses II had already had to fight sea raiders in the Delta, including Sherden 'who came in warships from the midst of the sea'. This may have been a major confrontation: the Delta 'now lies safe in its slumbers', says a source of 1278 BC, now that the King 'has destroyed the warriors of the Great Green Sea'. In fact so many prisoners were taken after this foray that Ramses was able to employ Sherden auxiliaries in his battle with the Hittites at Kadesh in 1274.

It seems likely then that the sea raiders had represented a growing threat to the Eastern Mediterranean for a century before the climactic raids. Where were they from, and who were they? These are contentious questions, but the general picture is reasonably clear: if some of the Peoples of the Sea were migrants, many were demonstrably traditional pirates. The Lukka, for instance, who lived on the Anatolian coast opposite Rhodes, made piratical raids by sea to Cyprus, then beyond to Phoenicia, and southwards to North Africa, where they participated in the Libyan attack against Merenptah. The term 'sea' in these sources, or 'Great Green', comes to mean the Eastern Mediterranean as a whole. Peoples like the Aqaiwasha, the Philistines, the Sherden and the Lukka have no original connection with Syria–Palestine, or with Egypt: they are from *outside* their world, over seas to the north-west. Very likely the 'islands' they are from are in the Aegean, and it is in this context that a fascinating suggestion has been put forward: could the Egyptian Aqaiwasha be Homer's Achaiwoi (despite being circumcised, as the Egyptians tell us – a custom which the historical Greeks did not practise)? Is it possible to detect Homeric Trojans, Teucrians, beneath the

Tjekeryu? Or Tyrsenoi (Lydians in western Anatolia who were later said to have emigrated to Italy) in the 'Tursha of the Sea'? In short, were the Sea Peoples a flood of migrating peoples who came through the Aegean world from the north on their way to Egypt, and helped bring down the world of the Mycenaean palaces? Or were they in part actually composed of Mycenaean Greeks – rootless migrants, warrior bands and *condottieri* on the move as other conditions, economic, social or whatever, broke apart the fragile stability of their world? Certainly there seem to be suggestive parallels between the war gear and helmets of the Greeks as depicted on, say, the warrior vase at Mycenae, and those of the Sea Peoples shown on Egyptian wall-carvings and tiles; and, remarkably, when the Philistines (Pulisati) were settled by the Egyptians in the Gaza Strip after their defeat, their pottery and weapons indicate close affinities with the Aegean. Furthermore, biblical tradition actually links the Philistines with Kaphtor (Crete) and the Aegean. Of the other peoples mentioned among the northern invaders, despite the tantalising similarities of name we have no means of making any secure identifications beyond the Lukka and Danuna. Some are quite obscure and likely to remain so, but, like the Philistines, the Sherden and Sheklesh *can* be traced later: the etymology of their names connects them with Sardinia and Sicily respectively. So perhaps elements migrated westwards after the convulsions of the early twelfth century BC. Interestingly enough, both Greek tradition and archaeology show that there *were* migrations of Greek-speaking peoples to the same places at this time.

We should not, however, think of these as great folk migrations in the style of the popular view of the 'folk wanderings' after the Fall of Rome. The Egyptian inscriptions give us what are clearly accurate figures for casualties among the Sea Peoples: in Merenptah's battle the dead included at least 6300 Libyans, 1213 Aqaiwasha, 742 Tursha and 222 Sheklesh; other figures are lost. Over 9500 people (including women and non-combatants, etc.) are counted as prisoners. The attack of *c.*1210 BC, then, was by a chiefly Libyan force supplemented by groups of 'Sea People' warriors, perhaps something like 20,000 fighting force in total, of whom maybe a quarter may have been Sea Peoples. Had Sea People bands actually formed settlements in Libya or were they operating from the Aegean? We do not know. A generation or so later Ramses III faced attacks of a similar size: over 12,000 were killed in the Libyan battle in his fifth year, over 2000 killed and 2000 captured six years later; for the Sea Peoples' attack of year 8 (c.1180) we have no figures, but a good guess might be a fighting force of 10,000 with women, children and non-combatants (travelling in ox wagons) to be added to that. These were big armies for the time – the Hittite army at Kadesh with all its allies numbered 35,000, but the armies of individual kingdoms cannot have numbered anything like that: as we have seen, even large Mycenaean kingdoms like Pylos or Tiryns with estimated populations of over 60,000 can only have had a military force of 2000 or 3000 *at most* – for offensive expeditionary campaigns.

WHAT HAPPENED?

The tale of this last attack is told on a magnificent relief on the Great Temple of Ramses III at Medinet Habu in Egypt.

... the foreign countries made a conspiracy in their islands. *All at once the lands were on the move,* scattered in war. No country could stand before their arms. Hatti, Kode [i.e. Kizzuwatna, the region around Tarsus in southern Turkey], Carchemish, Arzawa and Alashiya. They were cut off. A camp was set up in one place in Amor [Amurru: Syria, presumabbly the coastal plain]. They devastated its people and its land was like that which has never come into being. They were advancing on Egypt while the flame was being prepared for them. Their league was Puliset [Philistines], Tjeker, Shekelesh, Denyen and Weshesh, united lands. They laid their hands upon the lands to the very circuit of the earth, their hearts confident and trusting: 'Our plans will succeed.' ... I [Ramses] organised my frontier in Djahi [between Egypt and Palestine] ... I caused the river mouth [of the Nile], to be prepared like a strong wall with warships, transports and merchantmen, entirely manned from stem to stern with brave fighting men.... (My italics.)

Two battles followed, one by land, one at sea. The invaders had probably penetrated as far as the Egyptian frontier: perhaps they were taken by surprise, for the relief scenes at Medinet Habu show a confused mêlée with ox carts loaded with women and children caught up with the fighters; the unencumbered Egyptians were able to use their horse and chariots to advantage, boosted by mercenaries including Sherden auxiliaries. The land invaders were comprehensively defeated. The climax came in the Delta with a fierce sea battle against the Sea Peoples' fleet. Here, somehow, they were trapped and annihilated in a confusion of capsizing boats:

As for those who came on the sea, the full flame was in front of them at the river mouths, while a stockade of lances surrounded them on the shore [or 'canal bank']. They were dragged ashore, hemmed in and flung down on the beach, grappled, capsized and laid out on the shore dead, their ships made heaps from stern to prow, and their goods....

Many prisoners were taken from all the races, each delineated on the reliefs with their distinctive war gear, and among them were 'leaders of every country', who were executed: 'Like birds in a net ... their leaders were carried off and slain'. The rank-and-file prisoners were settled at strategic points on the frontier, rather as the Romans used Germanic federates in the Late Empire: 'I settled them in strongholds bound in my name,' says Ramses. 'They were numbered in hundred-thousands. I taxed them all, in clothing and grain from the shore-houses and granaries each year.' Among these were the Philistines, who in the twelfth century BC make their appearance in the 'way of Canaan', the line of Egyptian forts running up the Gaza Strip. Here their tombs have been found, revealing a strange mixture of burial customs: anthropoid coffins in the Egyptian style, pottery of a type similar to twelfth-century Mycenaean, and war gear resembling that on the warrior vase from Mycenae. Their ancient traditions stuck with them, if they were indeed originally from the Aegean world, as the Bible asserts: when the Philistine champion Goliath fights the boy David, he is wearing what is still recognisably Mycenaean war gear! So the climax to the great land and sea raid of *c.*1180 can be reconstructed with some certainty. But what had preceded it? Where had the league of Sea Peoples come from, and why was it on the move? Did they really exist as a unified movement? These are questions with which experts are still grappling.

The archaeological record perhaps enables us to corroborate the general picture of a period of instability and violent destructions. But Ramses names Hatti, Kode, Carchemish, Arzawa and Alashiya being 'cut off' by the Sea Peoples. Is this believable? Could it really be that all these places were actually destroyed by the attack of 1180? The date certainly agrees very well with the destruction of the Hittite capital at Boghaz Köy, the palace at Mersin in Cilicia (Kode), of Tarsus in Cilicia, and Carchemish. In particular there is this dramatic evidence from the last clay tablets written at the great city of Ugarit in northern Syria:

To the king of Alashia (Cyprus) my father, I say: thus speaks the king of Ugarit your son. Ships of the enemy have come, some of my towns have been burned and they have done wicked things in our country. My father clearly does not know that all my troops are deployed in Hittite territory, and all my ships are standing off the Lycian coast. They have not [so far] returned, so the country is at the mercy of the enemy. Let my father understand this! And that seven enemy ships have appeared offshore and done evil things. Now, if there are more hostile ships on the way, please inform me and of what kind – I *must* know about it!

This letter was still in the oven waiting to be baked when Ugarit was burned – perhaps from the sea, although the excavator attributes its final destruction to an earthquake. Destructions on Cyprus at the same time may be connected with the same troubles which had led to the Ugaritic fleet sailing westwards.

These last tablets from Ugarit give us another potentially crucial factor: at this critical moment the king of Ugarit is urgently sending grain from Mukish to Ura in Cilicia (southern Turkey) 'to alleviate the famine there'. If this was more than a local crisis, then it could suggest that climatic and economic conditions in the Aegean and Anatolia were encouraging migration southwards; this in its turn would enable us, for instance, to make sense of archaeological evidence for massive depopulation in Messenia. This kind of approach to the evidence has been pursued by climatologists with interesting results. Studies in climate patterns through tree rings and pollen deposits, examination of the fluctuation in growth phases in European peat-bogs and lake levels, have all suggested to experts that there was a crisis in the climate of the European and Aegean worlds in around 1200 BC which may have assisted in the movement of peoples from the Hungarian plain into Thrace, and thence into the Aegean. Depopulation in Messenia (and central Anatolia?) could then have been linked, with drought as a possible contributory cause. In this connection we may care to remember Herodotus' story that after the Trojan War Crete in particular was so devastated by plagues and pestilence that it became virtually uninhabited. These are wider questions which, though they have a great bearing on our story, cannot be examined within the scope of this present book, and the reader is recommended to look at the books and articles in the bibliography; but such considerations show how misleading it can be to use traditional methods of historical inquiry to answer what turn out to be very long-term questions of decline.

Our scattered indications – including the Ugaritic reference to famine – suggest that all was not well in the Aegean and Asia Minor at the turn of the thirteenth century BC. It does not allow us to say that the Sea Peoples were responsible for the fall of the Hittite Empire, though if we consider that what the Egyptians called Sea Peoples were only a part of larger movements, of widespread disruption in the Eastern Mediterranean, then they may not have been. However, though a number of Hittite centres, such as Boghaz Köy and Masat Hüyük, did fall around 1180 BC, the present excavator of Boghaz Köy is inclined to attribute the fire that destroyed them to internal revolt rather than external enemies. With a little licence, though, we can trace the track of the Sea Peoples through Amurru–Syria, which Ramses says they devastated. Tell Sukas on the Syrian coast was sacked at this time, as were Hamath, Carchemish, Açana, Sidon and Tell Abu Hawam, a great site near Haifa; several are associated with pottery the experts call LH III C 1, dating them to around 1180: their destructions certainly fit very well with the great land and sea raid. On Cyprus the catastrophe which overtook Kition, and the burning of Enkomi, likewise point to the Sea Peoples. Interestingly enough, these places were rebuilt by Greeks; for all their close contacts with Cyprus, actual Greek immigration into Cyprus begins only with the period of the Sea Peoples.

Were the Sea Peoples in part composed of Aegean warriors? It seems possible, even likely, but at present these events are shrouded in mystery. Where do they fit with the detailed history which has now been worked out for some of the mainland kingdoms? The depopulation of Messenia after the fall of Pylos, for example? Or the swelling of population in the Argolid around Tiryns at this time? And do the Egyptian accounts have any bearing on later Greek legends which speak of migrations after the Trojan War to Anatolia, to Sicily and southern Italy – curiously paralleled in our admittedly uncertain linguistic evidence for Sea People migrations to those parts? Could Odysseus' raid on the Nile Delta in the *Odyssey* even contain a dim memory of the terrible disaster which overtook the league of Aqaiwasha and the rest?

On the fifth day we came to fair-flowing Aegyptus, and in the river Aegyptus [i.e. the Nile] I moored my curved ships, then I told my trusty comrades to remain there by the ships, and I sent out scouts to

set up lookout posts. But my comrades ... set about devastating the
fair fields of the people of Egypt; and they carried off the women and
little children and slew the men. And the news went swiftly to the
city. Then their people came out at dawn and the whole plain was
filled with foot soldiers and chariots, and the flashing of bronzes ...
and then they killed many of us with the sharp bronze, and others
they led back to their city alive, to work for them as forced labour....

Odyssey, XIV, 245

Attractive and plausible as such speculations are, at present they are
no more than that. But there is one important connection with the
Sea Peoples' raid of 1180 which we have not yet examined – could
the fall of Troy itself be the work of the Sea Peoples?

TROY VIIA – THE SIEGE OF TROY LOST AGAIN

The reader will recall that we left the question of the sack of Troy
with Carl Blegen's conclusion, that the city called Troy VIIa, the
one with the shanties, the soup kitchen, and the storage jars in
the floors, was Homer's Troy; that its destruction by violence and
fire was the Homeric siege. We had our reservations about his
interpretation but deferred them for a while. Now we cannot put
off any longer tackling the problem of the date of the destruction
of VIIa, the one Late-Bronze-Age level of Hisarlik which looks
as if it fell to attack by an army. Was Blegen right? Here we
cannot avoid a few technicalities, and I hope the reader will bear
with me. The heyday of Troy VI (phases d–g) contains pieces of
imported Mycenaean pottery of the class known as LH III A. The
last phase, the city of the great towers (VIh), Blegen thought
contained both LH III A and III B. But new research suggests
Blegen was wrong: Troy VI had no III B pottery, and hence must
have been destroyed around 1300 BC or a decade or two later.
Troy VIh was therefore the city known to the Mycenaens at the
peak of the power of the palaces in mainland Greece in the
fourteenth and early thirteenth centuries, and the masses of
Mycenaean imports prove it. So the Troy of the shanties and soup

kitchen, VIIa – a continuation of the same settlement – begins some time after c.1300–1275. It contains almost no Mycenaean pottery of this period – only the odd sherd, in fact: most are Trojan imitations of Mycenaean styles. But how long did VIIa last, and when did it fall?

Blegen asserted that 'not a single piece' of LH III C pottery was found in Troy VIIa (when he wrote, the beginning of III C was thought to be c.1230–1200; it is now placed at 1190–1185 or later). However, it is now clear that several pieces of LH III C *were* found in Troy VIIa, which would suggest it was destroyed around 1180 BC. This is confirmed by the appearance of another kind of pottery, the so-called 'Granary Class', in the next phase of Troy, VIIb I: this phase can hardly have begun until the 'Granary Class' was widespread in Greece, that is, in 1170–1160. Troy VIIa, then, which Blegen thought Homer's Troy, is far too late for the Trojan War if it was fought by an expedition in the time of the Mycenaean palaces. Accordingly, if Blegen was right about the duration of the VIIa settlement, the fall of Troy VI could have been improbably late, say between 1250 and 1200. So Blegen was guilty of overenthusiasm in his 1240 date for the sack of VIIa, let alone 1270. This becomes obvious when we work back from the sack of VIIa: Blegen proposed a duration of only a few years, within a half century or 'even a generation of man' (clearly he was reluctant to say ten years!). If VIIa fell around 1180 BC, then the fall of VIh would be datable nearer 1200.

Was the life of VIIa so brief, though? This seems unlikely. Blegen's earlier statement, 'within a century', seems nearer the mark. Two houses had two successive floor levels and one three; not mere relayings (as we still find in rural Anatolia) but strata totalling up to a metre in depth, accumulated over some time; this surely takes VIIa well back into the thirteenth century BC but lasting long enough to receive III C pottery; forty or fifty years seems a plausible low estimate. It would appear, then, that Blegen truncated the life of Troy VIIa; its shanties and storage jars were not laid in for *one event*; they were a condition of a whole time, not a short-lived emergency at all: they are the architectural character of the whole phase of the settlement, and it is curious that this was not remarked on by critics at the time. In fact, the archaeology of Troy VIIa would fit very well with the disturbed period of *c.*1210–1180, the period of the invasions by the Sea Peoples, the upheavals in the 'islands of the Great Green' described in Egyptian texts; a time when all cities in Eastern Mediterranean lands were vulnerable to attack as central authorities were everywhere weakened. If we wish to pin down the brutal sack uncovered by Blegen to one particular event (and I should stress that there is no need to do this), it would be perverse to ignore the Sea Peoples' raid of 1180, which we know destroyed places in western Anatolia, precisely in the area of Troy, when it ravaged Arzawa and Hittite country before heading south. Troy VIIa *may* have fallen to Sea Peoples – whoever they were – like many places in Anatolia and Syria.

We can see, then, that Blegen was carried away by his desire to find a Homeric synchronism. His date of 1270–1240 BC for the life of Troy VIIa is far too early. Troy VIIa fell in around 1180, *after* destructions on the mainland which in some cases ruined the great palaces forever. It would appear that Troy VIIa *cannot* be Homer's Troy: Troy VIh *could be*. But if Troy VIh fell to an earthquake, does the Trojan War vanish? Is Schliemann's dream on the point of dissipating forever? In fact I do not think that these new discoveries about the date of the fall of Troy VIIa necessarily rule out VIIa as the model of the Trojan War.

ANOTHER TROJAN WAR?
'THE PEOPLES IN THEIR ISLANDS WERE ON THE MOVE'

Could not Troy VIIa have been sacked by Mycenaeans after all? Not by a great coalition under a Mycenaean high king, but by Mycenaean Vikings sending their corsairs through the Aegean world in the first half of the twelfth century during the time of upheavals of the Sea Peoples? The generic term 'Sea Peoples' should not deceive us into thinking that there was one organised movement. In a time of internecine upheaval and migrations we may well follow the Viking analogy: Mycenaean royal sons with their armed following, stateless kings, renegades and pirates may well have taken advantage of the general unrest to sack many cities in the Aegean world. Sackers of cities must still have sailed from Tiryns in the twelfth century. Is it conceivable that Troy VIIa fell to Sea Peoples who were in fact Mycenaeans? That the tale was sung in the declining years of the twelfth century BC back in the courts of Mycenae and Tiryns? This interpretation has no glorious Troy, no Mycenaean 'empire', but at least it has a siege in the archaeological record. The only alternative explanation takes us nearer the myth; that is to place the Trojan War in the period of the Mycenaean 'empire', at the time of the beautiful walls of Troy VI, just as the epic tradition asserts. But there the archaeological evidence says there is no siege. Can we reconcile these facts? Let us look again at the destruction of Troy VI. Here the archaeology tells us more than Blegen thought. The date may have been around 1275; there is no means of being more precise. The evidence of earthquake damage seems convincing, but only a small area of the city was examined by Blegen.

THE DESTRUCTION OF TROY VI BY EARTHQUAKE

Lying at the junction of the so-called African and Eurasian plates, the Aegean area is notoriously prone to earthquake. Troy itself is situated near the junction of one of the intermediate crust 'blocks' of this zone, and near the end of the major Anatolian fault; as a result there is a great deal of seismic activity: twenty-seven earthquakes are recorded in the area since 1912, some (1912, 1935, 1953, 1968) big ones at 6 or 7 on the Richter scale ('... general panic. Poor masonry destroyed, good masonry damaged seriously. Foundations generally damaged. Buildings shifted off foundations'). This is the scale of earthquake proposed for Troy VI; they can be worse, of course – the maximum recorded is 8.9, when damage to man-made structures was total.

The period AD 1939–68 seems to have been particularly bad, and it would appear that major quakes come in rapid succession to be followed by a period of relative quiet which can last up to 150 years, punctuated only by minor ones every twenty years or so in the Troy region: but one of the scale of 6 or 7 can be expected on the Troad on average every 300 years. That said, the 'region of Troy' is large; an earthquake of this scale 60 miles away (as are most of those cited) will not have affected Troy; to do so the shock would have to be directly underneath the city.

The earthquake history of Troy was detected at points by Schliemann. Blegen and his team were able to show that Troys III, IV and V all suffered major earthquake damage, and that in their opinion Troy VI, the most glorious of all, was very badly damaged. They assume that the mudbrick superstructure of the main wall was thrown down, and that the upper parts of all the excavated houses must have suffered likewise. As a result of this destruction, they implicitly suggest, economic problems were caused which determined the nature of the successor city Troy VIIa. Their major points are as follows.

The main wall of Troy VI was founded on a cushion of earth above the bedrock, presumably to protect it against earthquake. Tower VIh was, however, laid directly on the bedrock and here large cracks are visible today. The inner face of the great stretch of wall on the south, originally vertical, had been partially dislocated and slightly tilted towards the north. The shifting seemed to have been accompanied by a mass of stones falling from the wall's superstructure, and this occurred before the successor settlement was founded. House VIG fell in the disaster: at its northern end the east wall collapsed. Masses of squared stones fell inward into the citadel from the upper part of tower VIh. The east wall of house VIE collapsed. Everywhere in the areas examined by the Americans a thick deposit of debris dating from the last phase of the sixth settlement was encountered, up to 4½ feet in depth.

Blegen was convinced that Dörpfeld had been wrong in thinking that the destruction of Troy VI was due to a hostile army. Let us for now accept the fact of the earthquake.

Earthquake experts distinguish between 'total disasters' and less catastrophic evidence of architectural and structural damage, and the major earthquake proposed by Blegen comes close to the 'total disaster' category. Nevertheless we should first ask ourselves whether Blegen's conclusions about the economic and social consequences of such a destruction were entirely right. After all, the main city wall, as far as we can tell, still stood around its entire circuit. Even today, after the destruction wrought by classical builders, the walls and towers are an impressive sight and a major obstacle. The damage, then, was severe but not as catastrophic as has been claimed: a number of the great houses were ruined and the superstructure of the main circuit walls fell in places. There is, however, no sign that any of the main circuit wall was actually toppled. It still stands today and is intact (leaving aside later building damage) for almost all its surviving length; in some places there are cracks, and in one place the wall has shifted, but in essence the main wall was undamaged: nowhere did it open up or fall. Therefore it is not true to say, as has been alleged, that 'nothing [was left] standing intact, not even the circle of great wall and towers' (Denys Page). But consider what follows. This was a city at the height of its wealth and glory and architectural development, built by a race of great builders. Such disasters happen frequently in the Eastern Mediterranean; they had happened before at Troy. Usually the people pick themselves up, repair the damage, and build bigger and better than before. But why were the great houses of Troy VI never rebuilt? Why were dismal tenements and shanties built in the open streets between the once noble houses? Why were some of the houses themselves not merely left in ruins, but partitioned? There is no archaeological evidence that *any* of the Troy VI houses retained its original function after the earthquake. If we accept the premise that the great buildings of Troy VI were houses and temples for the royal clan and their immediate retainers, living around and below the palace, then a dramatic change has taken place. Why was it that the spacious mansions had been left in ruins or divided up; the 'wide streets' obstructed with small houses, some only 15 feet by 12, or even less – in one no fewer than 22 pithoi sunk into the floor? The character of the whole settlement is now so radically different that we are justified in asking whether an earthquake was not the only thing to have happened to Troy VI. It looks very much as if the powerful rulers who lived in houses like the Pillar House (we cannot speak for the palace itself) were no longer there: and surely no earthquake could be powerful enough to kill all the royalty whose citadel this was? Either the Trojans had lost the will to rebuild, or the ruling clan who had directed the magnificent constructions of VIh no longer existed. It is difficult to be speculative with so much of the site destroyed. We know, after all, that the Trojans *were* able and had the will to reconstruct the street in the south entrance, laying a new drain. We know also that the defences were patched up with a new outwork for the south-east gate. But in many places the wreckage lay where it fell, and on the whole it seems likely that the great houses had ceased to have their original function – ceased to shelter a powerful royal race.

Inevitably such a conclusion can only be speculative, for earthquake experts agree that it is *possible* for a severe earthquake to kill all the people in a city if it occurs at an inopportune moment (in the night, say, when people are sleeping, or at prayer time, as has happened in the modern Near East). But had Troy VI been attacked and sacked as it lay in its greatest weakness, crippled by an earthquake? If it had, then we would have an explanation for the extraordinary transformation in Trojan society after the earthquake. If there was no such attack, then there remains no archaeological evidence for the Trojan War, and if we wished to cling on to any belief in the epic tradition at all, we would have to conclude that the Greeks attacked but failed to take Troy, as many have suspected from Lechevalier onwards.

But did the excavators of Hisarlik find any evidence to point to a Mycenaean attack on Troy VI? Combing the accounts of Blegen, Dörpfeld and Schliemann (who of course had no idea that his Sixth or 'Lydian' City was contemporary with Mycenae) it is possible to find some support for such an idea.

First there is good evidence that Troy VI was thoroughly burned. Blegen brushed over this in his final report, but Dörpfeld's account leaves no doubt: 'The citadel was completely destroyed by enemy action,' he wrote in 1902. 'We distinguished *traces of a great fire in many places.*' (My italics.) He adds that the toppling of the *upper* parts of the walls and gates was hardly explicable either by fire alone, or even earthquake. Now Blegen dismissed this burning in his report, though he noted thick black carbonised debris throughout the deep 'earthquake' layer, but in an interview published in 1963 he affirmed that 'Troy VI had been burned – no doubt about that.' People had been killed too: in the street, west of the Pillar house, Blegen found a human skull.

More interesting than these vague hints is the presence of large numbers of Mycenaean weapons in the last phase of Troy VI. In the light of Blegen's emphasis on one 'Aegean' arrowhead in his version of the fall of Troy VIIa, it is worth listing the veritable arsenal found in Troy VI, some definitely assignable to the 'earthquake' layer. Blegen found a stemmed arrowhead from VIh which he thought Mycenaean on the basis of others he had discovered at Prosymna, near Mycenae; Schliemann found an identical one in his Sixth City. A barbed arrowhead found by Blegen between house VIG and the main wall was similar to others found by Schliemann and Dörpfeld; again Blegen could offer a mainland parallel from his own dig at Prosymna. Blegen also found a riveted Mycenaean knife with a flanged haft. In the Sixth City again – but we do not know how late – Schliemann found a Mycenaean lancehead with a hollowed socket; he remarked on the Homeric parallel, and mentions that he had found many like this at Mycenae (Dörpfeld found another example in Troy VI). Also in the Sixth City, Schliemann unearthed four double-headed bronze axes 'perfectly identical' to axes he had found at Mycenae; Dörpfeld found another of these, along with masses of terracotta slingshots, three bronze sickle-shaped blades, knives and celts, all with good mainland parallels. Now, most of these cannot be securely dated to the last phase of

Troy VI – not all are certainly Greek, though they look like it – but we may well ask whether they all came as a result of peaceful trading.

Apart from the clear evidence of burning, these finds do not amount to very much, of course, but they bring us to a last question which has not occurred to any commentator since Blegen announced his discoveries. *Was* Troy VI destroyed by earthquake? The evidence has seemed so rock-solid that it has been depended upon. But is it possible that the damage to Troy VI was, after all, the work of men, as Dörpfeld had thought when he uncovered the city in 1893? For Dörpfeld 'traces of a great fire were distinguished in many places', but the toppling of the superstructures of the walls and towers, he felt, 'could not be wholly explained either by a conflagration alone *or by an earthquake*'. (My italics.) The fire was unarguable: not indeed 'so universal or so striking to the eye as in Troy II, but only because the building material of Troy VI was not so combustible'. Blegen, we know, agreed: there was 'no doubt' about the burning of the city, even if he did not say so in his reports. Was it conceivable, then, that Troy VI had been deliberately demolished, 'slighted' after a siege? There are near contemporary parallels for this in the siege warfare of the Assyrians, who are known to have dismantled and devastated cities with which they had engaged in particularly bitter sieges. It is fascinating that Blegen seriously considered this idea. In *Troy, III*, 1953, he wrote:

A large force of determined men armed with crowbars and other equipment could in time demolish almost any wall that men have built; but if they set out deliberately to efface the site of Troy, they would surely have begun by razing the citadel wall to the ground. Furthermore, vindictive destruction after the capture of the town in war would almost surely have been accompanied by great conflagration. Here, however, only the upper parts of the walls have been overturned, and we found *no evidence of a serious fire*. (My italics.) It is true that carbonised matter occurred freely, but ... no widespread layer of burning was recognisable. Accordingly it seems safe to rule out human handiwork ... a violent earthquake shock will account more convincingly than any probable human agency for the toppling of the city wall.

There are weaknesses to Blegen's argument. Clearly any deliberate demolition of the walls *would* most likely have satisfied itself with the destruction of the superstructures of the walls and the ruining of the houses within. The massive bases of the walls were far too solidly built to be easily dismantled; they still stand today almost intact, and archaeology cannot tell us whether the few cracks and the one instance of tilting happened at this time. But the most damning argument against the earthquake comes from a study of the notebooks of the previous excavators of Hisarlik: evidence for the great earthquake of Troy VI seems to be confined to the south-eastern sector of the city, where there may have been a tendency to landslips in earlier settlements. In the opinion of earthquake experts, too, Blegen's evidence is dubious and his conclusion unproven. From a seismologist's point of view it is impossible to tell the difference between earthquake damage and man-made destruction; many archaeologists would agree.

The question of pottery dating should also be reconsidered here. Blegen presumably had already come to his conclusions about the dating of Troy VIIa – and hence its likely identification with Homeric Troy – before he looked at Troy VI, the stratum below. With hindsight we have seen that his conclusion about the dating of Troy VIIa was incorrect, and that it fell in the twelfth century BC, not in the mid-thirteenth. As for the date of the Troy VI 'earthquake', Blegen favoured a date soon after 1300, the transitional point from the LH III A to LH III B pottery styles. Here he was broadly correct, except for one important proviso. It now appears that no LH III B can be safely attributed to Troy VI; so the city may have been destroyed in the period *c*.1320–1275. Once again, though, we can see how the overall picture which the archaeologist hoped to prove tended to govern the evaluation of all the dating evidence around it.

It therefore seems permissible to bring the legend into this discussion. Greek tradition insisted that the Achaians deliberately demolished the walls of Troy before they departed. This was mentioned in the *Iliou Persis*, the lost epic which followed on Homer's *Iliad*. The razing of the walls was thereafter a constant feature of the story, down to the famous final scene in Euripides' *Trojan Women* where the captive women listen to the thunder of the towers being battered down, so frightening and turbulent that Hecuba compares it to an earthquake! In Aeschylus, too, the walls of Troy are 'dug down' and 'overturned'. Late as these testimonies are, they are nevertheless part of the tradition, and the archaeology *could*, astonishingly enough, show us this down to the last terrible detail.

Such a remarkable final convergence of archaeology and legend would be intriguing, but is probably beyond final proof. Nevertheless the ruin of Troy *is* the tradition, and Troy VI is certainly the city with which Mycenae had relations, the city which fits the indications of the tradition. 'Making the city into a mound and a ruin' was the frequent result of Assyrian sieges, and we may conjecture that this is what the Argives did to the city of Priam, just as the tradition says they did to Thebes: Pausanias confirms that the razed Cadmea of Thebes was still a taboo area in his own day. The tradition may after all be consistent with the findings of modern science.

There is a last point to be considered in connection with the fate of Troy VI. Could the story of the wooden horse actually go back to a Mycenaean siege engine? So Pausanias thought ('Anyone who doesn't think the Trojans were utterly stupid will have realised that the horse was really an engineer's device for breaking down the walls'), and the tale stresses that the wall was broken down when the horse entered the city. Could this be a garbled recollection of a siege machine? They certainly existed in Near Eastern warfare at this time: powerful 'wooden horses' containing many men to operate the ram which opened up city walls, they were developed most effectively in Assyria from the twelfth century BC onwards, but we have absolutely no indication that such devices were used in the thirteenth-century Aegean. Intriguing, but once more unprovable.

With hindsight, then, the fate of Troy VI is more open to debate than Carl Blegen thought, and though the site is dug out, further evidence may perhaps be revealed by the continuing detailed examination of the excavation notebooks of all three explorers of Hisarlik. Until then we should be aware of the problems surrounding the date and circumstances of the end of the greatest city on Hisarlik.

THE DATE OF THE TROJAN WAR

The pottery evidence allows us to make a general estimate of the date of the fall of Troy VI. The fall was followed by an almost complete cessation of imports to VIIa: only one sherd of thirteenth-century Mycenaean pottery can be safely attributed to the latter city (the site was so badly disturbed that Blegen felt other examples could be upcasts from Troy VI). If we tentatively suggest a date of 1275–60, it would fit in very well with the chronology of the Hittite letters. This would be the reign of Hattusilis III, during which Hittite relations with the kingdom of Ahhiyawa became notably hostile. At this time, too, we can say from Linear B tablets preserved at Pylos (c.1220 BC?) that the Greeks were making predatory forays towards the north-east Aegean, be it to the island of Lemnos (attacked by Agamemnon's army, according to Homer) or to the mainland in Aswija, an area south of the Troad where Homer has Achilles campaigning. The fall of Troy could then come into the lifetime of Alaksandus of Wilusa, whom we have seen reason to think could have some connection with Alexandros of (W)ilios. In any case, we can point to the likelihood that in Hattusilis' time the Greeks (Ahhiyawa) and the Hittites came to blows over 'the matter of Wilusa'. While admitting the difficulties surrounding the Wilusa question, these are noteworthy coincidences and they suggest that a memory, however dim, of these events underlies the tradition preserved by Homer. As we saw in Chapter 4, Greek epic was so very specific about where Troy was; the tradition had apparently already taken shape by the eighth century BC, incorporating elements which go back to the Bronze Age. If we can add to these facts the possibility that the great city of Troy VI was sacked and deliberately devastated, then we have gone some way towards upholding the basic accuracy of the tradition namely that Troy did indeed stand on Hisarlik, that Troy VI was the city of Homer, and that, as Homer told, Bronze-Age Greeks attacked and sacked it. It would be tempting to put it towards 1260, at the time of Hattusilis' crisis in the west (page 206).

A VISIT TO TROY IN THE HEROIC AGE

So we can at least feel certain about the Troy to which the tradition in Homer ultimately refers. The Troy celebrated in epic poetry – perhaps even before the end of the Mycenaean age – was Troy VI, in the last great phase of its life from $c.1375$ to $c.1275–60$. As we saw in the chapter on Homer, though some epithets applied to the city in the *Iliad* are merely stock descriptions, a number are so specific they must refer to the site on Hisarlik; the cumulative effect of the epithets strongly suggests that late Troy VI must be the 'Homeric' city. Now that we know the date of the fall of Troy VIIa is too late for the Trojan War, this is made all the more certain. These last phases, culminating in Troy VIh, were the heyday of the city architecturally, economically and in terms of trade and contacts: this was the time when Mycenaean contacts with Troy were at their most intense (to judge by the pottery imports). This, then, was the city which the Greeks knew at the height of the Mycenaean empire.

What would a Bronze-Age traveller – or a bard – have seen if he had visited Troy towards the middle of the thirteenth century BC? It is time for us to put together the evidence found by Schliemann (albeit unwittingly), by Dörpfeld and Blegen, to which we can add further lost details of Troy VI demolished by Schliemann but recoverable from his notebooks. We will journey there as we did to Mycenae (p. 165) with an eye for what it looked like in its heyday, but this time we will approach it from a distance along one of its trade routes reminding ourselves that archaeology has shown that Troy–Hisarlik was an important place irrespective of its role in Greek legend, and that its life to some extent depended on its contacts with the outside world, Anatolia in the first place, the Aegean, and even farther afield.

Our imagined journey is by sea, in a Bronze-Age Greek merchantman sailing with a cargo of copper ingots from Cyprus; perhaps there is some unworked ivory traded in Enkomi and a few crates of the Cypriot pottery favoured by the Trojans with its distinctive ladder patterns or cross-hatched lozenges. In the pots is opium, cumin and coriander. Ours is coasting traffic, clinging to the shore 'like a child to its mother's knee' as Alexander Kinglake put it, an ancient network of routes from island to island and promontory to promontory, tiny ports of call on the few coastal margins where Bronze-Age man had scratched out a living. It is the trade observed in later centuries by the Anglo-Saxon Saewulf, by the Spaniard Clavijo, by Edward Clarke; they all stopped in the same safe havens, traded the same goods and cooked the same food in the galley – in the case of our thirteenth-century-BC boat, fish kebabs on skewers grilling over a fire on ballast stones in the boat's belly: such detail the archaeologist can confirm (see p. 226).

The journey from Cyprus to Troy would have taken two months or more – no different from the eighth century AD when the Anglo-Saxon Willibald was at sea from 30 November until the following Easter (724–5), or, for that matter, the nineteenth century, when Alexander Kinglake spent forty days at sea between Smyrna and Cyprus in 1834. Only the arrival of steam and the telegraph altered the timeless realities of Aegean shipping. Our boat would have put into all of the stopping-places in the islands and the coast opposite: Rhodes, Kos and Miletus with their Mycenaean settlements, Cnidus and Zephyrus, Iasos on its peninsula with its cobbled streets and fisheries. Though thinly populated, the islands were naturally rich and by no means presented the barren aspect they do today – as late as the fifteenth century AD travellers speak of their extraordinary fertility.

From Miletus the Bronze-Age captain would have had to round Samos through the rough and windy straits opposite Icaria – exactly as Kinglake, Clarke and other travellers to Troy did in the nineteenth century. Then you steered along Chios, that most fertile and productive of all the islands off Asia Minor where, as anyone who has sailed it will know, the passage is sweetened by the wind-borne scent of orchards and olive groves. From Chios, according to the Pylos tablets, Asian slaves were shipped back to work in the mainland palaces, and by 'Chios' the Bronze-Age scribes doubtless meant the fine natural harbour of Emborio on the southern tip of the island, where a Mycenaean settlement stood on a steep promontory over a sheltered bay with magnificent views across to the hills of Asia Minor. (The name of the island, *Ki-si-wi-ja* in the Linear B tablets, it has been suggested, is the Phoenician word for mastic, the resinous gum of the lentisk tree which was highly sought after in the ancient world.)

After Chios another important port of call was Thermi in Lesbos. Lesbos has always been an intermediary between the Aegean and Asia Minor, so close to the shores of the Troad. It shared the culture of Troy VI and was sacked at the same time, around 1250 – by Achilles according to Homer, by Pijamaradus according to the Hittite Foreign Office! The port lay halfway along the eastern side of the island, well fortified with a double wall behind which were packed narrow houses and streets paved with beach pebbles. Thermi was one of the biggest towns in the Aegean; its people worked copper, wove textiles and made their local red and grey pottery; they fished with bone fish-hooks, and, so far as the archaeologist can tell, they liked oysters and sea-urchins: one more city of the Bronze Age whose end was fiery. In the centre of the island in classical times was a shrine to the Bronze-Age god Smintheus, a powerful inflicter and averter of plague. His perhaps were the idols sent to the ailing Mursilis II; to him, according to Homer, the Greeks at Troy prayed for relief (*Iliad*, I, 456). Smintheus was also later worshipped in Tenedos and the Troad, where he had a temple at Hamaxitus, and it may have been for him that the custom began among sailors of making food offerings into the sea off Cape Lekton where his temple stood, a custom which survived into modern times – transferred to an Islamic saint.

Approaching Troy and the mouth to the Dardanelles the Bronze-Age sailor's feelings were no doubt the same as Edward Clarke's in 1801: 'No spectacle could be more grand than this corner of the Aegean Sea ... *Tenedos* upon the west, and those small *Isles* which form a group opposed to the *Sigean* Promontory. Nothing, excepting the oars of our boat, ruffled the still surface of the water: no other sound was heard. The distant Islands of the *Aegean* appeared as if placed upon the surface of a vast mirror ... (ahead) the mountainous Island of *Imbros*, backed by the loftier snow-clad summits of Samothrace. ...' (*Travels*.) It is often difficult to sail against the wind into the Dardanelles – this was why Lord Byron spent so long kicking his heels in 1810, in company with a score of other vessels (p. 53), but in the Bronze Age the bay of Troy must have been a magnet for seafarers, who had a safe haven once they had turned 'inside Ilios'. The mouth of the bay between the headlands was about 1½ miles across. Inside, in front of Troy, it opened out to about 3 miles of shallow sea, fringed by the alluvial flats of the rivers, salt marshes, lagoons and wind-blown sand-dunes.

The city stood on a ridge sticking westwards into the bay; below it was perhaps a mile of alluvial plain stretching to the sea-shore, much of it marshy in winter but otherwise dry; in this respect it must have resembled the plain of Argos, well watered and green in the spring, russet brown in high summer except around the marshes: ideal horse-raising country. There would have been no real harbour, just a trading shore where boats tied up to stakes or stone anchors on a sandy beach. Among the small local craft we might imagine fishing-boats, especially at the time of the seasonal migrations of mackerel and tunny which come through the Dardanelles each autumn; perhaps like the Turks after them the Trojans had wooden watchtowers on the straits to alert them for the harvest, and its slaughter in the offshore nets.

The bay must also have been especially rich in shellfish, oysters and sea-urchins.

At any one time there would have been only a handful of boats in the bay, though from the archaeology we might be permitted to imagine the odd seagoing Greek 'tramp' from Tiryns or Asine with a cargo of pottery – stirrup jars full of perfumed oil, alabastros cups and bowls for use in Trojan noble houses. But this was a small trade to judge by the local wares. Troy had been, and remained, an Anatolian city. Nevertheless, as mentioned earlier, the Mycenaean captains had a few things to offer the Trojan royal supervisor – carnelian beads, ivory boxes, an ivory gaming-board with counters, pins of electrum or silver, even perhaps a decorated ostrich egg: such were the luxury products of the Age of Bronze!

The Trojan king presumably had his own ships, not only to protect his shores from the perennial raiders and pirates, but to raid in his turn, to seize slaves and loot, and also to sell some of his own products which went wider afield. He perhaps exported bales of wool, spun yarn and made-up textiles, for, like Knossos, Troy was a sheep town with (we may guess) 'state-run' cottage factories in the outlying villages which sent their renders in to the palace stores. The Trojan local grey pottery found its way in small quantities to Cyprus and even to Syria and Palestine, though 'export' is doubtless too grand a word for the process which took it there. Lastly, as we have seen, horse breeding may have been a major element in the Trojan economy, not only foals but fully grown warhorses being exported; we may then imagine horses grazing on the lower plain and corrals for breaking and training nearer the town.

From the sea it was a short walk to the city across a mile of alluvial plain. Troy stood on the northern edge of a plateau which fell away precipitously on the north to the marshy valley of the river Dumrek Su (classical Simois). Whether there was an outer town around the citadel on Hisarlik is still not known. Blegen found traces of houses on the south and west and located a cremation cemetery for Troy VI 500 yards south of the city walls on the southern slope of the plateau. But test pits sunk by Schliemann and Blegen on the plateau revealed no Bronze-Age remains. Perhaps the later building of New Ilium destroyed any trace, and it is at least possible that Troy VI had a sizeable outer town, comparable in area with, say, Eutresis (500 yards square enclosed by the outer walls, the built-up centre 200 by 150, similar to the citadel of Troy VI). If this was so, then the place will have looked far more like a regional capital than would appear today from its ruins. The royal citadel on Hisarlik stood on the western eminence of the plateau and rose in three concentric terraces, the uppermost about 130 feet above sea-level, the lowest about 100 feet. It enclosed an area of 200 yards by 120 – comparable with the 'capital' sites in Greece – within which water-supply was ensured by a deep well in the eastern bastion (though there was a spring outside the walls to the south-west). The fine walls of Troy VI had twice been remodelled, the final phase with its towers the product of three or four generations of rulers after 1400. The landward approach was, naturally, the heaviest defended, where the roads from the interior and the western Anatolian states led to the city: here were the tallest walls and the most massive gates and towers.

The visitor to Late-Bronze-Age Troy would have arrived at the south gate past the houses which lay outside the fortress. This gate was the main entrance to Troy and from it a paved street ascended the terraces of the city to the entrance of the king's palace. To the left of the gate was a great square tower of limestone blocks standing about 50 feet high and projecting 10 yards out from the gate. In this tower was one of the principal altars of the city and in front of it was a line of six stone pedestals on which stood the images of the Trojan gods to greet the visitor. On the right-hand side of the gate stood a long house where burnt sacrifices were performed; here we might imagine the Trojans making offerings before they went on journeys or campaigns, and likewise strangers sacrificing before they entered the city. These cult areas outside the gate and its great tower perhaps help account for the later Greek traditions of 'holy Ilios'.

To the right of the gate as we look at it Dörpfeld thought there had been two great flagstaffs peeping over the wall. Troy had three main gates, on the south, east and west, all perhaps fronted by idols, and a postern gate by the great eastern bastion. The technique of the masonry distinguished Troy from citadels of the Aegean world, and from Hittite work. The closely fitted limestone blocks, with their characteristic batter going up the first 12 or 15 feet, surmounted by a vertical stone superstructure; the vertical offsets worked out of limestone blocks of many shapes and sizes with the jointing alternated from one course to the next and the cutting of the offsets finished on the wall: all this seems to reflect a native north-west Anatolian style of work which goes back many centuries on Hisarlik, and is later found at the nearby Phrygian site of Gordion.

Of these great walls enough survives today on the south side to gain an impression – particularly at the projecting tower on the south-east, so finely jointed though no mortar is used, and above all at the eastern bastion, 60 feet wide and still standing nearly 30 feet high, once perhaps a watchtower which dominated the plain of the Simois and the eastern approach along the plateau. From this bastion a 200-yard stretch of wall ran along the northern crest of the hill, a 'splendid wall of large hewn limestone blocks', as Schliemann put it; already badly damaged by classical builders this was demolished by Schliemann between 1871 and 1873. Just how massively this was constructed was discovered by Carl Blegen when he examined the north-western corner in the 1930s. Here the wall took a sharp turn round the hill, descending 8 yards in a mere 15, and here Blegen found stepped foundations, which had been sunk no less than 23 feet below the Troy VI ground-level to provide support for a bastion which must have been well over 60 feet high: the visitor can still see the bottom courses of this structure which must have been dug out by the builders of Ilium Novum.

Such were the walls of Troy, which were certainly 'well built', 'finely towered' and 'lofty-gated' as later Greek tradition had it. Only on the western side was a small segment of the older circuit still not replaced. This archaic wall, which can still be seen today, was only half as thick as the new wall and far less strongly constructed, made of smaller, rougher stones and not as deeply founded. Here the city's defences were weakest and easiest to attack.

Inside Troy all the roads seem to have led up to the western summit of the little hill, where we may assume the palace stood. On the terraces below the palace were about twenty-five large houses or mansions in which the immediate retainers and kinsmen of the royal family must have lived, with perhaps separate houses for kings' brothers and sons. The biggest were quite impressive large two-storeyed buildings nearly 30 yards long, resembling the megara at Tiryns and Mycenae though entered by side-doors. One of them, the so-called Pillar House near the south gate, was 28 yards long and 13 wide with a main hall and kitchen area, its roof supported by large central columns of stone, one of which survives today; presumably the upper storey was wood-framed with mudbrick and plaster, with windows, or possibly a clerestory roof (a style of architecture still to be seen in north-west Anatolia). Interestingly enough, Blegen thought that this building was converted into an arsenal or a barracks in the last phase of Troy VI, for a hoard of slingshots was found inside, along with evidence that large quantities of food had been consumed there; and, as we have seen, in the street to the west, Blegen also found – 'inexplicably' – a human skull.

What of the palace itself? The conventional view since Dörpfeld has been that no trace survived of the top of Hisarlik, sheared off when the civic centre of Roman Ilium was built. But modern research has shown that the left summit of the hill was still partly preserved when Schliemann began his dig in 1870, for there he came upon the footings of the archaic temple visited by Alexander the Great with parts of Troy VI buildings close to it. Conceivably, then, the Greek colonists who founded Ilion in c.730 BC built their temple over the ruins of 'Priam's palace'. Furthermore, 10 yards or so to the south-east, almost in the centre of Hisarlik at a height of 120 feet, in investigating an 'island' left by Schliemann and Dörpfeld, Carl Blegen found a shabby 5-yard stretch of wall with another running parallel to it: these lay directly under the footings of a Roman colonnade of shops. This fragment of late Troy VI stood immediately to the west of where we would expect the palace entrance to have been, at the top of the road which curves up from the south gate. Tiny remnant as it is, this may be our only surviving fragment of the palace of Bronze-Age Troy.

Of the appearance of the palace we know nothing, but it must have resembled the characteristic megara of Troy VI (a style going right back to the great buildings of Troy II – there is remarkable architectural continuity on Hisarlik). Like Pylos it must have been surrounded by storerooms and domestic accommodation. There, presumably, like all Late-Bronze-Age rulers, the king of Troy had magazines and workshops, stores of hundreds of jars for oil, grain, figs, wine. Perhaps, as at Pylos, there was a chariot workshop with craftsmen and stores of axles, bodies and wheels; there must also have been a smithy where bronze weapons were made, in styles influenced by both Aegean and Hittite forms. Potters there must have been in numbers, making the masses of local wares and local imitations of Greek pots; presumably their kilns lay outside the citadel. As befitted a textile town there were workshops inside the walls, where thousands of spindle whorls were found by all three diggers of Hisarlik; it is not unreasonable to imagine a royal store of cloth and wool with made-up cloaks like those at Pylos: ordinary ones, 'cloaks for followers', royal garments and 'cloaks suitable for guest gifts'. If we wish to push our speculations a little further, on analogy with the Hittite and Linear B tablets we might assume that the king of Troy employed a goldsmith in addition to his bronze-smiths. He may have had a craftsman to make the fine sword pommels of alabaster or white marble which were evidently prized in Late-Bronze-Age Troy. He must have had dyers to colour his linen and wool: this job, like the spinning and weaving, and the grinding of grain, would have been done by women. In addition to his potters he must have had a fuller, a cutler, unguent boilers, bakers, huntsmen, woodcutters, priests to tend his shrine, a soothsayer – even perhaps a physician (such as the *i-ja-te* in Linear B). Like the kings of Mycenae he may have had a singer of tales who could tell of the deeds of his ancestors; he will certainly have had royal messengers and heralds, and may even have employed a scribe who could write in Hittite on tablets of clay or wood. All these ideas are plausible, but we simply cannot prove them. Looking at the surviving houses we may guess that the total population of Troy VI can hardly have exceeded 1000 within the walls; how many more lived in the lower town and plain we do not know, but 5000 would seem roughly right. However, archaeology could suggest that a still wider area shared the culture of Troy VI – including, for instance, settlements on Gallipoli; Thermi on Lesbos clearly also had links. So we may yet find that Troy VI was a greater power in the north-east Aegean than has been supposed. On his own, however, the king of Troy could hardly have raised an armed force of more than a few hundred heavily armed warriors. If he could call upon his Arzawan neighbours for help in a crisis – or even the Great King of Hatti himself – we do not know it. So much of the history of Hisarlik remains a mystery, though it is exciting to think how much new discoveries could change this situation: especially if (as must surely happen) an archive is discovered of one of Troy's western Asiatic neighbours.

Troy–Hisarlik, then, was an Anatolian culture in contact with the Aegean world. Troy VI and Troy VIIa were just two of the settlements which were destroyed in Anatolia and the Aegean at the end of the Bronze Age. If we wish to link their destructions to the later Greek traditions about 'Troy', we should not forget that they also have a context in the wider historiographical problems posed by the destruction of cities in Mediterranean lands in the Late Bronze Age. In one sense there were many Troys and many Trojan wars, and it is to that broader picture that I shall turn in my final chapter.

EIGHT

THE END OF THE BRONZE AGE

After diligent inquiry I can discern four principal causes of the ruin of the Roman Empire, which continued to operate in a period of more than a thousand years. I. The injuries of time and nature. II. The hostile attacks of the barbarians … III. The use and abuse of the materials [i.e. raw materials, commodities and their markets]. And IV. The domestic quarrels of the Romans.

GIBBON, *Decline and Fall of the Roman Empire, VI,*
Chapter LXXI (AD 1787)

*In the later years of dynasties, famines and pestilences become numerous. As far as famines are concerned, the reason is that most people at that time refrained from cultivating the soil. For, in the later years of dynasties there occur attacks on property and tax revenue, and through customs duties, on trading. Or, trouble occurs as the result of the unrest of subjects and the great number encouraged by the senility of the dynasty to rebel. Little grain is stored. The grain and harvest situation is not always stable from year to year. The amount of rainfall in the world differs by nature. The rainfall may be too little or too much. Grains and fruits vary correspondingly. Still for their food requirement people put their trust in what it is possible to store. If nothing is stored they must expect famines. The price of grain rises. Indigent people are unable to buy any and perish. If for some years nothing is stored, hunger will be general. The large number of pestilences [which follow] are caused by these famines; or by the many disturbances which result from the disintegration of the dynasty. There is much unrest and bloodshed, and plagues occur …
as there is now overpopulation.*

IBN KHALDUN, *An Introduction to History,* III, 49 (AD 1377)

The sufferings which revolution entailed upon the cities were many and terrible, such as have occurred and always will occur, as long as the nature of mankind remains the same; though in a severer or milder form, and varying in their symptoms, according to the variety of the particular cases. In peace and prosperity states and individuals have better sentiments because they do not find themselves suddenly confronted with imperious necessities; but war takes away the easy supply of daily wants and so proves a rough master, that brings most men's characters to a level with their fortunes.

THUCYDIDES, *History of the Peloponnesian War*, III, 82 (*c.*400 BC)

WHY DO CIVILISATIONS DECLINE? What happens when they do? These questions have always been at the centre of historical research as my quotations above show. In our attempts to isolate the causes of the collapse of the Greek world at the end of the Bronze Age we have found in different areas different explanations being put forward: earthquake, disease, famine, climate, war, drought, de-population, plague, attack from outside: in many places the archaeology has suggested a complex interrelation of such factors rather than any one cause. This is in keeping with the way we have been encouraged to look at the past by modern historians like Braudel: 'in historical analysis … the long run always wins in the end … annihilating innumerable events − all those which cannot be accommodated in the main ongoing current.' This view would have been largely accepted by the great historians quoted above, even if they would have been reluctant to relegate events to the 'ephemera of history' and to see individuals as 'imprisoned' in a destiny in which they have little hand, as Braudel would have it. But Polybius and Thucydides would have agreed on this modern emphasis on the interrelation of climate, geography, weather and patterns of cultivation on to which civilisations are grafted. Thucydides' remarkable 'anthropological' account of prehistoric Greece (p. 32) shows how economic factors could have determined the rise and fall of Minoan and Mycenaean civilisation. The *World History* of the great medieval Arab scholar Ibn Khaldun gives full play to the relation of political decline to disease, overpopulation, climate, rainfall and crop failure. In the past, however, there was no means of scientifically quantifying such factors. It is in the last few decades that archaeological techniques have been developed which are enabling modern historians actually to measure factors such as the depopulation of Messenia, and to estimate, say, the population of the Argolid against land use and crop yield. Much work remains to be done, and undoubtedly there will be important new discoveries in the future, but the effect of this geographical approach is to emphasise the role of the long term against that of the individual event, to diminish the role of the Hectors and Agamemnons of the Bronze-Age world, and to look instead at the roles of people like the women flax workers at Pylos, the silent masses who supported such societies. This will be the line taken by the next 100 years of Aegean scholarship. In this view the Trojan War – even if it occurred – is of little significance, being merely one of hundreds of Troys, that is one of hundreds of cities in the Late-Bronze-Age world whose fates as a whole need to be understood before we can make general deductions about this important phase of human history. It could even be argued that we need to understand all these other places and their fates before we can fully understand the site of Troy itself. Indeed, should the destruction of the city of Troy *only* be approached in this way, and the tale of Troy ignored? Such ideas have now come into play in recent work on the decline of the Aegean Bronze Age. Are the destruction of cities, the incursions of invaders like the Sea Peoples, only symptoms rather than causes? Was the economy of this world already in decline before the 'glorious' period of thirteenth-century Mycenae began? Archaeology can rarely give us unequivocal answers to such questions, and historians are tempted to look at other civilisations as models. In this case a most interesting model was put forward not long ago by American archaeologists working on the mysterious decline of the Mayan civilisation in Central America, for which there seemed no external explanation at all. The conclusion they arrived at was that early societies of any kind of complexity of organisation often decline because the systems they have created to make their social structures work simply fail in the end to cope with the variety of natural factors which determine their means of production. As Khaldun noted, this can be triggered off by many things – a succession of bad harvests, drought, plague, rapacious rulers: in the face of such factors the very basic structures of society are too fragile to cope and they break down, their resistance gone like a living organism which has lost its immunity.

SYSTEMS COLLAPSE

The American archaeologists listed the factors they thought pertinent to the decline of the Maya, which can be convincingly applied also to the fall of Mycenaean Greece (and, incidentally, to the end of the Roman Empire in Dark-Age Britain too). The signs are as follows (the reader will immediately note that these are what we would call symptoms rather than causes):

1. The central political organisation collapses or breaks up; its central places ('capitals') decline; public building and work ends; military organisation fragments; palaces and magazines are abandoned; temples and cult places are eclipsed and only survive as local shrines; literacy is lost. This has obvious application to Mycenae over the thirteenth to the twelfth centuries BC.

2. The traditional ruling élite, the upper class, disintegrates; kings, as in Greece, vanish and the important local men, in this case the *korete* ('mayor') and *basileus* ('headman') take their place; their rich burials cease; their residences are often reused either by squatters or by cottage industries; the supply of luxury goods they bought or made dries up. This is not only applicable to a number of Mycenaean centres, but strikingly fits the transition between Troy VI and Troy VIIa, as against the hypothetical interpretation put forward on (p. 123).

3. The centralised economy collapses. Just how centralised this was in Greece can be seen in the Knossos and Pylos tablets (p. 132). Now there is no more large-scale trade, exchange or

estate management; crafts and specialised industries vanish; specialised and organised agriculture ends; people fall back to local homesteads, small-scale cultivation and a barter economy.

4. There is widespread abandonment of settlements and ensuing depopulation. Towns and cities are frequently left to be taken over by the lower classes; there is often a flight to the hills, to isolated defensible spots – like Karfi in Crete, for example, or Bunarbashi near Troy.

5. Particularly interesting with regard to Homer's story are the cultural tendencies evident in the aftermath of such a collapse. In the 'Dark Age' which follows, a romantic myth develops concerning the 'heroic world' which has vanished. The new power groups which emerge – for whom in Greece the *basileus* is now the 'king' – legitimise themselves by constructing genealogies linking them to the states of the 'Heroic Age'. Thus Ionian princelings of Homer's day, like Hector of Kyme and Agamemnon of Chios, took the names of, and claimed descent from, the heroes, just as in Dark-Age Britain, Celtic kings made up genealogies with Roman names, and Anglo-Saxon new-comers fabricated regal lists linking themselves to the mythical kings of their continental Germanic past, even incorporating Roman names too. Early chroniclers and poets then tend to tell of the collapse of the old world in terms of a heroic struggle with outside invaders – whether it is the Dorians in Greece or the Saxons in Britain – and the tale is personalised in terms of deeds, heroes and battles. In the end, as much in *Beowulf* as in Homer, a confusion develops between the Golden Heroic Age of the past and the new Heroic Age. The function of the bard, if anything, is to equate the two.

To this account we should perhaps add a final note which connects with some of our earlier thoughts about the nature of archaeology as a science. The reverberations of the 'Dark-Age' and 'Heroic-Age' myths can be traced down to modern historians, who accept as evidence these romantic traditional narratives which were orally transmitted and only set down in writing centuries after the collapse. As we have seen, the slow development of scientific archaeology has tended to be shaped by the acceptance of the myth in a way that the writing of history has not. It has, for example, focused on the larger and more obvious sites of the vanished states, like Mycenae, Tiryns or Troy, at the expense of the hundreds of 'insignificant' sites not mentioned in the myth but where the real life of the people persisted. This can be paralleled in Britain with claims for the historicity of the Arthurian tale and the digs at Tintagel, Glastonbury and 'Cadbury–Camelot'. Like the Arthurian legend, the tale of Troy is a Golden-Age myth, made all the more potent because of an assumed kernel of historical truth.

THE TROJAN WAR: AN ATTEMPTED SYNTHESIS

So when I think of the individual, I am always inclined to see him imprisoned within a destiny in which he himself has little hand, fixed in a landscape in which the infinite perspectives of the long term stretch into the distance both behind him and before.... As I see it, rightly or wrongly, the long term always wins in the end.

FERNAND BRAUDEL, *The Mediterranean*, p. 1244 (1973)

Such conclusions about the importance of the individual in history will not appeal to those interested in great events and battles, to those who wish to believe in a real Agamemnon or Hector, a real Trojan War. In fact in this 'structuralist' view it would be pointless to write a work of history on a 'historical' Trojan War, a contradiction in terms; even if we could prove beyond all doubt that it were a real event, it would still be of minor importance compared with the long-term deep structures touched on in this chapter. As it is, with ambiguous evidence at our disposal, it is easy to agree with the strictures of Sir Moses Finley, who has not only denied that the war ever happened, but insists, in *The World of Odysseus*, that 'Homer's Trojan War ... must be evicted from the *history* of the Greek Bronze Age'. And it is true that, like it or not, the Trojan War has long since transcended the strict analysis of the Bronze-Age historian: so much so that the work of Schliemann, Dörpfeld and Blegen, who dug Hisarlik, and of the hundreds of commentators, though to a lesser or greater degree scientific in method, is in one sense as much an illumination of the *myth* as are the works of Berlioz, Virgil or Aeschylus mentioned in Chapter 1. The myth in each case conditioned the interpretation of the evidence. The reason is that for most people Lord Byron's remark is true: 'We do care about the authenticity of the tale of Troy ... I venerate the grand original as the *truth of history ... and of place*; otherwise it would have given me no delight.' Faced with this paradox, the strict historian has to agree with Schliemann's friend Charles Newton who said, in reviewing Schliemann's *Mycenae* in the *Edinburgh Review* in 1878:

How much of the story is really to be accepted as fact, and by what test we may discriminate between that which is merely plausible fiction and that residuum of true history which can be detected under a mythic disguise ... are problems as yet unsolved, notwithstanding the immense amount of erudition and subtle criticism which has been spent on them.

But it would be unfair to end on such a note in a book of this kind. As I hope we have found in this search, there is an immense amount of circumstantial evidence which suggests that a kernel of the tale of Troy goes back to a real event in the Bronze Age; how much we cannot yet be sure, but it cannot do any harm to end with a plausible reconstruction of what might be reasonably adduced from that mass of evidence: a piece of political journalism, if you like, which can be taken with a pinch – or stirrup jar – of salt, according to taste. Here, then, is my version of the presumed 'historical' Trojan War and its background.

The fourteenth and thirteenth centuries BC were the heyday of Mycenaean civilisation. The chief power was at Mycenae: there the dynasty extended its influence over the whole Peloponnese by military conquest or by dynastic alliance of a kind common in the Bronze-Age Near East. This extension may be reflected in the archaeological record by the rebuilding of Pylos (*c*.1300 BC) and of the Menelaion (*c*.1300–1250) and by the first destruction of Thebes, the great rival in central Greece (*c*.1300?). Archaeology also shows us that the palaces at Mycenae, Pylos, Tiryns and the Menelaion shared the same material culture, the same artistic traditions, and the same bureaucracy down to the smallest detail. Tiryns, like Pylos, had some sort of archive and thus may have been independent of Mycenae, but it is more likely that it recognised the overlordship of Mycenae and was its port. Orchomenos, the enemy of Thebes, may also have been part of this world, employing the same artists and architects. Knossos, too, seems to have been occupied at this time by a Greek dynasty that had intimate relations with Mycenae and the mainland, importing stone from the same Spartan quarries, using the same art and sculpture, and a bureaucracy identical in every detail. This was one world, then: its city states may have had independent traditions, their own kings, but at certain times they acknowledged a 'Great King' in the same way as other kingships in the Near East. The overwhelming balance of evidence suggests that the Greeks, the Achaiwoi of Homer, were the people known to the Hittites as the people of Ahhiyawa throughout the fourteenth and thirteenth centuries BC, and that in the thirteenth century they were at times acknowledged as 'Great Kings' by the Hittite Foreign Office, in the same way as the kings of Egypt, Babylon and, later, Assyria. I assume that at this time the seat of the king of Ahhiyawa was at Mycenae, and that he was a member of the dynasty remembered by Greek tradition as the Atreids. At this time the Greeks extended their influence throughout the islands of the Aegean; their trade routes led west to Sicily and eastwards via Cyprus to Syria; they controlled settlements on the coast of Asia Minor at places like Iasos and Miletus, whose regions were acknowledged by the Hittites as Greek territory with agreed frontiers. To a limited extent the Greeks were involved in the diplomacy of the time, exchanging gifts and ambassadors with the Hittites, sending cult idols to the Hittite court, and entertaining Hittite royal kinsmen. That they were known to the Egyptians and had direct ambassadorial contacts is shown by the inscription recording an Egyptian visit to Mycenae and Crete in around 1380.

For the mainland palaces, the period between 1300 and *c*.1250 BC was the greatest period of Mycenaean building; it was a period either of great confidence or of great defensiveness. At this time tremendous fortifications were completed at Gla, Tiryns, Mycenae, Athens, and at scores of lesser sites like Eutresis, Araxos, Krisa and Tigani. That the most superb monuments of the civilisation should come so soon before its observable decline is not unusual, as Ibn Khaldun noted:

At the end of a dynasty there often appears some show of power that gives the impression that the senility of the dynasty has been made to disappear. It lights up brilliantly just before it is extinguished, like a burning wick the flame of which leaps up brilliantly a moment before it goes out, giving the impression it is just starting to burn, when in fact it is going out.

Here we are entitled to take into account the traditions enshrined in Greek legends which are known to have a basis in the Bronze Age. It was the uniform belief that palaces like Mycenae were places of blood, ruled by violent men, prey to internecine struggle, and constantly engaged in warfare. The archaeology of palaces like Mycenae and the details in the Linear B tablets confirm that this was indeed a militarist and aggressive world. Theirs was at base a subsistence economy. A large subordinate population, probably including many slaves, was tied to the land, producing the food for their masters and enough surplus oil, pottery, grain, textiles and flax for export. Similarly in the tablets the emphasis on war gear should be noted. At Knossos and Pylos there are massive quantities of very expensive materials which, in the case of the copper, tin and gold, could only be obtained through war or trade. In other words, both the labour force and the means of coercion could only be sustained by trade or violence: a truly vicious circle, and no doubt kings like

Agamemnon were cruel and ruthless, as kings had to be in this kind of culture. It is a case of self-defence as much as anything else, for only by violence could the ruling élite preserve themselves. As Ibn Khaldun put it:

Any royal authority must be built upon two foundations. The first is might and group feeling, which finds its expression in soldiers. The second is money, which supports the soldiers and provides the whole structure needed by royal authority. Disintegration befalls the dynasty at these two foundations.

Kings like Agamemnon, then, needed to reward and equip their war host with loot – treasure, raw materials, precious metals, cattle and women. This is true of all so-called heroic societies. In Homer, as we have seen, the greatest praise is to be called a 'sacker of cities'. This is the reality of Bronze-Age power; it has to do with the very structure and ideals of the society. This is entirely borne out by the Linear B tablets from Pylos. The presence there of slaves from Lemnos, Chios, 'Asia', Miletus, Halicarnassos and Cnidus, working in highly organised 'state industries', shows us that the world of Agamemnon was one which constantly needed to seize slaves in war, or buy them from its slave ports. It was a society where surplus expenditure at the top – treasure, royal cult, royal graves, war gear – was so enormous that a great pyramid of labour was needed to sustain it, labour which had to be constantly replenished – even though the women slaves bred children – for the life expectancy of such people must have been very low. Nothing drives this point home more clearly than the contrast in the Pylos tablets between the lengthy descriptions of the stocks of ornate furniture in the palace stores at Pylos, and the curt lists of foreign slaves and their rations. Imagine the expenditure and craftsmanship lavished on this: 'one chair of spring type, inlaid with [blue glass paste] kyanos and silver and gold on the back, which is inlaid with men's figures in gold, and with a pair of gold finials, and with golden griffins and griffins of kyanos' – this is merely one item in scores listed on surviving tablets (as we would expect, the same loving attention to detail is evidenced in the descriptions of war gear, for example in chariot bodies 'inlaid in ivory, painted crimson, equipped with bridles with leather cheek straps and horn bits').

By contrast, look at the 'twenty-one Cnidian women, twelve girls, ten boys.... At Eudeiwelos: eight women, two girls and three boys; [rations] 336 litres of wheat, 336 litres of figs....' Experts have guessed that each of these people received a ration of 24 litres per month, a little less than the classical soldier's ration; supplemented by figs, the wheat could be decreased: the Roman agronomist Cato recommends a reduction in the ration of bread for slaves 'when they start eating figs'. Such was the world of Agamemnon.

With that background, the peculiar conditions of the thirteenth century now need to be taken into account. Mycenaean society was already under stress. Soon after 1300 the Mediterranean had started to witness the widespread raiding and instability which would later engulf it. There may have been economic problems, overpopulation, crop failures, drought and famine – these are questions the experts have yet to resolve; similarly we cannot yet answer the question of climate change. Was there perhaps also a cessation or diminution of Mycenaean trade with the Near East later in the century? All these factors may have played a part. We should not rule out the possibility of internecine feuds within kin groups of dynasties, and fighting between rival city states, as in the legend of the Argive sack of Thebes in the generation before the Trojan War. Events on the coast of Asia Minor may also have played their part: at just this time the Hittites seem to have taken Miletus, one of the greatest towns in the Aegean, and it may be that Greek interests were squeezed out of south-western Anatolia, forcing them to look further northwards for their slaves and raw materials – towards Troy.

Hypotheses these may be, but a combination of some or all of these factors *must* be true; we have to account somehow for the changing economic fortunes of the Peloponnese, and we have to assume that Agamemnon and his fellow kings and élites did what they could to remedy the situation. Their rule needed booty, slaves and treasure, and frequent predatory forays must have been the way they sustained themselves: in fact such hostings could have gone out yearly. Most likely these forays were to the north and east, especially on the coast of Asia Minor where the Hittite tablets show that the Greeks were increasingly active in the early decades of the thirteenth century. Seen in this light, an attack on the citadel which controlled the Dardanelles seems so obvious that if we had no tale of Troy we would have had to postulate it. Undue worry about the motives for such an attack is unnecessary – this kind of warfare is, as I have said, in the very nature of Mycenaean society and kingship.

Here we can attempt to bring in the evidence of the Hittite tablets, if only speculatively. As we have seen, the kings of Ahiyawa mentioned, but not named, in the Hittite texts may be those remembered in Greek tradition as the dynasty of Atreus and Agamemnon. But in Anatolia we are on sounder historical footing. We are in the days of the Hittite kings Muwatallis (1296–1272), Urhi Teshub (1272–1265) or Muwatallis' brother Hattusilis (1265–1235). Of the dynasty in Wilusa/Troy we also know something. The Wilusan king in Muwatallis' day (and perhaps considerably later) was Alaksandus, who is surely the model for Homer's Alexandros–Paris (Anatolian Pariya). His is the likely time in which the war took place, and the Hittite archive provides a broad context for the war in its portrayal of the increasing influence of Mycenaean kings in western Anatolia.

The Greeks had been growing in strength and influence over the previous two generations. Miletus had been sacked by the Hittites in c.1320, but by Hattusilis' day (1260s) Miletus was acknowledged as Ahhiyawan territory with an agreed border delineated by treaty. Greek influence over its ruling family is taken as real by the Hittites, who were aware of the presence there of a brother of the Greek king. But both Muwatallis and Hattusilis needed to keep the west pacified at a time when they were obliged to fight wars on several fronts. They had the growing might of Assyria to contend with in what is now northern Iraq, pressing westwards towards the rich trading cities of the upper Euphrates and Syria; they also had the Egyptians continuing to push northwards in Syria. In 1275 Muwatallis fought a drawn battle at Kadesh against Ramses II with troops of eighteen subject peoples, client states and allies. Evidently these included armed élites from some of the Arzawan states because Dardani (Wilusans) were present, presumably under King Alaksandus. Wilusa then was still intact in 1275.

Move on ten years though: in 1262/1, Hittite territory right up to the gates of Carchemish fell to the Assyrians, a major disaster to Hattusilis. At that very moment he was threatened to the south by Ramses, and struggling in the west with the Ahhiyawan king and his ally the renegade Arzawan Pijamaradus, who was sowing discord and dissension on the Aegean seaboard. The network of client states built up by Hittite diplomacy over two centuries was now under threat. It may have been during this period that the Trojan War was fought. It was an uneasy time when, as the Hittite tablets show, in western Anatolia kings were deposed, pretenders set up, and lands ravaged, with political exiles seeking refuge 'overseas' in Ahhiyawa, in Miletus, or further afield (the exiled former 'Great King of Hatti' himself, Urhi Teshub, indeed was still plotting away in the Egyptian court).

To a Bronze Age political analyst, it must have looked as if the 'domino theory' was working itself out in western Anatolia. And always in the background was the shadowy presence of the king of Ahhiyawa, with whom the Hittites now, for the first time, felt the need to be conciliatory. The evidence of the Hittite archives clearly shows us the predatory nature of the Achaian presence in western Anatolia, just as the later legend said; let us then accept what the archives are telling us.

The war, therefore, could have taken place between 1274 and 1263 BC, between Kadesh and Hattusilis' campaign down the Maeander valley to subdue the renegade Pijamaradus. Then, after Hattusilis has chased all the way to the Aegean at Miletus, and made his conciliatory noises to the king of Ahhiyawa, he speaks revealingly of the troubles of the past few years. In particular he is almost apologetic about an earlier quarrel with the Ahhiyawan king, and of 'the war with Wilusa over which we have now made peace': So the war was either right at the start of his reign (*c.* 1265) or else during his time as general of the ageing Muwatallis (1275–72; he was out of favour with his brother Urhi Teshub).

Let us speculate a little further. The conflict had arisen on several fronts. The Greek king had been aiding a faction in the Arzawan royal family who were hostile to Hatti. He was in league with the nabobs of Miletus on the shores of Asia Minor, who acknowledged his overlordship and provided him with raw materials and slaves. He had also been instrumental in other west Anatolian kings renouncing the overlordship of Hatti; the ruler of the Seha River land, for one, had 'relied on the king of Ahhiyawa,' and provoked a confrontation with Hattusilis. Into these events the king of Troy/Wilusa was sucked. Though in the north-eastern extremity of the Aegean world, his ancient citadel was well-known to the Greeks; it may have sheltered a colony of Mycenaean merchants; the kings may have exchanged embassies. Troy was the strongest fortress in the northern Aegean. It had a dominant position at the intersection of ancient trade routes by land and sea. It was an ancient dynastic seat with royal treasure accumulated over generations. A great prize for the sackers of cities.

Perhaps there was some pretext, some diplomatic incident, which triggered it off (Homer says the seizure of a royal woman); but it was a pretext sufficient to enable Hattusilis and the Greek king subsequently to patch things up. Exactly who sided with whom we do not yet know, but the Greek Great King launched a seaborne expedition to the Troad, doubtless with his allies and confederates. But here is the crucial factor: in attacking Wilusa, the Greeks would inevitably draw in the Hittite king or his generals. For just as the Wilusans were bound to provide troops for the Great King of Hatti for his expeditionary campaigns (as they did at Kadesh in 1275), their treaty with Muwatallis required the Great King of Hatti in his turn to help them if they were attacked; this was the duty of an overlord. Perhaps indeed

Homer preserves a dim memory of this in the Trojan Catalogue which lists the considerable force of west Anatolian allies who came to help Priam and Paris – Alexandros in their hour of need.

A Mycenaean expedition to the north-east Aegean would not have been difficult to mount. They had the resources in terms of ships, even if Homer's catalogue has magnified the numbers. The Thera frescoes show us what may be a Mycenaean overseas expedition to the Libyan coast, with long-oared and sailed vessels containing heavily armed warriors with boar's-tusk helmets, long spears and oblong tower shields. The manner in which such forces were raised is shown in the Pylos tablets, where their equipment is enumerated in every detail. For an overseas expedition it would have been an élite force: the main kings with their retinues and the armed followings of their chief barons, at most a few hundred from each kingdom. Troy was obviously not the only, or even the main, objective. The tradition in Homer in fact asserts that Troy was one incident in a series of forays into Teuthrania and Mysia, with attacks on Lemnos, Lesbos, Pedassos, Lyrnessos and other places, in all of which cities were sacked, cattle and women seized. The archaeological evidence for the destruction at just this time of Thermi on Lesbos, one of the biggest towns in the Aegean, fits very well with the Homeric tale of Achilles' sack of Lesbos.

The Trojan story, then, takes in a long period of Mycenaean aggression in the coasts and islands of north-west Anatolia. Troy was not the only place sacked, but it was the best known to the Greeks, the best built and the most difficult to defeat. It is even possible that, as Lechevalier suspected, and as the Hittite texts might suggest, the whole expedition was a failure, its events magnified back home by the bards of threatened dynasties as their world grew increasingly shaky. But the city was surely destroyed. A plausible version of the story would be that, as at Phylakopi and Knossos, the Greeks descended on golden Troy after it had been damaged by a natural catastrophe, the severe earthquake which Blegen believed struck Troy VIh. But as we have seen, there is no compelling evidence for the earthquake, and the legend may after all be correct in asserting that Troy was deliberately demolished after a bitter siege. The place was plundered, and its women carried back to work on the estates around Mycenae and Pylos; it is even possible that along with the captive Lemnian and Asian women we have one of these people named on a Pylos tablet written down a generation or so later: 'a servant of the god, *To-ro-ja*' ('Trojan woman'?).

What about the details? Did Agamemnon really exist? Possibly: we know from Germanic and Celtic epic poetry that the names and pedigrees of the ancient kings are often preserved in some form; thus the Mercian overlord Offa could cite his ancestors back to kings who ruled before the English ever came to Britain. There is nothing intrinsically unlikely in the idea that the names of the last great kings of Mycenae, Atreus and Agamemnon, were handed down by the bards.

Did Helen really exist, and was her seizure the cause of the war? There is a parallel for the abduction of a royal woman being used as a pretext for war in the Norman invasion of Ireland in the twelfth century AD; on the other hand the attack on a castle or town to recover a captured princess is an ancient theme in epic, a stock story for bards whether they be in medieval Ireland, early India, or even thirteenth-century-BC Ugarit, so we would be unwise to insist on it. Nevertheless our evidence has shown that the seizure of women on overseas raids was indeed a common feature of this world, and the more beautiful the better. Of Helen we can at least conclude that she is possible!

We might also add a word about the other famous woman in the tale of Troy: young Iphigenia (or Iphianassa in Homer), whose sacrifice at Aulis was the prelude to the expedition and which has been the theme of so much later art, literature and music. There is no reason to think that she really existed, but one of the most remarkable of recent finds in archaeology has revealed evidence of human sacrifice, and even ritual cannibalism, in the Bronze Age. The discovery at Knossos of the remains of two children aged eight and eleven (the age of Iphigenia in the tale), who seem to have been ritually killed and partially eaten prior to the catastrophe which overtook the palace and its suburbs in around 1420 BC, gives some substance to the idea that child sacrifice could have taken place elsewhere in the Late-Bronze-Age Aegean at moments of crisis. That sacrifices also preceded the fall of Pylos could be suggested by one of the last of the Linear B tablets from the palace, but this is by no means certain (see p. 234). Nevertheless, the Knossos find invites a new look at famous tales such as the cannibalism of the children of Thyestes (Agamemnon's uncle) and the sacrifice of Iphigenia herself.

As for the Trojan heroes, it is an interesting fact that of the names in the Linear B tablets which are found in Homer, twenty of them (one-third) are applied to Trojans: in other words, Greek names have been invented for Trojan heroes, Hector among them. But two names may not fit with this, and they are significant ones: Priam's name looks like the Anatolian name Pariamu, found in Hittite texts, and Alexandros of Wilios does seem to have a connection with the Alaksandus of Wilusa named in Hittite tablets of the early thirteenth century and his alternative name Paris is very likely the Anatolian Pariya. More than that we cannot say. Evidently Greek tradition in the Dark Ages had only the dimmest notion of Asia Minor in the Heroic Age.

And what of the wooden horse? It has been explained as a simple fairy-tale motif, and as we have seen it has been rationalised as a wooden ram in a horse-shaped housing in which men could be contained. Recently, however, an intriguing explanation has been offered which is at least worth discussing, if only to be rejected. In this version, the tale of the horse has been connected with the god Poseidon, who we know existed in the Mycenaean pantheon. In Arcadia Poseidon was always worshipped in the shape of a horse, in other parts as a horseman or master of horses. For country folk he was Hippos, the horse. But Poseidon, even in historical times, was also regarded as the only originator of *earthquakes*. Here let us remember the alleged destruction of Troy VI by earthquake, and how in the tale Laomedon cheated Poseidon and was punished by the demolition of his beautiful walls. Did a later bard invent the thrilling device of the wooden horse with the Poseidon connection in the back of his mind, transferring the older traditions to an earlier sacking by Herakles? To me such an explanation seems over-ingenious and frankly implausible, but if the Greeks did indeed sack Troy only after it had been shattered by an earthquake, can we still perhaps retain the connection of a cult idol of Poseidon, the god of earthquakes, in the shape of a wooden horse – left by the Greeks as a thank-offering? On the whole, it is best to admit that there is something unfathomably mysterious about the wooden horse story; it was evidently in existence long before Homer's day, as we know from artistic representations, but more than that we cannot say.

Our search is nearly over. The sack of Troy was remembered because it was the last fling of the Mycenaean world; no other king of Mycenae would claim 'Great Kingship'. As in medieval Ireland the best bards sang the latest stories, and Troy was the latest. A generation or so later the cracks appear in their world. The fate of all cities was not necessarily the same; Mycenae and Tiryns were damaged by earthquakes; Pylos may have been sacked by local rebels; Messenia suffered large-scale depopulation, as possibly did Lakonia; the Argolid experienced a new influx; there were migrations overseas; no great single collapse, but progressive decline, disintegration, weakening of powerful authorities meaning less and less rebuilding (though in some places, such as Tiryns, the reverse would be true). Many centres were abandoned for good, and around them there was a steady influx of Greek-speaking peasantry from outlying areas, settling in abandoned countrysides like impoverished immigrants from the Third World, a kind of gold-rush remembered by tradition as the arrival of a new people, the 'Dorians'. In some places a recognisably Mycenaean life lasted through the twelfth century; Mycenae was abandoned around 1100 BC. The peasantry and local leaders still lived on, but a complex series of events had led to the failure of the developed palace civilisation of the Late Bronze Age. So specialised was the literacy devised to run this system that the knowledge of writing vanished with the end of the palaces and the death or dispersal of their tiny literate élite; their society no longer had any need of the written word.

In summing up these factors let us not forget the legends, at least as models for what *might have happened*. They tell us of constant rivalries within the royal clans of the Heroic Age – Atreus and Thyestes, Agamemnon and Aigisthos, and so on – and we can certainly say that such feuds are characteristic of this kind of society at all times. The legends of the Epigoni and Herakles also may preserve traditions of wars between the city states of the Mycenaean world and the feuding clans of the great royal families. Historians and anthropologists of the Dark-Age west can point to exactly similar feuds in the royal clans of Carolingian, Merovingian, Ottonian and Anglo-Saxon society: one of the chief functions of royalty there was to resolve the internal strife which in such societies is the norm. Bronze-Age Greek kingship cannot have been any different. The epic told of how on his return from Troy the 'Great King' Agamemnon was murdered by a rival kinsman, and other kings faced deposition or rebellion; these legends go back to the end of the Bronze Age, and, though we cannot prove them, they are plausible: studies of kingship in the Near East offer many parallels and suggest that the large kin groups of Bronze-Age royal clans must have continually brought up rival claimants. Where the royal person is so important, much rested on his security; if he fell, internal dissension could follow – 'political' power advanced and receded swiftly. Thucydides' account, then, seems basically acceptable: the long duration of the war against Troy and 'the late return of the Hellenes from Ilium caused many revolutions, and factions ensued almost everywhere … and it was the citizens thus driven into exile who founded the cities [overseas]': Thucydides dates the overrunning of the Peloponnese by the 'Dorians' eighty years after the fall of Troy; only after that, he says, did the main migrations take place to Ionia, the islands, Italy and Sicily: 'all these places were founded subsequently to the war with Troy'. However simplified, this basic picture has been confirmed by archaeology.

As for the preservation of the story through the 'Dark Age', it may well have been sung in the courts of Mycenae and Tiryns during the twelfth century BC. The 'catalogue of ships' was probably constructed by a bard in the twelfth century out of a genuine list of the famous places in the Mycenaean kingdoms of Greece; it was intended to be a backward-looking work, harking to the Golden Age of the heroes. An audience in the 1100s knew that places like Pylos no longer existed: Nestor represented the Golden Age of old-fashioned kingship, fatherly and stern, but 'fair': this was what a great *wanax* was like (the word, as *anax*, is preserved by Homer). They were the kings who held the 'empire' together – the twelfth-century-BC equivalent of 'Victorian values', one might say. Memory of the sites of many of the key places was preserved orally on the spot, so that in the eighth century we have tales enshrined in a rich and detailed bardic tradition fostered in émigré communities in Ionia. In Lakonia and the Argolid, where the heartland of Mycenaean power had resided, hero cults developed, centring on Mycenaean tombs where offerings were left to the heroes of that marvellous age; at the Menelaion site the memory survived, sponsored by numerous pilgrims who came leaving offerings for Helen and Menelaos; at Amyklai, another Bronze-Age palace site in Lakonia, there seems to be continuity of cult right through to classical times. In Sparta, surprisingly, as well as Mycenae, we find a cult of Agamemnon. In Orchomenos the great treasury became a shrine for 'King Minyas'; the same process was repeated at countless more obscure Mycenaean tholos tombs, especially where they could be identified with places in the catalogue of ships. Homer is the culmination of this development, the high point – though by no means the end – of a long bardic tradition. If we say he composed around 730 BC we may not be far off; but how much later the *Iliad* was set down in writing is unclear; as we have seen, the seventh century may be the most realistic guess. But long before then the tale had developed on the site of Hisarlik itself, where possibly from before 700 BC the people of Lokris sent their maidens to serve Trojan Athena. By then the fact, whatever *that* was, had become a legend, and in turn the legend had become a fact. Which is where we came in.

THE LATER HISTORY OF ILION, NEW ILIUM

The power of tenacious survival on the inherited ground is one of the most striking characteristics of the people who flourished on the Trojan acropolis through the Bronze Age.

CARL BLEGEN, *Troy and the Trojans*

We cannot leave the story of Troy without looking at its subsequent history. The city is after all the centre of our story, and as we said at the start, it is a city which existed for over 4000 years. The destruction wrought by the Greeks from Mycenae in the thirteenth century BC (if ever it happened) was but one destruction among many, and, as before, the inhabitants returned to the ruined city and rebuilt it. But the people of the succeeding city, VIIa, as we have seen, lived through violent and unstable times; their shanties and storage jars perhaps testify to that. The brief life of that phase of the city ended in terrible violence: the city was stormed and burned down; many citizens were killed, some even left dead in the streets. But after the raiders had gone, even then some survived to make the wrecked city habitable, to build their huts on the calcined stumps and blackened debris. What we call Troy VIIb 1 was still the home of descendants of the founders of Troy VI who had first settled on Hisarlik in around 1900 BC. Evidently the fortification wall still stood high enough to offer protection, and to build houses against: the south gate was still the city's main gate. They still made their Grey Minyan ware; even contacts with the Mycenaean world are still there: there are quite a few examples of twelfth-century ware (LH III C). But the Aegean world had suffered great changes. After half a century or so newcomers came to live on the hill of Hisarlik: their arrival left no marks of violence, so perhaps the impoverished inhabitants of VIIb 1 offered no resistance. The newcomers are marked by a dramatic change in pottery style, for they were makers of a crude handmade pottery called Knobbed Ware after its decorative knobs or horns: 'a strange phenomenon on a site where the potter's wheel has been familiar for many centuries,' said Carl Blegen. It looks primitive and perhaps the older inhabitants of Troy thought so: the Knobbed Ware is characteristic of the Late Bronze Age in Hungary and the Danubian culture, but probably came to the Troad over the Dardanelles from Thrace; they came, too, bearing hammer axes, pointed hammers, socketed and flat celts – all well-known Hungarian types – which were found by Schliemann in his digs.

But the previous inhabitants still seem to have survived: enough of the local Grey Minyan continued to be made and used in some quantity, so part at least of the earlier people lingered on in VIIb too. Had a Thracian warlord with his retainers and women perhaps come here for security during the movements of peoples north of the Aegean, the troubles of the time of the Sea Peoples, and taken control without a struggle? Had he perhaps been accepted by the Trojans, who had no king of their own?

Troy VIIb 2 received the odd pot from the Mycenaean world, but otherwise was a poor backwater. Towards 1100 it ceased to exist. Evidence of burning in several houses suggests that this settlement too was destroyed by fire, presumably put to the torch and looted. This marked the end of ancient Troy, though not, perhaps, the end of the Trojans. New evidence suggests that even now a tiny settlement hung on around the shrines below the west wall. Also at this time a considerable body of Trojans may have taken refuge on the summit of Bunarbashi, high above the gorge through which the Scamander flows down from the mountains into the plain of Troy: a site farther inland, more remote from the sea and the perennial sea raiders, easier to defend; there they might hope that the terrors of the passing of the Age of Bronze to the dismal Age of Iron would pass them by. (These heights of Bunarbashi, it will be remembered, were the site which Lechevalier thought was that of Troy in Chapter 1.) Whoever they were, these people carried with them the tradition of making Grey Minyan pottery and maintained it down to the end of the eighth century BC, a span of nearly 300 years. Then Bunarbashi was abandoned in its turn. Now it is an extraordinary fact − noticed by Carl Blegen − that at the end of the eighth century, when Bunarbashi was abandoned, the site on Hisarlik suddenly is lived in once more, and by people who could still make Grey Minyan pottery! Had some of the descendants of the original inhabitants returned to their old home? It is an intriguing thought, but Blegen's archaeological evidence is tenuous in the extreme; in essence the new Troy − Ilion − was a Greek colony, looking west, and for more than 1000 years it would form part of the *oikoumene* − the common world − of the classical Hellenic civilisation.

The Greek colony was founded before the year 700 BC by colonists from Aeolian Lesbos. It is just possible that Homer himself visited the new colony, though what role it played in the formation of the epic we do not know. Did the citizens of the city in 700 BC have stories about the Trojan War, for instance, carried down by oral tradition? It is not impossible. From about 700 BC the strange custom of the Lokrian maidens (see p. 31) began in Troy, which carried on until the Christian era: the altar and area of sacrificial burnings Blegen found on the west side of the city may have been their sanctuary. The place was never a great success, merely a small market town for the sale of the produce of the plain. But such was the fame of the tale, and so uniform was the belief that this was its true setting, that many famous pilgrims came to worship on the spot, and this rather unprepossessing little place enjoyed a brief heyday from the end of the fourth century BC which we might count the beginning of Hellenistic Ilion. Then it was adorned by wealthy patrons. Its chief landmark was a Doric temple of Athena on the old acropolis, site of Troy VI. At this time Alexander the Great's general, Lysimachus, built fine walls around the site, enclosing a city 1200 yards by 800. In the lower town there were a few handsome buildings, an agora and basilica, and a theatre which could hold 6000 (though the city's population can never have reached such a figure). But without its great bay, now silted up, it was really a nowhere place: it soon declined again till it was 'so decayed that there were not even tiles on the roofs' (c.190 BC). Devastated in the fighting of the Mithridatic Wars in 83–82 BC, the city may have lain largely ruined for some time: the story of Caesar's visit in 48 BC certainly implies it, and from then on the town existed as a poor country town with a few hundred people, superseded by the wealthy town of Alexandria Troas situated on the coast with its grand basilica, fine baths and its population of some 40,000. It cannot have helped when Ilium was sacked by the Goths in AD 259. By the Late Roman Empire it was, one imagines, a bit of a backwater, a hick town, not one that any self-respecting would-be rhetor or governor would like to be coupled with. By then, too, it had a Christian bishop and a little Byzantine church, probably a typical whitewashed redbrick affair of the kind you see all over the Greece of today. But it still had its pagan ghosts, as Julian discovered when he went round it with its bishop in 354 (p. 39). When did city life finally die out on Hisarlik? Clearly the old place was in decay in Julian's day (one imagines geese in the streets, crumbling walls with pigsties in among them, and many abandoned houses). Schliemann thought the city was abandoned in the fifth century AD, basing his belief on coin finds – that is, when did coins cease to be used? It was a commendable try: in fact subsequent finds have generally corroborated him, suggesting, if anything, that it survived well into the sixth century. The last citizens of classical Ilion perhaps lived long enough on the hill to see the apotheosis of Justinian's renewed Hellenic empire. But of the lives of those individual citizens in the last phase of Troy's existence we know nothing. In fact the fifth and sixth centuries AD were a very flourishing period for the Troad, especially in the villages, for there was a kind of move to the countryside. This last breath of prosperity may have touched the town, if we can go by the finds of coins of Theodosius I and II at Ilium: people still had money to spend and things to buy. But from Justinian's time such finds die out. We do not have to search far for a reason. In 542 the empire was ravaged by a terrible plague, and whole villages and cities were wiped out in Anatolia. We cannot prove that Ilium was among them, but from then on the record is silent for centuries.

From the sixth century the history of the place is virtually a blank; presumably it was a deserted and overgrown ruin – but it may just be that some sort of village continued on the site which was not traceable in the archaeological record. Our evidence for this comes in the work of the Byzantine emperor and administrator Constantine Porphyrogenitus who says that there was a bishopric at Ilium in the 930s, at the time of the Anglo-Saxon empire in Britain. Was the bishopric actually on Hisarlik? If so it would indicate that the church of the fourth century (or its successor) had survived.

Blegen found another hint that a Byzantine building had stood on the site, in a large cutting inside the south gate. This could suggest a small village with a still working population, a church, and perhaps some sort of wall. But these were grim times. Byzantium by now was a beleaguered state, 'waiting for the barbarians': Saracens from the south, Slavs from the north and west, Turks from the east. Arab attacks deep into the Aegean had been severe since the seventh century AD, and in the early tenth century they had been able to devastate Lesbos and sack Salonica. At this time smallholders were settled in many villages in Asia Minor to provide local levies for the Byzantine defence forces; perhaps little Ilium felt these events too. Later in the tenth century the growing pressure of Slav incursions on the northern frontier (the Greek mainland had already been inundated) caused the government of Constantinople to transfer part of the population of Asia Minor to the Slav borders, dispossessing smallholders. Disasters during the Turkish occupation of the Troad in the eleventh century caused a further loss of population, but the decline had clearly been a long time coming. It can only have bean a tiny and impoverished community – perhaps just a small group of families with their priest – which defended itself on Hisarlik from the eleventh to the late thirteenth centuries AD. Then the rich life which had existed from the fourth millennium BC ceased.

The last phase of the history of the Troad is Turkish. In fact the area was overrun by the Seljuk Turks as early as the 1070s and occupied for a quarter of a century until the Byzantines took it back. Finds of coins and pottery on the site show that occupation continued on Ilium for the next 200 years on a small scale, perhaps sustained as ever by the alluvial soil of the plain and seasonal fish, though archaeology suggests that the villagers could no longer afford any luxuries. In 1306 the Troad fell to the Ottoman Turks, and has been Turkish ever since. Our first detailed accounts of the plain come in fiscal surveys of the fifteenth and sixteenth centuries: these show it dotted with villages, mainly tiny ones of only half a dozen families. Ilium is evidently finally abandoned.

What happened to all the Greeks who had lived in the Troad until the Turkish conquest? The history of the Greek element in the population has yet to be sifted – Greeks are surprisingly absent from the surveys – but it is likely that they remained with their churches, with which the Turks, unlike the Roman Catholics, did not interfere. Greeks were frequently met by sixteenth-and seventeenth-century western travellers in the Troad, such as Belon and Lithgow at Alexandria Troas. In the eighteenth and nineteenth centuries there were Greek speakers in the interior of the Trojan plain, usually isolated craftsmen, travelling dealers, or *han* keepers. Then surprisingly after Greek independence, as Alexander Kinglake noted, a big influx of Greeks came into Asia Minor, and in Schliemann's day there was a handful of landowners, oil merchants and householders who were Greek. At that time the main Greek village was called Kallifatli, just over a mile to the south-west of Ilium; the modern village of this name in fact lies a few hundred yards away from the site of old Kallifatli towards the river Menderes. The old village was abandoned after the war of 1922, and the modern one founded by Turks from Bulgaria. Kallifatli was apparently a tiny place in 1574, with only six adult males named as taxable; Gell says it was large and prosperous in his day (1801), perhaps through immigration; but the plague of 1816 took away 200 people, leaving it in ruins but for a dozen houses. It had recovered a little in Schliemann's day, and he hired workmen from its population of 100 or 200. As a result the villagers were able to carry off much marble from Ilium, and their old cemetery has numerous carved stones. Kallifatli in a sense is the last living link with Ilium, though perhaps there is a village somewhere back on the Greek mainland with a family who came from Kallifatli after 1922. Given the tenacity with which the ancient Trojans clung to life, it would be pleasing to think that somehow the descent of the people of Troy – in however small a drop – ran in someone's veins somewhere, but that doubtless is taking the concept of the 'collective memory' too far!

Hisarlik is now of course an archaeological site, which is where we began. Most of its secrets have been given up, though there are small areas still unexcavated. The rest of the plateau of New Ilium, which remains to be explored, is now cultivated fields strewn with rubble, with groves of oaks inhabited only by squirrels – and perhaps, ghosts?

POSTSCRIPT:
THE TROJAN WAR
FOUND AGAIN?

THE FIRST EDITION OF THIS BOOK told the story of the three great excavations of Troy, by Schliemann, Dörpfeld and Blegen. It concluded that there was now little hope of further information coming out of the site of Hisarlik itself, which had been so devastated by the archaeologists and by Schliemann in particular. What remained to be explored was the extensive lower town of the Roman city where excavation might prove whether Bronze Age Troy had a town too.

In 1988, less than five years after I wrote that conclusion, a new excavation of the site began under the direction of Manfred Korfmann, whose name will now take its place alongside the greats of the past. The site was cleared of undergrowth and made more intelligible to visitors; the eastern defences were freed from their tangle of fig trees: Schliemann's great trench was cleaned out, crumbling walls were restored, and key features such as Schliemann's 'great ramp,' the east gate, and Dörpfeld's northeast bastion were dismantled, consolidated and rebuilt. In the lower town the Hellenistic and Roman theatres were explored and mapped, and the grid plan of the Roman streets was discovered. In addition a wide-ranging geophysical survey of the plateau and the Trojan plain was undertaken.

A very dramatic find had already taken place in preliminary excavations at Besik Tepe, five miles southwest of Hisarlik. This cone-shaped tumulus is one of the oldest and most prominent on the plain; it stands nearly 50 feet high on a natural platform above the sea in sight of Tenedos at the northern edge of the wide sweep of Besika Bay. It was investigated by Schliemann in 1879 and again by Dörpfeld in 1924, who demonstrated that an earlier prehistoric mound had been transformed into the striking shape we see today at some time in the Late Bronze Age. In other words the tumulus had been raised into its present monumental cone before Greek settlers arrived in the Troad in Homer's day, the eighth century BC; perhaps indeed it is the great tumulus by the seashore mentioned by Homer.

Modern scholarship has shown that Besik Tepe is almost certainly the mound which the classical Greeks regarded as the tomb of Achilles, scene of the famous visits by Xerxes and Alexander. Close to it Korfmann was able to locate the original seashore at the time of the Trojan War, when the bay was deeper, and the tumulus stood on a promontory which went nearly a mile into the sea. Only yards from the line of the ancient seashore a potentially critical discovery was made: over fifty cremations and burials with Mycenaean Greek grave goods and pottery datable to the early thirteenth century BC (late Troy VI). One stone-lined chamber tomb contained funeral offerings, including a fine pedestalled vase, and the dead man had been cremated with his sword. Most significant, five seal stones were found in the burials, two of which were certainly of mainland Greek provenance. Such stones are thought likely to have been personal seals of Mycenaean aristocrats. Had Korfmann then found the long-sought-for evidence of the Greek camp, and even some of the Greek dead? Or was this the cemetery of a Mycenaean merchant colony (perhaps the likeliest solution, as the remains included women and children)? It was not a question on which Korfmann would be drawn. 'I can only express an intuitive impression,' he wrote, 'a feeling I have, that the cemetery we have just laid bare at the harbour of Troy should belong to the very time when the Trojan War ought to have occurred.'

The presence on the Trojan coast of cremations from the Heroic Age, close to the mound the ancients believed to be the tomb of Achilles, raises fascinating questions about the survival of traditions of a Mycenaean presence in the Troad. (Does this find, for example, have some connection with Homer's story of a cemetery by the seashore near the Greek camp?) As we shall see, the very latest discoveries at Hisarlik now suggest continuity of population on Hisarlik from the thirteenth to the eighth century

BC, from the time of the Trojan War to the time of Homer; the tale could after all have been handed down orally on the site itself.

The finds at Besik Tepe have also given substantial support to the idea that the Greek fleet would have anchored in Besika Bay, and not in the bay of Troy as Schliemann and most modern scholars had supposed. Situated on the coast known in classical times as Achaiion ('the Achaean shore'), Besika Bay is wide and shallow, with a good protected anchorage; it lies right opposite the island of Tenedos, which is only six miles away. Could it have been the harbour of Troy? In the late eighties Korfmann's team made an attempt to determine the bay's topography in the late Bronze Age, taking over seventy drill cores from the land behind the beach.

They were able to prove that at the time of the Trojan War the bay was much more deeply indented than now, with the sea coming 600 yards further into the bay (the old line of the dunes is marked today by a slight tree-lined ridge curving round the shore). Analysis of the core samples showed that behind the beach there had been a large freshwater lagoon half a mile long and 400 yards across; though long silted up, the area still gathers some water in wet winters. This may perhaps explain an enigmatic feature of Homer's story (*Iliad*, VI, 4; see p. 144) which has never been satisfactorily elucidated: the *stomalimne*. This was a lagoon which apparently lay between the Greek ships and the Scamander river; according to scholars' marginalia recorded in the great Venice manuscript of the *Iliad*, this reading was in some older manuscripts of the epic, but was excised by the critic Aristarchos because it contradicted his theories about the topography of the plain and the location of the Greek camp. Once again archaeology seems to have shown that the Homeric text contains detailed local knowledge.

The presence of the lagoon underlines the point that, unlike the Trojan plain, Besika Bay has an abundance of fresh water even in the height of summer. In fact, it has been an important anchorage on this coast for centuries, probably for millennia. Navigational texts and shipping records from the Middle Ages onwards show that traffic going up into the Dardanelles would usually be compelled to wait here, the last anchorage before the narrows, because the currents and winds coming down the Dardanelles were so strong. The British and French fleets did so on several occasions in the nineteenth century, and as we saw on page 53, Lord Byron was detained in Besika Bay for seventeen days in 1810. Even into our own century, the Black Sea pilot for 1908 says it was not uncommon to see two or three hundred ships waiting for a favourable wind in the Tenedos channel and nearby anchorages.

In prehistory, with only oars and primitive sails, the bulk of maritime traffic heading towards the Dardanelles and the Sea of Marmara probably unloaded at Besika Bay and transshiped its goods by land past Troy. (Schliemann, for example, mentions that his supplies and tools were always unloaded at Besika Bay.) From there they would have been carried by cart or pack animal along the old track from Besika Bay to Troy. This route leads over a pronounced rise where the tower of Yerkesik stands today; from here Besika Bay and Troy are both visible, though neither can be seen from the other. This may be the *throsmos* or 'rise in the plain' recorded by Homer on three occasions when the Trojans deploy their army in a threatening position above the Greek camp. From the rise the road leads down to the ford of the Menderes (Scamander) on the line of the nineteenth-century causeway and then ascends from the river in a northeasterly direction towards the Trojan plateau and Hisarlik: this most likely is the axis of the battles envisioned in the *Iliad*.

Manfred Korfmann's archaeological explorations have now shown a long continuity of occupation on the Besika site, with Byzantine defences and warehouses, Hellenistic port installations, Troy VI material, and a substantial settlement from as early as the third millennium BC. It is almost certain, then, that Besika Bay, and not the marshy and malarial flats below Hisarlik, was the harbour for Bronze Age Troy, and presumably also the site of the Greek camp. This is precisely what we would infer from Homer:

> Their ships were drawn up far away from the fighting.
> Moored in a group along the gray churning surf –

first ships ashore they'd hauled up on the plain
then built a defense to landward off their sterns.
Not even the stretch of beach, broad as it was,
could offer berths to all that massed armada,
troops were crammed in a narrow strip of coast.
So they had hauled their vessels inland, row on row,
while the whole shoreline filled and the bay's gaping mouth
enclosed by the jaws of the two jutting headlands.

Iliad, XIV, 35–44, translated by Robert Fagles

Originally a deep and wide embayment between two prominent headlands, Besika Bay fits the Homeric description perfectly. The discovery of the Mycenaean cemetery on its shore probably clinches the matter.

Then Korfmann's team turned to the site itself. On the plateau south of Hisarlik, they began to examine the Roman town, looking for Bronze Age remains below it. Unfortunately the bedrock is less than six feet below the soil, and the Roman builders who liked to found their buildings on bedrock cleared away much of what lay beneath. But wherever they dug south of the citadel, in between the foundations of the Roman buildings and streets, remains of the Bronze Age were still disclosed. Right against the south wall were well-built houses of stone and wood, some very large. Two hundred yards from the south gate of Troy VI they uncovered the footings of six houses with such large quantities of Mycenaean pottery that the excavators wondered whether they had not found evidence of a small trading colony of Mycenaean merchants. Troy VI, then, certainly had a town.

Korfmann was anxious to define the limits of this town, and geomagnetic readings suggested the presence of a thick wall of mudbrick enclosing a large area extending towards the southern edge of the plateau. Excavating along this line, 400 yards south of the Troy VI walls, his team subsequently found a rock-cut ditch 3 metres wide, behind which there would probably have been mudbrick fortifications. There were also indications of two gates in this southern part of the circuit. Also, in the middle of the plateau, a long cutting in the bedrock was excavated with rear post holes suggesting the presence of a massive timber palisade with a wall walk supported by posts: this may have been part of the eastern defences of the Troy VI lower town. Further geomagnetic surveys have yielded evidence of two more gates not yet excavated.

Troy VI was not just a fortress. The outer town formed an elliptical shape south of the citadel across the end of the plateau, occupying most of the western third of the Roman city. Covering an area of about 200 hectares, it was comparable in size with the Mycenaean towns of the Argolid and, if the whole area was occupied, it may have had a population of five or six thousand people.

An important gap in our knowledge of Troy VI has always been the lack of evidence about religious cults. Dörpfeld thought he had found a shrine in one of the pillared houses inside the wall, but it was always assumed that the town's main shrine was destroyed when the Romans levelled off the top of the hill to build their Athena temple and civic centre. However, new finds below the Troy VI wall on the western side have offered a different possibility. Here a Mycenaean cult figurine was unearthed, the first such discovery on Hisarlik. Had this come from the shrine of a foreign community in Troy? Or was it a foreign god in a Trojan shrine? Either is possible – it was around this time that the sick Hittite king Mursilis had requested idols to be brought to his bedside from Lazpa (Lesbos) and from Ahhiyawa itself (see p. 205).

Along with the Mycenaean idol was a very traditional Anatolian cult object, part of a bronze stag of a kind known from central Anatolia at Alaca Huyuk. It is fascinating that both these pieces were found in the area which was a cult area in Hellenistic times and where that most mysterious of all Troy stories, the weird custom of the Lokrian maidens, was enacted supposedly for a thousand years after the war until their ancestor's crime had been expiated (see p. 31). If there was a Bronze Age shrine in this area of the town, it would form a parallel with Mycenae where the main cult building was below the hill and outside the palace area.

Finally, it was here on the west that Korfmann's team found indications contrary to what has always been believed, that there may have been no break in settlement on Hisarlik between the end of the Bronze Age and the Ionian Greek settlement in the eighth century. In the area of the shrines, traces of a new stratum were uncovered, between Troy VIIb2 and Troy VIII, which suggested that an impoverished population hung on at least in this part of the lower town. This raises the possibility of continuity on Hisarlik from the late Bronze Age to Homer's day. If the site was not after all a deserted ruin when the Ionian Greeks settled there in the eighth century BC, Homer could have had access to local traditions of the story which had been handed down orally on the site.

So now we can be clear that the Troy excavated by Schliemann, Dörpfeld and Blegen was the citadel of a sizeable town, which itself probably went back at least as far as 1500 BC. Troy VI then was the royal stronghold, the residence of the ruling clan. In this light we should remember that no other site in western Anatolia compares with Hisarlik. With more than forty strata and nearly seventy feet of deposits, it was in its region a uniquely long-lasting and massively fortified place. Nowhere north of Mycenae do such fortifications exist in the Late-Bronze-Age world. Bearing that in mind, it can surely now be assumed that Troy VI was the seat of an important Anatolian kingdom, quite possibly one of the regional capitals mentioned in the Hittite archives. This is all the more clear when we remember that Troy/Hisarlik was also one of the most ancient settlements in western Anatolia, with an impressive continuity of traditions on the site, especially in architecture. All in all, this suggests a long-lived dynastic seat: in short, a line of strong Trojan kings. Such of course was the Greek tradition.

If Hisarlik/Troy was indeed a major regional 'capital' in between the Greek and Hittite worlds, we may predict that it does appear in the Hittite tablets, just as Emil Forrer deduced so long ago (see p. 199). As yet we cannot recognise it for certain because the interpretation of the Hittite geography of the region is as yet controversial. But one place in the Hittite archives still stands out strongly as the likeliest candidate for Troy: Wilusa. This is a state about which a fair amount is now known, and what is known points towards the Troad for its location. As we saw in Chapter 6, Wilusa was a long-lasting kingdom in western Anatolia, once independent of the Hittites but a loyal (though distant) client state from around 1600 BC. In the treaty of about 1280 BC, perhaps shortly before the Trojan War, it undertook to furnish troops to the Hittite king for his military expeditions – and may have done so on the Kadesh campaign. It was an Arzawan state and presumably lay on, or near, the northwest Anatolian seaboard. The recent decipherment of a strange poetic or ritual text from thirteenth-century-BC Boghaz Köy has provided us with an interesting gloss on this question. Written in the Luvian language, which was spoken in west Anatolia (and perhaps in Troy?), the text gives this formulaic opening line to some lost work: 'When they came from steep Wilusa …' So the same epithet was applied to Hittite Wilusa as to Homeric (W)ilios (*Ilios ophruoessa, Ilion aipu*).

A further insight into Wilusa may also be offered by the Alaksandus treaty. For in its coda it gives the names of the Wilusan gods. First is the Anatolian storm god (like the Greek sky god, invincible with his thunderbolt). There follows one lost name (perhaps female), then an Appaliunas, who can hardly be other than Apollo (Apeilon in Cypriot Greek); the tablet concludes with 'the male and female gods, mountains, rivers, springs, and the subterranean stream of Wilusa.'

This suggests that Apollo was one of the chief deities of the Wilusans. Now it is a remarkable fact that in Homer Apollo is not the god of the Greeks, but the chief deity of the Trojans with his temple in their citadel. At the very beginning of the *Iliad*, of course, he is the god whom Homer sees as responsible for the ten years of suffering experienced by the Greeks, the 'countless losses' of the Achaians before Troy:

What god drove them to fight with such fury?
Apollo the son of Zeus and Leto ...

So the theme of the *Iliad* is set out at the start. It may contain more than a vestige of Bronze Age fact. The cult of Apollo is now thought not to be Greek but Anatolian or Cypriot in origin (Homer calls him 'Lycian-born'). Interestingly enough his name does not appear in the Linear B tablets so far unearthed. In classical times his cult was particularly strong in the Troad: according to the geographer Strabo 'his worship extends all along this coast.' In addition to his island shrines on Lesbos and Tenedos, he had several important cult centres, most famous of which was the Smintheum at Hamaxitus/Chrysa where there are traces of occupation as early as the third millennium BC. It is possible then that the proto-Apollo was indeed the god of the Troad in the late Bronze Age and that Homer has preserved a genuine memory of Trojan religion.

Before we leave this question of the possible identity of Troy and Wilusa, there is one last clue to be drawn from the treaty of Alaksandus: if Wilusa was indeed in the Troad, then where was the shrine of the deity of the 'subterranean stream of Wilusa' which the treaty singles out for special mention? There was a subterranean spring deep under the site of Troy itself, and another underground spring which rose outside the walls. But if the holy underground stream of the treaty was in the Troad, it can hardly be other than the famous Ayazma, two miles below the summit ridge of Mount Ida, the throne of the Trojan gods. This is the source of the Scamander river, whose sanctity is stressed by Homer above any other river (it is 'divine,' 'born of the gods,' 'descended from Zeus'). Homer also says the river was worshipped with sacrifices, that bulls and, especially, horses were sacrificed to it; he says that a priest was maintained by the Trojans specifically to perform the rites for the river.

At the Ayazma, the river emerges into a picturesque basin under a limestone cliff, pouring out of a natural subterranean tunnel which is walkable for 220 yards into the mountain and which in its early part is four or five yards high. It is one of the most famous natural features of the Troad; as Lord Aberdeen described it in 1803, 'one of the grandest and most picturesque scenes ... the water rises in a vast cavern and gushes out forming a magnificent spectacle.' Charles Maclaren, who came here in 1847, attributed the ancient sacredness of the river to the fact that it springs from the very foot of Zeus's throne:

Instead of collecting its water like other rivers from obscure, feeble and scattered sources, it bursts out at once into day in a magnificent cascade, clear as crystal, issuing forth in mystery and sublimity from a deep cavern in the hidden recesses of the mountain amidst thundering echoes, and encompassed by scenery of extraordinary beauty and grandeur.

The place is still visited by pilgrims today. Early this century, before the Greeks were expelled from the Troad, it had a great local reputation for the cure of fever (important in the malarial conditions of the Scamander valley) and a special service was held here by the Greeks on the festival day of Hagios Elias. In those days, the trees around the basin were hung with votive rags, and oil lamps and incense were burned. Indeed, in the remoter past the reputation of its sanctity spread far beyond the Troad. In 1803 Lord Aberdeen met pilgrims here from as far away as Constantinople and even, remarkably, people from Kula in central Anatolia who had come on a thirteen-day journey to bathe and drink the water. Here then the evidence from topography and ethnology, from Homer and the Hittite tablets may perhaps converge in a most striking way. In the Mediterranean world the immemorial sanctity of such places has often survived all changes of peoples and faiths, and although over three thousand years have elapsed since the treaty of Muwatallis referred to the sacred places of Alaksandus' kingdom, it is not inconceivable that the 'sacred subterranean stream of Wilusa' has survived as a place of worship up till our own times.

The identification of Wilusa with Troy would be more likely

if we could be sure that the troublesome king of Ahhiyawa in the Hittite texts is indeed Mycenaean Greek, as I argued ten years ago. This identification is now stronger. In the early 1980s some scholars had postulated a Thracian or Bulgarian Ahhiyawa; this had little to recommend it, and is now seemingly ruled out by new inscriptions discovered at Xanthus which tend to confirm the picture of west Anatolian geography adopted in Chapter 6 above. In any case the Thracian theory had the further major drawback of leaving a disagreeable void in reconstructing the history of the period (namely, why at the height of their power and influence, did the Mycenaeans thus appear to be unknown to the Hittites?).

The Hittites, it is true, exhibit a curious lack of information on what was obviously a power to be reckoned with. This certainly suggests the seat of Ahhiyawan power was overseas, even though boundary texts and letters show Ahhiyawa had a foothold in western Anatolia. There are clear hints of sea journeys to reach it; one text refers to an exiled Arzawan prince, an ally of Ahhiyawa, going 'to the islands,' before exile, apparently in Ahhiyawa itself. Now a new translation of an important Hittite letter mentions the Ahhiyawan king seizing islands which had been in the Hittite sphere of influence. Most would now accept that such islands, off the shore of western Anatolia, are in the Aegean (probably, as we shall see, Lesbos and its smaller neighbours).

The strong likelihood is that Forrer was right after all, and that the Ahhiyawans and Homer's Achaiwoi are indeed the same. The Hittite tablets suggest that around 1300 BC the Greeks extended their power over islands close to the Anatolian shore and also recaptured Miletus (Hittite Millawanda) and its hinterland. In the process their forays became a real threat to the network of Hittite client states in western Anatolia, a threat which the Hittite Foreign Office acknowledged and attempted to deal with. Subsequent letters catalogue cases of Ahhiyawan interference among the Hittite client states in Arzawa, the fomenting of alliances with these states against the Hittite king, and the giving of support to troublesome renegades like

Pijamaradus. Finally, on one tablet there is talk of war with the Great King of Hatti. All in all, it is hard to see who else can have caused all this, if not the Mycenaean Greeks.

It is at this time that we find the Ahhiyawan king being addressed by the Hittite chancery as 'great King.' Could a Mycenaean *wanax* ruling in the Argolid and over some Aegean islands really have been called 'Great King' by the rulers of central Anatolia? Many have doubted this, but it is clear now that he could. He does not appear in the list of Muwatalli's day in the Wilusa treaty, but he does appear subsequently in documents of Hattusilis and later. This fits with other evidence that the Greeks extended their power in the Aegean in the early thirteenth century BC. Now further parallels for the use of the title of 'Great King' are available, for example in a newly discovered bronze tablet from Boghaz Köy, and in other material which shows that during the thirteenth century 'great kingship' was bestowed upon the rulers of lesser states (such as Tarhuntassa and Carchemish). These were kings directly involved in the Hittite hegemony, in one case inside Anatolia. In this light we can see that Hattusilis' conciliatory and flattering diplomacy towards 'my brother the great king of Ahhiyawa' is more likely to be a sign of his need to control the fringes of his empire by negotiation rather than by war: a hazardous gamble given the shifting sands of west Anatolian politics.

So are we any nearer pinning down the exact date of the Trojan War? In the first edition of this book, it was pointed out that the Hittite tablets describe the king of Ahhiyawa intervening directly or indirectly on the shores of western Anatolia in at least two instances, in the Seha River land and in Wilusa (see p. 216). In the latter case the Hittite king says 'we made war' or 'we were in enmity.' Plainly this now has to be taken seriously by scholars. Two further points may be relevant here. Hittite hegemony in western Anatolia collapsed at least twice in the early thirteenth century BC: once at the start of Muwatalli's reign in 1296; again some time early in Hattusilis' reign (*c.*1263–1261). Then, as I pointed out, Hittite troubles in their western regions may have coincided with a major attack by the Assyrians in the upper Euphrates which took them right up to the gates of Carchemish: this took place in around 1262/1 BC and could be referred to in a fragmentary text which mentions Egypt, Carchemish, Ahhiyawa and Pijamaradus (perhaps then from the same time as Hattusilis' campaign to Miletus).

Now the paleography and orthography of the Hittite tablets are not yet certain, and because of the fragmentary state of many tablets, their authorship is still debated; for example, the most crucial document in the whole series, the Tawagalawas letter, has lost its top, so we cannot be sure of its date. If the king in the letter is indeed Hattusilis as I suggested in my first edition – and *if* Wilusa is Troy – then we might indeed speculate that the Trojan War took place in the period 1275–1260. If, though, the letter were from Muwatalli, then we would have to put the fall of Troy VI back perhaps to the 1280s, and certainly pre-1272 (which is still acceptable on the earlier date now proposed for the beginning of LH III B pottery, namely before 1300 BC).

This last solution has some points in its favour. It is suggested by the letter of Manapa-Tarhundas, king of the Seha River land, which, as we have seen, most likely lay south of the Troad in the Caïcus valley; the letter dates from Muwatallis' reign but possibly the latter half, i.e. some time between 1285 and 1272. As it stands, the tablet is badly damaged, and does not mention the king of Ahhiyawa, but the main personalities mentioned in the Tawagalawas letter appear here too, which suggests it is describing the same events. Important in this is the island of Lazpa (Lesbos), which is coveted by both sides in the dispute, Hittites and Pijamaradus, and which may be one of the islands 'given by the Storm God' to the Ahhiyawan king. In the letter, seven thousand prisoners have been shipped from Lazpa to Millawanda/Miletus, probably with the help of Ahhiyawan ships; at the same time the Seha River land, which is clearly adjacent to Lazpa, has been attacked. This is the background to the beginning of the letter: the king writes that a high-ranking Hittite general has arrived in his country with a Hittite army:

Gassus arrived and brought along the Hittite troops and when they set out again to the country of Wilusa in order to attack it [or 'to attack it again' or 'to launch a counterattack'] I however fell ill, I am seriously ill, unable to move ... When Pijamaradus had humiliated me, he set Atpas against me: he [Pijamaradus] attacked the land of Lazpa.

Later the king mentions 'raids and counter-raids' but the text is too broken for us to determine the outcome. Now Gassus appears in other letters of this time employed in the military sphere; he is a high-ranking general reporting on fortress inspections and detailing attacks on enemy fortresses; he appears in the company of kings and may even have been the C-in-C of the Hittite army. Clearly General Gassus has come west on the orders of the Hittite king, the now-ageing Muwatalli. He has come to the Seha River land in order to attack Wilusa; or (given that Wilusa is a loyal vassal of Hatti in the contemporary Alaksandus treaty) to attack a pretender to the throne of Wilusa; or to confront an enemy who is in possession of Wilusa (for example, Pijamaradus and his allies, who include the king of Ahhiyawa).

The events in this letter could well be those referred to in the Tawagalawas letter, even if it was written some time later. (Pijamaradus' career, for example, may well have lasted many years; the troubles over Wilusa may have been prolonged over the reign of more than one Wilusan king). But the facts given here about Gassus' expedition give considerable support to the idea that the hostilities over Wilusa mentioned in the Tawagalawas letter may have taken place late in Muwatalli's reign. In my first edition I suggested a date of 1275–1260 as a working hypothesis, with Hattusilis involved, directly or indirectly, either as Great King of Hatti, or in his youth as his brother's generalissimo soon after the battle of Kadesh. This is still possible, but the Manapa-Tarhundas letter suggests a date no later than 1272, and possibly up to a decade or so earlier. This alternative would fit with the archaeology, with the details in the Tawagalawas letter and even with the strange tradition from Caria that 'Motylos,' that is

Muwatalli, was the ally of Paris–Alexandros. Further research will no doubt clarify these matters.

In conclusion, then, the hypothesis of a historical Troy and Trojan War is now stronger. On this reading of the evidence, Hisarlik was a long-lived city at the mouth of the Dardanelles. It lay at the intersection of the great tin route across the Hellespont between the Balkans and Anatolia. It controlled a rich agricultural plain, and dominated the sea route to the Sea of Marmara, with its large bay which was a natural gathering place for ships making the slow journey against current and wind into the narrows. Finally, it may also have controlled Besika Bay, the last anchorage for boats before the Dardanelles, and the unloading point for merchandise to be transshipped by land to the Sea of Marmara.

This strongly fortified and ancient city was evidently ruled by a long-lasting dynasty throughout the Late Bronze Age. It stood on the edge of the Hittite and Aegean spheres of influence, quite far removed from both. The Hittite archives show that the emperors in Boghaz Köy sometimes claimed suzerainty over these western lands – and on occasions reached the Aegean Sea in person; sometimes, though, their hegemony receded and the best they could manage was rule through alliances with friendly states who made treaties and 'sent ambassadors.' This was not an empire in our sense then, but a segmentary state whose authority declined rapidly towards its outer fringes.

As the Hittite records show, it was on these outer fringes that the King of Ahhiyawa's influence was felt: in the coastlands, archipelagos and peninsulas of the eastern Aegean; in cities such as Millawanda and Wilusa; in islands such as Lesbos; in the fertile valleys of the west Anatolian rivers, Maeander, Cayster, Hermos, Caïcus and Scamander. Slowly extending this influence, taking 'your islands which the Storm God has given to me,' the Ahhiyawan king made himself a force to be feared in Hatti when he began to interfere directly with Hittite client states on the Aegean shore. According to the Hittite diplomatic archive, they and the Ahhiyawans came to blows over Wilusa in the first half of the thirteenth century BC, the period of the height of Mycenaean power. This is precisely the time when Greek Linear B tablets record Asiatic women seized on plundering raids from these shores, and as we have seen, this may be part of the context of the war: a 'heroic' warrior society replenishing its slave workforce and rewarding the heavily armed followings of its kings and sub-kings. The attack on Troy, though, was not merely to seize captives from the countryside, but part of a major campaign against the ancient and strong citadel of a powerful dynasty. Of any other motive we are none the wiser, and are likely to remain so.

But, in conclusion, it is safe to say, given the progress of the latest excavations in the Troad, that the search for the Trojan War is far from over. Exciting discoveries will no doubt continue to be made. In particular, the new exploration of the site offers the real possibility now of the identity of the place being decided. We know that the kings of the Hittites exchanged letters with Ahhiyawa and Wilusa; we know merchants in Greece and Hatti also used written archives. The find of a perfectly preserved bronze copy of a treaty at Boghaz Köy in 1986 only underlines the likelihood of further texts turning up which will reveal more about events in western Anatolia in the thirteenth century BC. It is not even beyond the bounds of possibility that tablets will be discovered in the lower town by Hisarlik itself, which may at least establish the name of the site first excavated by Schliemann. It is of course premature to suggest that the long search for the historicity of Troy and the Trojan War may be nearing a climax; but we may now be reaching the point where the intersection of history and myth can be firmly delineated.

BIBLIOGRAPHY

This list makes no pretence to be comprehensive, for the literature on this subject is truly vast. I have found the following books helpful, and I hope they may also help readers interested in pursuing this fascinating subject.

On early travellers to Troy, there is a useful survey in *The Troad: an archaeological and topographical study* by J. M. Cook (Clarendon Press, 1973). There is an important article on eighteenth-century travellers by T. J. B. Spencer, 'Robert Wood and the problem of Troy', *Journal of the Warburg and Courtauld Institutes*, vol. 20, 1957, pp. 75–105.

On Heinrich Schliemann, apart from his books mentioned in the text, there are selected letters, many in English, in *Briefwechsel* edited by E. Meyer (2 vols, Berlin: E. Gebr Mann, 1953–8), and also 'Schliemann's letters to Max Müller in Oxford', *Journal of Hellenic Studies*, vol. 82, 1962, pp. 75–105. His historic 1890 report is in Carl Schuchhardt's *Schliemann's excavations: an archaeological and historical study …* (Macmillan, 1891). Two recent important articles, 'Schliemann's discovery of "Priam's treasure": two enigmas' by Donald F. Easton and David A. Traill, appear respectively in *Antiquity*, vol. LV, 215, November 1981, pp. 179–183, and vol. LVII, 221, November 1983, pp. 181–6; this periodical is in most big libraries. Of Schliemann biographies all are marred by the myth, but that of Emil Ludwig, *Schliemann of Troy* (Putnam, 1931), is still very readable. The best is the compilation by Leo Deuel, *Memoirs of Heinrich Schliemann: a documentary portrait drawn from his autobiographical writings, letters and excavation reports* (Hutchinson, 1978).

Wilhelm Dörpfeld's great work *Troja und Ilion* (Athens, 1902) is untranslated, but there is a good summary of it with maps and photographs in Walter Leaf's *Troy: a study in Homeric geography* (Macmillan, 1912).

Along with Sir Arthur Evans' *The Palace of Minos: a comparative account of the successive stages of the early Cretan civilisation …* (Macmillan, 1921–36), the *Annual of the British School at Athens*, vol. 6, 1900, and an article in *Monthly Review*, March 1901, are useful. Joan Evans' *Time and chance: the story of Arthur Evans and his forebears* (Longmans, 1947) and Sylvia L. Horwitz's *The find of a lifetime* (Weidenfeld and Nicolson, 1981) are, as yet, the sum of Evans' biographies. Two useful paperback publications are available from the Ashmolean Museum in Oxford: *Sir Arthur Evans 1851–1941, a memoir* by D.B. Harden (1983) and *Arthur Evans and the Palace of Minos* by Ann C. Brown (1983). For those with strong nerves the controversy over Knossos can best be read in *On the Knossos tablets. two studies* by L. R. Palmer and J. Boardman (OUP, 1963); in Mervyn R. Popham's *The last days of the Palace of Knossos: complete vases of the Late Minoan III B period* (Studies in Mediterranean Archaeology, vol. 5, Lund, 1964) and *The destruction of the Palace at Knossos: pottery of the Late Minoan III A period* (Studies in Mediterranean Archaeology, vol. 12, Gothenburg, 1970); in L. R. Palmer's *A new guide to the Palace of Knossos* (Faber, 1969) and Erik Hallager *The Mycenaean Palace at Knossos: evidence for the final destruction in the III B period* (Stockholm: Medelhavsmuseet, 1977). Two articles which I have found particularly helpful are L. R. Palmer's 'The

First fortnight at Knossos', *Studi Micenei*, vol. XXI, 1980, pp. 273–301, and W.-D. Niemeier's 'Mycenaean Knossos and the age of Linear B', *Studi Micenei*, vol. XXIII, 1982, pp. 219–287, which seems to me to put the case for the revisionists beyond reasonable doubt – but be warned, the whole controversy is very technical!

On Mycenae there are great introductory books by Chrestos Tsountas and J. I. Manatt, *The Mycenaean age: a study of the monuments and culture of pre-Homeric Greece* (Macmillan, 1897); A. J. B. Wace's *Mycenae: an archaeological history and guide* (Princeton University Press, 1949) and G. E. Mylonas's *Mycenae's last century of greatness* (Methuen, 1968). Wace's loving description of the place should be savoured. The key article by Wace and Blegen mentioned on page 121 is 'Pottery as evidence for trade and colonisation in the Aegean bronze age', *Klio*, vol. 32, 1939, pp. 131–47. C. W. Blegen also wrote a popular introduction, *Troy and the Trojans* (Thames and Hudson, 1963). His yearly reports are in the *American Journal of Archaeology* (1928–38). The supplementary monograph, 4, *Troy: the archaeological geology* by G. Rapp and J. A. Gifford (Princeton University Press, 1982) contains information about the existence of the bay in front of Troy.

On the controversy surrounding Blegen's 'Trojan War' there is the famous discussion in the *Journal of Hellenic Studies*, vol. 84, 1964, pp. 1–20. The 'dissenter', Sir Moses Finley, has encapsulated his views in *Schliemann's Troy – one hundred years after* (British Academy, paperback 1975) in *The World of Odysseus* (Chatto, 2nd rev. edn, 1977; Penguin Books, 1972) and in 'Lost: the Trojan War' in *Aspects of antiquity: discoveries and controversies* (Penguin Books, 1972).

On Linear B, in addition to Michael Ventris's and John Chadwick's *Documents in Mycenaean Greek: 300 selected tablets from Knossos, Pylos and Mycenae with commentary and vocabulary* (Cambridge University Press, 1956), there is a highly readable introduction by John Chadwick, *The Mycenaean world* (Cambridge University Press, 1976).

On Homer, G. S. Kirk's *The songs of Homer* (Cambridge University Press, 1962) is still the best introduction (there is a shortened version from the same publisher, *Homer and the epic*, 1965). Also to be recommended in paperback are J. Griffin's *Homer* (OUP, 1980) and J.B. Hainsworth's *Homer* (Clarendon Press, 1969). I have found particularly helpful Minna Skafte Jensen's *The Homeric question and the oral-formulaic theory* (Copenhagen: Museum Tusculanum Press, 1980).

On the catalogue, R. Hope Simpson's and J. F. Lazenby's *The catalogue of the ships in Homer's 'Iliad'* (Clarendon Press, 1970).

On modern Mycenaean and Cretan archaeology there are excellent broad introductions by Sinclair Hood, George Cadogan, Lord William Taylour and O. T. P. K. Dickinson and an interesting geographical approach by John L. Bintliff, *Natural environment and human settlement in prehistoric Greece* (Oxford: British Archaeological Reports, 1977). An exciting synthesis is J. V. Luce's *Homer and the heroic age* (Thames and Hudson, 1975). *A companion to Homer*, edited by A. J. B. Wace and F. H. Stubbings (Macmillan, 1962), is still invaluable. Very useful, though bulky, if you are footslogging round the sites is *Mycenaean Greece* by R. Hope Simpson (Park Ridge, NJ: Noyes Press, 1981).

On Hittites and Greeks, *History and the Homeric Iliad* by Sir Denys

Page (Cambridge University Press, 1959) is now superseded because of
the redating of the texts – see this in the revised edition of *The Hittites* by
Oliver Gurney (Penguin Books, 2nd edn. revised 1981). Important new
developments are noted in articles by Itamar Singer in *Anatolian Studies*,
vol. XXXIII, 1983, pp. 205–217, 'Western Anatolia in the thirteenth
century BC according to the Hittite sources', and by H. G. Güterbock,
'The Hittites and the Aegean world 1. The Ahhiyawa problem reconsidered', *American Journal of Archaeology*, vol. 87, 1983, pp. 133–8. Opposition
to the Ahhiyawa identification can be found in J. MacQueen's *The Hittites
and their Contemporaries in Asia Minor* (Thames and Hudson, 1975). J. D.
Muhly's 'Hittites and Achaeans: Ahhijawa redomitus', *Historia*, vol. XXIII,
no. 2, 1974, pp. 129–45, and in James Mellaart's many articles in *Anatolian
Studies*, 1961–70, along with his piece in a forthcoming Festschrift for
George Mylonas. The Greek theory now looks increasingly solid.

On Greeks in Anatolia see C. Mee's 'Aegean trade and settlement in
Anatolia in the second millennium BC', *Anatolian Studies*, vol. XXVIII,
1978, pp. 121–155. Nancy K. Sandars's *The Sea Peoples: warriors of the
ancient Mediterranean, 1250–1150 BC* (Thames and Hudson, 1978) is the
only general introduction to that shadowy subject. Matters should be
clarified when the Sheffield Sea Peoples' Colloquium papers edited by
R. A. Crossland are published. There are some fascinating items in the
Proceedings of the First International Colloquium on Aegean Prehistory held in
Sheffield in 1970, *Bronze Age migrations in the Aegean: archaeological and
linguistic problems in Greek prehistory* edited by R. A. Crossland and A.
Birchall (Duckworth, 1974). A future volume will include the papers of
the Troy conference. *Pharaoh triumphant* by K. A. Kitchen (Aris and
Phillips, 1982) is an extremely informative and interesting look at the life
and times of Ramses II, the Egyptian view of the thirteenth century BC.

Travellers' guides – of course the greatest pleasure of all is seeing
these places for oneself, but there are some helpful general books: *The Blue
Guide to Greece*, edited by Stuart Rossiter, includes Crete (Benn, paperback
1981); he also edited *The Blue Guide to Crete* (Benn, 1980). George Bean's
guides to Asia Minor are all published by Benn – *Aegean Turkey: an
archaeological guide* (1979), *Lycian Turkey* (1978) and *Turkey Beyond the
Maeander* (1980) are indispensable for later remains though they do not
concern themselves with the Bronze Age. Ekrem Akurgal's *Ancient
civilizations and ruins of Turkey* (Istanbul: Haset Kitabevi, n.e. 1983) is
extremely useful, with plenty of site plans. The fascinating work of J. M.
Cook *The Troad: an archaeological and topographical study* (Clarendon Press,
1973) is absolutely indispensable for detailed field-walking around Troy,
but unfortunately lacks a good map. Good site guides include Blegen for
Pylos, Mylonas for Mycenae and Kurt Bittel for Boghaz Köy.

The artefacts described in *In Search of the Trojan War* are mainly in the
great museum collections in Athens, Heraklion and Ankara, but there are
some excellent local museums which should not be missed, especially at
Thebes, and Chora near Pylos. There are small site museums at Troy and
Miletus. In the United Kingdom, the British Museum has a small Anatolian
section and some interesting Mycenaean material, including of course
Elgin's loot from Mycenae and Minos Kalokairinos' pithos. In Oxford, the
Ashmolean Museum has the best Cretan collection outside Crete; there

too, incidentally, are kept the archaeological paintings of Thomas Burgon, the Smyrna merchant who set the ball rolling in 1809, and who is buried in St Giles Church, a stone's throw from the Museum door.

Last but not least, Homer himself. There are fine translations of *The Iliad* in prose by Walter Leaf (2 vols, 1886–8) and Andrew Lang, W. Leaf and E. Myers (1883–9); there is a *Compact Homer* translated by A. Lang (Barron's Education Series, US, paperback 1981). Another fine translation in verse is by Richmond Lattimore (Routledge and Kegan Paul, 1951). The translation by E.V. Rieu published in the Classics series by Penguin Books, 1951, which had sold a million copies by 1984, is in readable but unpoetic prose. Christopher Logue has done a tremendous adaptation of Homer, *War music: an account of Books 16 to 19 of Homer's Iliad* (Cape, 1981).

On Homer I leave the last word with Alexander Kinglake who in 1834, standing on the Trojan plain, fondly recalled his childhood teaching 'that the Iliad was all in all to the human race – that it was history – poetry – revelation, that the works of men's hands were folly and vanity, and would pass away like the dreams of a child, but that the Kingdom of Homer would endure for ever and ever', *Eothen, or traces of travel … brought home from the East*, 1844, (Century, 1982; OUP, paperback 1982).

ADDITIONAL BIBLIOGRAPHY

On the new excavations *Studia Troica*, vols. 1–14 (Mainz, 1991–2004) is indispensable. This is a yearly account with beautiful new maps of the city plus numerous site plans and photographs; the important examination of Besika Bay is by Ilhan Kayan in vol. 1, with detailed reconstructions; in the same volume is Donald Easton's 'Troy before Schliemann.' The project website is www.uni-tuebingen.de/troia

Troy and the Trojan War, ed. M. Mellink (Bryn Mawr College, PA, 1986) comes out strongly for a real basis to the Homeric tale. Manfred Korfmann's excavation of the cemetery at Besik Tepe is summarised in English in this book, and more fully documented (in German) in *Archäologischer Anzeiger* for 1984–6 and 1989. *The Trojan War*, ed. L. Foxhall and J. K. Davies (Bristol, 1984) is divided over its historicity; but some contributors have revised their ideas since this symposium was published, for instance D. Easton in his review of my book (*Antiquity*, vol. LIX, 1985, pp. 188–96) and James Mellaart on his reconstruction of Hittite geography ('Hatti Arzawa and Ahhiyawa' in the Festschrift to George Mylonas, *Philia Epe*, vol. 1, Athens, 1986, 74–84).

On the problem of the end of Troy VI, in addition to Easton's review, is S. Hiller's account in *Studia Troica*, 1, 1991, pp. 150–54.

On Aegean archaeology in general see *The Greek Bronze Age*, ed. E. French and K. Wardle (valuable papers including C. Mee on Mycenaean finds in western Anatolia, and an up-to-date summary of the evidence for Mycenaean Miletus). On Troy, Michael Siebler's *Troia* (Mainz, 1994) is a beautifully illustrated distillation (in German) of the new material.

On the Jewels of Helen, the full story can now be told: D. Easton, *Anatolian Studies*, vol. XLIV, 1994 (citing a vast bibliography since 1984). Dr. Easton is also preparing a popular book on Troy (Thames & Hudson).

On Frank Calvert: the unpublished material in the first edition of this book helped to spark a renewed interest in Calvert; see Marcelle Robinson (*Anatolian Studies*, vol. XLIV, 1994) and Susan Heuck Allen, *Finding the Walls of Troy* (1999) (full of fascinating family material and photographs).

On Homer and the epic: there are excellent new translations of the *Iliad*, in verse by Robert Fagles and in prose by Martin Hammond (Penguin). G. S. Kirk's *The Iliad: a commentary* is now published, the first large-scale commentary on the *Iliad* for nearly a hundred years (Cambridge, six vols. 1985–93); in it there is much of archaeological and historical interest: Kirk's comments on the historicity of the war (vol. II, 1990, pp. 36–50) are the best summing-up at present available; his detailed analysis of the catalogue of ships in vol. 1, pp. 168–263 is also of great interest. On Homer as an artist see, among many, the sparkling book by Oliver Taplin, *Homeric Soundings* (OUP, 1992). On the origins of the tradition, M. L. West, 'The Rise of the Greek Epic' in *Journal of Hellenic Studies*, vol. CVIII, 1988, p. 151ff. and replies by J. Chadwick in CX, 1990, p. 174ff. and W. F. Wyatt, vol. CXII, 1992, p.167ff. Wyatt postulates direct descent from Mycenaean epic. On possible Anatolian influences on Greek epic: J. Puhvel, *Homer and Hittite* (Innsbruck, 1991). *Greek Religion* by Walter Burkert (Blackwell, Oxford, 1987, paperback) offers many insights into the Mycenaean (and Anatolian) origins of Greek religion.

On the Hittites: the source material here is expanding by the year. For general problems concerning the Greeks, see H. Guterbock's exciting piece in the Mellink symposium. On specific points: an essential discussion of some of the crucial documents is P. H. J. Houwink ten Cate, 'Sidelights on the Ahhiyawa question' in *Jaarbericht Ex Oriente Lux*, 28, 1983–4, pp. 33–79. The new bronze tablet was published by H. Otten, *Die Bronzetafel aus Bogazkoy* (Wiesbaden, 1988), and reviewed (in English) by P. H. J. Houwink ten Cate in *Zeitschrift für Assyriologie*, 82, 1992, 233–70.

On 'Great Kings' in Carchemish and elsewhere, J. D. Hawkins in *Anatolian Studies*, vol. XXXVIII, 1988; see too, on Hittite treaties, the articles by R. H. Beal and O. Gurney in vol. XLIII, 1993; on the Greeks in the Hittite tablets, generally accepting the line in this book, T. R. Bryce in *Historia*, vol. XXXVIII, 1989, p. 1ff. On a possible Hittite trade embargo on the Greeks: E. Cline in *Historia*, XL, 1991, p. 1ff.

For the most recent survey of the question see T. Bryce, *The Hittites* (Oxford, 1999) and Joachim Latacz, *Troy and Homer: Towards a Solution of an Old Mystery* (Oxford, 2004), though Latacz's identification of the kingdom of Ahhiyawa as Thebes is based on a very dubious reading of one letter.

Picture Credits

All photographs by Michael Wood except:

Picture section 1
Page 1 (below) By permission of The British Library
Page 2 (above left) Science Photo Library

Picture section 2
Page 1 (above) Ashmolean Museum, University of Oxford, UK
Page 8 Troia Projekt, University of Tuebingen

INDEX